MAY   2008

Conversations with Thomas McGuane

Literary Conversations Series

Peggy Whitman Prenshaw
General Editor

D1215556

Photo credit: Audrey Hall

Conversations with Thomas McGuane

Edited by
Beef Torrey

University Press of Mississippi
Jackson

www.upress.state.ms.us

The University Press of Mississippi is a member of the Association of American University Presses.

Copyright © 2007 by University Press of Mississippi
All rights reserved
Manufactured in the United States of America

First edition 2007

Library of Congress Cataloging-in-Publication Data

Conversations with Thomas McGuane / edited by Beef Torrey.— 1st ed.
    p. cm. — (Literary conversations series)
  Includes bibliographical references and index.
  ISBN-13: 978-1-57806-886-9 (cloth : alk. paper)
  ISBN-10: 1-57806-886-X (cloth : alk. paper)
  ISBN-13: 978-1-57806-887-6 (pbk. : alk. paper)
  ISBN-10: 1-57806-887-8 (pbk. : alk. paper) 1. McGuane, Thomas—
Interviews. 2. Novelists, American—20th century—Interviews.
I. Torrey, Beef. II. Series.

PS3563.A3114Z64   2006
813'.54—dc22   2006042165
[B]

British Library Cataloging-in-Publication Data available

Books by Thomas McGuane

The Sporting Club. NY: Simon & Schuster, 1968.

The Bushwhacked Piano. NY: Simon & Schuster, 1971.

Ninety-two in the Shade. NY: Farrar, Straus & Giroux, 1973.

The Missouri Breaks: An Original Screenplay. NY: Ballantine, 1976.

Panama. NY: Farrar, Straus & Giroux, 1978.

An Outside Chance: Essays on Sport. NY: Farrar, Straus & Giroux, 1980.

Nobody's Angel. NY: Random House, 1982.

Something to Be Desired. NY: Random House, 1984.

In the Crazies: Book and Portfolio, with Russell Chatham. Seattle, WA: Winn Books, 1985.

To Skin a Cat. NY: E. P. Dutton/Seymour Lawrence, 1986.

Keep the Change. Boston: Houghton Mifflin/Seymour Lawrence, 1989.

"Tenth Anniversary Edition" of *An Outside Chance: Essays on Sport.* Includes four new essays and an introduction by Geoffrey Wolff. Boston: Houghton Mifflin/Seymour Lawrence, 1990.

Nothing but Blue Skies. Boston: Houghton Mifflin/Seymour Lawrence, 1992.

Sons. Northridge, CA: Lord John Press, 1993.

Live Water. Stone Harbor, NJ: Meadow Run Press, 1996.

Some Horses: Essays. NY: Lyons Press, 1999.

The Longest Silence. NY: Alfred A. Knopf, 1999.

Upstream: Fly Fishing in the American West. NY: Aperture Foundation, 2000.

The Cadence of Grass. NY: Alfred A. Knopf, 2002.

Gallatin Canyon: Stories. NY: Alfred A. Knopf, 2006.

Contents

Introduction

"All things come to him who goes after them" could easily be an apt credo for maverick novelist Thomas McGuane. Besides being a highly acclaimed novelist, McGuane has nearly done it all: an MFA from Yale, a former Wallace Stegner Fellow, an accomplished essayist, an editor, a screenwriter, a movie director, a world-class angler, a rancher who raises prize cutting horses, a son, brother, father, stepfather, husband (and twice ex-husband), and gloating grandfather. All of which have profoundly influenced his craft.

The oft-interviewed McGuane has assembled a productive, diverse, and highly visible writing career. Praised for its technical luminosity, McGuane's savagely comic vision of American culture and fanatical, fertile imagination has fathered a cast of unforgettable, existentially blundering protagonists to the elation of his loyal literate readers.

This first volume of selected interviews spans the metamorphosis and trajectory of McGuane's writing life to date. His compelling and captivating story will bear witness firsthand to McGuane's self-determination, wit, warmth, candor, passion/s, and penetrating intelligence—as well as his insecurities, pratfalls, headaches, and heartaches—in both his life and his life work. Furthermore, these discussions expose the intriguing evolution of a mature, literary writer and monitor the growth and transformation of a complex, creative, and fully engaged mind, and his unique contribution to American letters.

In a 1976 interview with Toby Thompson, McGuane frankly tells us, "I have absolutely one major theme, which is: Why go on? It's been rephrased by lots of people. I almost think it's the master theme of literature." [1]

McGuane's life has had lots of goings-on. As he readily admits to the *Detroit News Magazine,* "I've done some things right and some things wrong, but I've done a lot of things." [2] These experiences have directly impacted his livelihood. He yearned to become a writer at an early age, notions of which were both aided and abetted by his parents. "My mother and my father, especially my father was not only not sympathetic to my aspirations, they were absolutely hostile to them," he mentions in a 2005 interview with the editor of this volume.[3] He adds that being a writer seemed to him "the most splendid thing he could be in the world—it's still true—to me being a writer is the way some people feel about making the New York Yankees. I just wanted to be one so badly; it was a literal, absolute burning, consuming thing with me."[4] "It struck me as a very romantic life. It wasn't so much that I wanted to write. It was that I wanted to be a writer. . . . I'd gradually begun to see the life of the writer as being the ultimate kind of free life."[5]

But there was also another *raison d'être* entrenched within this feral passion and desire. "I had this thing about authority—which I am not jacking up for autobiographical interest. I am totally incapable of dealing with authority. Teachers, police officers, political figures, everything. It's been a huge force in my life. So I began at a very primordial level to try to figure out a way of never having to have a boss of any kind . . ."[6] This adversarial relationship with authority figures clearly extends to yet another major theme found within McGuane's fiction—"the father and son relationship" (and the obvious autobiographical underpinnings). As McGuane confesses to the *Paris Review*, "This is plainly so. If you'd been around me while I was growing up, you'd have clearly seen that my relationship with my father was going to be a major issue in my life."[7]

It's obvious that McGuane's early desire to become a writer (at least the identity of such) led him to great writers and a disciplined (and "intense") work ethic, which over time have dramatically altered both him and his work. In a 2005 interview with this book's editor, he states: ". . . Somebody interviewed Gerald Chapman and asked him what I was like when he was my writing teacher at Harvard and his remark was, 'He was so intense it was frightening.' Well, you know you can't live like that your whole life. And also it causes you to neglect a lot of things. And if you're working hard and you're driven by fear of failure and all those things, your peripheral vision goes all to hell."[8]

Discussions of McGuane's great love of literature are plenteous within nearly all the interviews, and one could compile an exhaustive reading list. As McGuane contends, "I have been sloppy in my approach to being an artist, but one thing I will say for myself. I read like a son-of-a-bitch."[9] The depth and breadth of which is visibly exhibited in the sophistication of his early prose, which has shifted considerably as he continued to hone his remarkable skills, as he states, "Writing, in my view, is the by-product of reading."

Early in McGuane's development as a writer he claims that "I don't think of myself particularly as a storyteller. My passion is language and human perception, not necessarily in the form of stories."[10] McGuane expands the idea:

> I want to write a novel that contains important information which I can conceivably represent as being important. I want to write a novel that will represent whatever it is I've learned about living. . . . I'm not interested in writing a novel to dazzle or entertain right now. Reading Jim Harrison's novel *Farmer*—was like a glass of ice water being thrown in my face. It had the pleasant quality of cleansing my eyes about literature at a time when it seemed like everything I picked up was sort of anticipatable or dull. . . . [A] piece of work written straight from the heart, without any cheating, by my best friend, had not a little of the quality of reproach about it. There are books that remind me immediately of the extreme importance and dignity of the profession of writing. To me the novel improved the world. . . . I feel that they've opened eyes, or . . . perceptions. And that's kind of what I want to do.[11]

Both McGuane and Harrison, often dubbed as bad boys of American literature, have vigilantly nurtured and cosseted their independence and preferred to live in relatively isolated rural locales that supply physical lives separate from but informing their writing lives. Their friendship of over forty years encompasses an unrestrained passion for literature, and what Harrison calls "the sporting life."

Although McGuane wrote about Montana in his comic novel *The Bushwhacked Piano*, it was "the thinking man's Western" *Nobody's Angel* that cast him as "the authentic voice of the New West." McGuane declares in 2005:

> As I have made too clear at times, I think regionalism is a bit of a snare. The region becomes an official place for literature, a bad thing, and I believe some of this has happened in the West, producing a queer, Kabuki atmosphere with somewhat stylized players and concerns. Stegner lived most of his life outside the West, his family compound was in Vermont, but had little to say about that part of his life. Norman Maclean spent a half-century in Chicago without much to say about it. Guthrie didn't return to Montana until he was in his fifties and what happened to that life? Much writing about the West takes up the old business of claiming the place, especially in the form of what I call prior appropriation memoirs. Another method, much practiced by academics is the business of claiming the place through canon-building

and list-making, "The Twenty-three Finest Montana Love Poems," et cetera. Our poor state has been festooned with these college follies. I much prefer the sort of frankness you find in Roth, say, where his work pushes on to reflect his increasing wordliness, but Newark is always there; or Updike for whom New England is increasingly and eloquently present but rural Pennsylvania casts its truthful shadow.[12]

Despite McGuane's academic background and credentials, as well as short-term academic appointments, he repeatedly voices a discernible scorn and distrust for academe in general, English departments and MFA programs in particular, and remains skeptical of most writers who have elected to live within the ivory tower (with Tobias Wolff and the late Saul Bellow noted exceptions). McGuane specifically views "Scared Cow writer's in residence" (McGuane's term) as "greatly underworked" and his fear is that in his own life, this secure existence would be "homogenizing and narrowing . . . eliminating the sinew from his fiction."[13] As he continues: ". . . Teaching ideally requires considerable pedagogical abilities and just because you're not making a living from your writing does not mean you have to become a teacher. I've had miserable writer-teachers; they thought they were of purely totemic value sitting at head of the class monosyllabically reacting to students' questions."[14] To the contrary he voices admiration for writers like Norman Mailer, Gabriel García Márquez, and Walker Percy, whom he feels engage with the real world.

In a similar stratum, McGuane does not embrace the widely held cultural perspective that "negative publicity" is an oxymoron. Clearly the media coverage of his life and work radically differs from his own perceptions. As McGuane explains: "It may be endemic to people in this job but I have felt that my critics have been mostly clueless about what I'm actually trying to do. The famous Hemingway lashup has never withstood an examination of my work, but it goes on. Even McMurtry tried to air it out one more time and I have been polite enough not to point out his taking on the mantle of Edna Ferber these past many years."[15]

Both the public and the press may have a great deal of difficulty relinquishing its long-held flashy tabloid persona or the macho mystique of McGuane as a young, long-haired, hard-drinking, drug-addled, womanizing wild ass. That McGuane is long since gone. As he discloses,

I'm not a rugged "man's man." I am an anxious artist, plagued by ambivalence and terrified by the responsibility of proposing to make a little literature. My anxiety about trying not to repeat myself has been confirmed by the catastrophes I've sometimes experienced at the hand of critics. It does no good to point out that the East Coast literary scene is like a kennel where all the dogs have rabies because some great writers, like the properly esteemed Philip Roth, find ways of flourishing there.[16]

McGuane recently illustrates such with the following anecdote. He writes:

I had a turning point in regard to the literary officials of New York. I read an excellent book about animals and what they know by Vicki Hearn, then a poet in residence at Yale, and a trainer of dogs and horses. On the dust jacket of the book was a passionate recommendation by Susan Sontag. When I met Susan Sontag at a writers' conference I thanked her for the recommendation. "That was a very bad book," she said baldly. But what about her quote on the jacket? "I thought it would be a good exercise for people to find out how bad it was for themselves." There you have it. In Mrs. Sontag's purse were reprints of an essay she had published in the *New Yorker* which she passed out to people she thought influential.[17]

He further expounds:

I'm a strong believer in the idea that the only legitimate criticism of a work of art is a better work of art. We live in a hurricane of opinions, and in a world like literature that is chronically subjected to self-appointed tastemakers, it is important to try to focus on one's work as strictly as possible. In other words, life is short.

My take on the art of fiction, which I do not intend to be exclusive, is that the task is to illuminate the writer's own times.

I have little interest in genre fiction, historical fiction, or fantasy fiction—though to feel more "au courant" or as they say in Spain, "mas actual," I have sardonically proposed writing a novel about a remorseful straying husband, set in the Hamptons during the Civil War. It also seems that meta-fiction has gone nowhere and has not even left the good residue afforded us by minimalism in such splendid hands as Raymond Carver's.[18]

Just as McGuane's fiction has changed over the years, so has his presentation of himself to the media. In correspondence with this volume's editor, McGuane notes:

I hope my interview persona has changed over the past thirty years, but can't really say how. All younger writers have a strong Hamlet streak, of course, and other forms of displaced narcissism and a proclivity for making statements that really translate as "make way for me." In recent years, I've felt that all I could do was the work in front of me and there was no sense in twisting in the wind over how it was received or how it sold. . . . I'm not uncomfortable talking about most things in my life, except those which are the normal purview of privacy. Even those no longer seem sacrosanct in a confessional age. When I open my e-mail in the morning, there are always several strangers offering to help me enlarge my penis or send me a Russian whore. That I once drank too much sour mash bourbon seems paltry in such a world.[19]

There you have it, the "goings on"—from reveries of the writer's life by a late-blooming, underachieving boy to a cocksure, determined, and ambitious adolescent; to a swashbuckling, twenty-eight-year old who bedazzled the literary world with his debut novel; to a one-time Hollywood typecast "Gonzo Cowboy"; to, finally, the ebullient and introspective sexagenarian still progressing toward the tantalizing closeness of wisdom, never quite achieved in the writer or his characters. As McGuane concludes, "I think I am getting more control of the craft. Writer and protagonist are always on the verge of wisdom. They struggle to find it, but they don't always. It's a terrible struggle to find language. I have to keep doing this."[20]

In the summer of 1982, I met Tom McGuane, during my first stay at El Rancho Brautigan in Pine Creek, Montana, at the invite of its part-time *patrón*, our mutual friend, the late Richard Brautigan. Richard didn't drive, didn't own a drivable vehicle, or have a driver's license, hence he depended (imposed) upon his friends for portage. So, by default, I became Richard's defacto designated driver for the weekend. That first morning following my arrival, with Richard riding shotgun, we hit the trail for Chico Hot Springs. Our first stop, just a couple miles south of Richard's homestead, was Tom McGuane's second Raw Deal Ranch.

Brautigan had made recurrent reference to McGuane during late night phone calls, and it was at his incessant recommendation that I first read him. This is where it all began . . . my consuming interest in McGuane's life and work.

Among McGuane's vast community of writing friends and associates, he is particularly noted for his enthusiasm, encouragement, and magnanimity. Foremost among them is his former classmate at Michigan State—the aforementioned writer Jim Harrison. In a 1985 interview with Bonetti, says McGuane of his friendship with Harrison: "I'm sure we've had an impact on each other's lives and thinking. We've managed to bolster one another in a fairly high view of the mission of writing, so that in lean years and blocked times it still felt that it was kind of a religious commitment . . . I am sure that the fact that Harrison and I have been writing back and forth for a quarter of a century almost entirely about writing has been one of the things that keeps the thread intact."[21]

Novelist, former Yale classmate, longstanding friend, and neighbor Gatz (William Hjortsberg) shares his fond recollections:

> Tom McGuane and I first met in the fall of 1962 when we were both graduate student playwrights at the Yale School of Drama. United by a shared passion for fly fishing and writing fiction, we become fast friends and spent countless hours discussing literature, wandering the aisles of second-hand bookstores, and fishing for trout in the Mill River, a small Connecticut brook just outside New Haven. . . . Tom's invitation in the summer of 1969 to come out and go fishing in Montana . . . brought me to the place I've more or less made my home ever since.
>
> Our writing careers . . . followed roughly parallel courses. We both received Wallace Stegner Creative Writing Fellowships at Stanford (although in subsequent years). . . . I've told the story of how Tom brought my first novel, *Alp*, to Simon & Schuster and helped get it published. . . . In the early seventies when Tom had his first success selling screenplays in Hollywood, he urged me to give it a try. "It's like taking candy from a baby," he said. I decided to follow his advice and pitched a story idea to Tom, a supernatural detective tale. . . . When I finished, Tom told me I should not use it as a script proposal. "It's much too good," he said. "You should write it as a novel." Such a notion had never occurred to me but, inspired by Tom's enthusiasm, I began chapter one. . . . The end result was *Falling Angel*, my most successful novel, still in print after twenty-seven years . . . and eventually was made into a movie. Without Tom's encouragement, it probably would have remained a near-forgotten bit of juvenilia . . .[22]

McGuane likewise is also the person attributed with introducing then-struggling artist Russell Chatham to the Hollywood jet set—Jack Nicholson, Harry Dean Stanton, Peter Fonda, Jeff Bridges. Chatham reflects on meeting McGuane in 1967:

> . . . I had a good friend named Rudi Ferris. . . . Tom and Becky [Crockett, McGuane's first wife] rented a house across the street from Rudi's parents, and so it was natural for them to get acquainted . . .

I was told by Rudi that Tom was a writer, and there were certain times during the day when he could not be disturbed due to the practice of this craft. I found that interesting for a couple of reasons, the first being that I'd never known a writer before, and second, I had no discipline in my life whatsoever, and pretty much did whatever the hell I wanted twenty-four seven, which is why I was penniless, and would remain so for the next quarter century . . .

One of the things I liked best about Tom in those early days was that unlike myself, who lived in the shadow of self-doubt, Tom was on the move, living among an ever larger circle of friends. If I could put it in a word, it would be that he showed me the way to engage the world.[23]

Writer, filmmaker, and photographer Guy de la Valdene chimes in as well:

I met Tom in the spring of 1969. He and his wife Becky and baby son, Thomas, were living on Summerland Key. We had coffee together, introduced by our mutual guide friend by the name of Woody Sexton. Later that summer Tom published "The Longest Silence" with *Sports Illustrated* and I did an interview/article with Al McClane for *Field and Stream*. We both wrote each other "I liked it" notes (his was superb) and a few weeks later Tom invited me to visit him in Montana, which I did. The first time we fished the Yellowstone he caught two five-pound brown trout in so many casts. We have been close friends ever since, and if I were to be thankful to anyone for changing my life, it would be him. . . . He introduced me to literature and to the close friends I have spent the last thirty-five years with . . .[24]

It was also Thomas McGuane who persuaded Robert Redford to read Norman Maclean's novella, *A River Runs Through It*, a work that Redford later turned into the critically acclaimed film, starring the then-little-known actor, Brad Pitt.

As mentioned before, McGuane and Harrison have deeply influenced each other's careers, and the writers have collaborated on screenplays and in films. Through Harrison's contacts in the publishing industry, he assisted in getting McGuane's *The Sporting Club* published at Simon & Schuster, and Harrison has mentioned in repeated interviews that he wrote his first novel, *Wolf* (which is dedicated to McGuane), upon McGuane's urging, while he was convalescing from a serious fall sustained during a hunting trip. Moreover, McGuane, who entered Hollywood screenwriting (and directing) in the mid-1970s, got Harrison involved in the business as well. McGuane also co-scripted with Harrison the film, *Cold Feet* (1989), and earlier both took part in *Tarpon* (1974), a respectable, pioneering (but little-known) low-budget documentary film about tarpon fishing in the flats of Key West co-directed by their mutual friend, Guy de la Valdene.

In Jim Fergus's 1989 essay, "The Sporting Club," Harrison states: "What I thought was marvelous about McGuane . . . was that he turned it all around at age forty-some. He just said, 'I'm not going to be that way anymore.' I used to say to him, 'You've gone from being my outstanding negative example, to being my outstanding positive example, from being this fierce street fighter, crazed drunk, to being kind and wise, and I'm not sure how to handle it.' " [25]

It's fitting that a 1971 conversation between Harrison and McGuane begins this volume. Also included are interviews from obscure literary reviews such as the Berkeley-based broadsheet cultural journal *Threepenny Review*, the short-lived *Rocky Mountain Magazine*, *Firestarter* ("news and revue, celebrating the cultural diversity of Southwest Montana"), and the *Tributary Magazine*.

Combined with lengthy interviews from the *Paris Review*, *Inrockuptibles* (the French equivalent of *Rolling Stone*), an online venue, and a new 2005 interview conducted by the editor especially for this volume, *Conversations with Thomas McGuane* is the most comprehensive and diverse collection of pieces on the writer. The term "interview" is employed rather loosely within this collection. Not all of the selections follow the traditional question-and-answer format, but include author profiles, informal literary discussions, or edited conversations, all of which employ direct quotations from McGuane (sometimes edited, others verbatim). The interviews took place in various locales (during book promotional tours, at McGuane's various residences, etc.) and were conducted in-person, via telephone, or written correspondence. As customary with all books in this series, the interviews herein have not been altered from the form of their initial publication. Consequently, there is some repetition, but this allows for McGuane's personality and reflections to come through unfiltered.

In all, the interviews provide valuable insight into the depth and range of McGuane's intellectual preoccupations, his personal interests, and his consistent and engaging conversational voice, intensity, candor, ever-present sense of humor, articulate/eloquent style, and demeanor. As McGuane concludes, "One of the great things to be is an unsuccessful writer, when all your life is in dreams. You have spiritual and mental freedom which is unparalleled. Eventually, you get more professionalized. You have a phone, you have a fax. And you look back to when nothing was at stake—except the dreams."[26]

This book would not have been possible without the unrelenting assistance and encouragement of numerous individuals, in fact, far too many to name. In short, I've amassed tremendous personal indebtedness in the completion of this project, which has been years in the making.

For the inspiration and friendship of Dr. Bob DeMott at the University of Ohio in Athens.

A special heartfelt appreciation to Tom and Laurie McGuane, his son and daughter-in-law, Tom and Michelle McGuane, and daughter, Maggie McGuane.

Special tributes to Dr. Dick and Sally Jenkins, and Dr. Lewis Parkhill formerly at Murray State College in Tishomingo, Oklahoma; Dr. Stan Vasa, my mentor, advisor, and former colleague at the University of Nebraska–Lincoln, and Dr. John Maag and Dr. Sue Kemp. The assistance and expertise of two former colleagues and professors at Doane College: Dr. Liam Purdon and Jay Kreimer.

For the interviewers and publishers who granted their permission to reprint the interviews selected for this volume. Leslie Edwards, the archivist at Cranbrook School in Bloomfield Hills, Michigan; Peter Berg, Director of Special Collections at Michigan State University Libraries, and my childhood friend Jim Lee for the English translation of the French selection in *Les Inrockuptibles*.

My former college classmates J. R. Hansen and Kevin Simonson, who provided sound input and proofed various drafts/revisions, and Niamh Murphy for enduring our endless literary banter. Additionally, Foof, Lana, Cole, Conner, Cason, and Callie Christensen; Chonie, Leslie, Whitney, and Alex Allbery; Ed and Liz Schulenberg, David Stamm, Bruce Weible, Rerrie Dake, Tom Ruth, Trout Heckman, Kevin Colerick, and many more, who all in some way have impacted this result.

For my very special friends and their unstinting support: Sy Settell, Jan Seng, Gregg Orr, David Harrison, David Bishop, and my former muse and trail buddy forever, Emily C. Hunter.

To the contributions of Keith Abbott, Guy de la Valdene, Bill Kohlhaase, Jim Fergus, Doug Stanton, Dr. Patrick Smith, among a host of others.

My Deadrock cronies: Jim Harrison, Gatz, Russell Chatham, Sally Epps of Clark City Press, Greg Keeler, Doug and Andrea Peacock, Elwood Reid, John Fryer, Dan and Robby Lahren, Steve Dennison, Suzanne Dennison, Tim Cahill, Max Crawford, Patty Kiderlen, my friend the late Richard Brautigan, and many more.

UPM staff, Director Seetha Srinivasan, my editor, Walter Biggins, and production editor, Shane Gong, for insuring the manuscript progressed from start to finish (and the indexing by Valerie Jones).

A special note of appreciation to the delightful Audrey Hall for the use of the cover photograph, and Gloria (In Excelsis Deo) Thiede—the finest and fastest transcriptionist in the West.

My brother, Kurt Milo Torrey, who will most likely never read this volume, but will certainly skim the acknowledgments to see his name in print.

Lastly, this book is dedicated to my mother, Marian Hoy, who patiently taught me a true love for words, the printed page, books, and literature. It is your exemplary faith, continual prayers, profound love, and active concern for which I will be forever grateful.

BT

Notes

1. Toby Thompson, "Art," in *The '60s Report* (New York: Rawson, Wade Publishers, 1979), p. 239.
2. Kathleen Stocking, "Hard Cases: Conversation with Jim Harrison and Tom McGuane, Riders of the Purple Sage," *Detroit News Magazine*, August 12, 1980, pp. 14–15.
3. Beef Torrey, "A Dialogue with Tom McGuane," 2005.
4. Thompson, p. 226.
5. Ibid., p. 225.
6. Ibid., p. 225.
7. Sinda Gregory and Larry McCaffery, "The Art of Fiction LXXXIX: Thomas McGuane," *Paris Review* 27, no. 97 (Fall 1985), p. 47.
8. Torrey, 2005.
9. Martha Duffy, "Papa's Son," *Time*, August 6, 1973, p. 70.
10. Gregory Morris, "Thomas McGuane," *Talking Up a Storm: Voices of the New West* (Lincoln, Nebraska: University of Nebraska Press, 1994), p. 210.
11. Thompson, pp. 239–40.

12. Correspondence with Beef Torrey, 2005.

13. Dexter Westrum, *Thomas McGuane* (Boston: Twayne Publishers, 1991), p. 15.

14. Kay Bonetti, "An Interview with Tom McGuane," *Missouri Review* 9.1, 1985–86, p. 81.

15. Correspondence with Beef Torrey, 2006.

16. Ibid.

17. Ibid.

18. Ibid.

19. Ibid.

20. Westrum, p. 131.

21. Bonetti, p. 82.

22. Correspondence with Beef Torrey, 2005.

23. Ibid.

24. Ibid.

25. Jim Fergus, "The Sporting Club," *Outside Magazine*, March 1989, p. 114.

26. Mary E. Iorio, "Literary Cowboy," *Cranbrook Journal*, Fall/Winter 1995, p. 8. Courtesy of Cranbrook Archives.

Chronology

1939	Born, December 11, in Wyandotte, Michigan, to Thomas Francis McGuane II and Alice (Torphy) McGuane. He was the eldest of three children, who grew up in Grosse Ile, Michigan, to a middle-class, Irish Catholic household—although his family was all from Massachusetts.
1945	Spends summers during his childhood at his Grandmother Torphy's home in Fall River, Massachusetts, and at the family's summer retreat, a fishing camp in northern Michigan on the Pere Marquette River.
1953–55	Attends Grosse Ile High School, and is retained in the ninth grade. Repeated behavioral and academic concerns prompt the principal to encourage his father to enroll him at Cranbrook Schools, a private boarding academy in Bloomfield Hills, Michigan.
1955	McGuane begins attending Cranbrook Schools, during which time he meets fellow student and future writer Edmund White. Joins JV and varsity soccer teams, the United World Federalist Club, and the Pre-Med Club, and becomes the "humor editor" for the *Crane* (school newspaper, where he writes an "advice column" called "Mother McGuane's Helps and Hints").
1957	Leaves home in the summer to live and work on a ranch, owned by the father of his girlfriend, in Sunlight Basin on Clarks Fork in northern Wyoming.
1958	Graduates from Cranbrook on June 14. In the fall, he enrolls at the University of Michigan in Ann Arbor but flunks out with a 0.6 grade point average.
1959	Transfers to Olivet College in Olivet, Michigan, in the spring, but returns to the University of Michigan in the fall. During the summer he studies fiction writing with literature scholar Gerald Chapman at Harvard University.

1960   Returns in the spring once again to Olivet College. Transfers in the
          fall to Michigan State University in East Lansing. Fellow students
          at Michigan State include writers Jim Harrison and Dan Gerber.
1962   In the fall, begins graduate work at Yale's Drama School.
          September 8: marries Portia Rebecca Crockett. Awarded a BA
          with Honor from Michigan State University, East Lansing
          (English Major) in December.
1963   Co-founds *Red Cedar Review*, an annual literary magazine edited
          by Michigan State University undergraduates, published in
          collaboration with the Michigan State University Department
          of English and Michigan State University Press.
1964   Travels to Ireland in the summer.
1965   Receives an MFA, majoring in playwriting from Yale University
          School of Drama, in May. Completes the three-act play *Islanders*.
          Begins corresponding with fellow Michigan State alum, Jim
          Harrison.
1966   Lives in both the port city of Malaga, Spain, and Florence, Italy,
          where he attends the Scuola per Stranieri.
1966–67   Awarded a Wallace Stegner Fellowship in Creative Writing, at
          Stanford University. July 2, 1967: his son, Thomas Francis IV,
          is born.
1968   Publishes his first novel, *The Sporting Club*. With the proceeds he
          purchases the first Raw Deal Ranch on Deep Creek, south of
          Livingston, Montana. In the fall he is named Fiction Editor,
          Sumac Vol. II, No. 1 (through the Fall 1971, Vol. IV, No. 1 issue),
          with fellow classmates and editors Jim Harrison and Dan Gerber.
          Named special contributor to *Sports Illustrated* (1969–73).
          Divides his time between his ranch in Montana and various
          homes in Key West, Florida. *The Sporting Club* is adapted into a
          full-length film, directed by Lorenzo Semple, Jr., released by Avco
          Embassy Pictures.
1971   Publishes *The Bushwhacked Piano*, which is awarded the Richard
          and Hinda Rosenthal Foundation Award in Fiction from the
          American Academy and National Institute of Arts and Letters.
          In March he completes the screenplay of the adaptation of *The
          Bushwhacked Piano*, written for Robert De Niro but never
          produced.

1972   Survives a near-tragic car accident outside Dalhart, Texas.

1973   Publication of his novel *Ninety-two in the Shade*.

1974   National Book Award fiction nomination for *Ninety-two in the Shade*. Writes screenplay and directs movie version of *Ninety-two in the Shade*, filmed in Key West. Also appears in the documentary film *Tarpon* (directed by Guy de la Valdene and Christian Odasso), featuring early footage of McGuane, Jim Harrison, Richard Brautigan, Jimmy Buffett, and Valdene. McGuane's sister Marian dies of a drug overdose.

1975   Writes the screenplay for the cult classic *Rancho Deluxe*, filmed in Livingston, Montana.

1976   McGuane's father dies. McGuane is divorced from Becky. June publication of *The Missouri Breaks*. October 28: birth of his daughter, Maggie, by actress Margot Kidder. Marries Margot Kidder. Completes the screenplay for *The Missouri Breaks*, a film produced by United Artists, which stars Marlon Brando and Jack Nicholson.

1977   Divorces his second wife, Margot Kidder. Marries Loraine (Laurie) Buffett, sister of the popular singer/songwriter Jimmy Buffett. Purchases the second Raw Deal Ranch, south of Pine Creek, Montana, in Paradise Valley. In the fall, wins Team Roping Championship at Gardiner, Montana Rodeo, teamed with Albert Howard Carter III. Completes first draft of screenplay *Flying Colors*.

1978   Publication of his novel *Panama*. In September, completes the screenplay for *Tom Horn*.

1979   Release of the movie *Tom Horn*. Completes the screenplay *Tropical Wholesale*, which was never produced. December 17: birth of his daughter, Anne. Named contributing editor for *Rocky Mountain Magazine*, edited by Terry McDonell, through the November/December 1980, Vol. 2, issue.

1980   Publishes *An Outside Chance: Essays on Sport*.

1981   January 1: McGuane gives up alcohol. Becomes co-owner of his father's company, Thomas McGuane, Inc. in Detroit, Michigan, which he manages with his brother for five years. McGuane's mother dies. In the summer he wins the Montana-Wyoming Cutting Horse Championship. Participates in the Berkeley Writers'

| | Conference at the University of California–Berkeley and teaches there with Robert Stone and Elizabeth Hardwick in the fall. |

1982   Publication of his novel *Nobody's Angel* and screenplay of the same title, which was never produced. Publication of *Vanishing Breed*, photographs of contemporary working cowboys of the West by Albert Allard, with an introduction by McGuane.

1984   Publication of his novel *Something to Be Desired*.

1985   Publication of the signed, limited-edition *In the Crazies*, a literary and artistic collaboration with Montana artist, writer, and friend Russell Chatham, edited by Terry McDonell.

1986   Sells the seven-hundred-acre second Raw Deal Ranch and moves to Sweet Grass Country, near McLeod, Montana. Publication of the short story collection *To Skin a Cat*. Wins cutting horse championship at the Houston Stock Show.

1987   Sells his late father's manufacturing business.

1989   Awarded the Montana Governor's Centennial Award for Literature. Release of movie *Cold Feet*, an original screenplay he co-wrote with Jim Harrison in 1976, in which McGuane has a cameo appearance. In the summer he wins Montana Cutting Horse Championship for the fourth time. Publication of his novel *Keep the Change*. Participates in the University of Michigan's Visiting Writers Series. McGuane's select manuscripts are displayed in an exhibition of books and manuscripts celebrating forty years of the Creative Writing Program at Stanford. The catalogue for such, *First Drafts, Last Drafts*, contains individual essays of those writers exhibited.

1990   Publication of the tenth-anniversary edition of *An Outside Chance*, which includes an introduction by Geoffrey Wolff and four new essays by McGuane.

1992   Publication of his novel *Nothing but Blue Skies*. June 9: Premiere of *Keep the Change*, a made-for-TV movie on TNT, based on McGuane's 1989 novel, adapted by John Miglis, directed by Andy Tennant, and starring Jack Palance, Buck Henry, and William Peterson.

1993   Awarded the Arnold Gingrich Angling Award, for his literature and conservation ethic by the Theodore Gordon Flyfishers. Publication of the signed, limited-edition of *Sons*.

1995   Chairs the Fiction Committee for the National Book Award. Awarded the Distinguished Alumni Award from Cranbrook Academy.

1996   Participates in the Paris Book Fair. Publication of *Live Water*.

1997   Named director of the American Rivers and the Craighead Wildlife Institute.

1998   In January, serves as a panelist at the 14th Annual Key West Literary Seminar entitled "American Writers and the Natural World," with fellow writers Jim Harrison, Russell Chatham, Dan Gerber, Doug Peacock, Annie Dillard, Gretel Ehrlich, Richard Nelson, Fredrick Turner, James Welch, Terry Tempest Williams, John Nichols, Rick Bass, Judith Minty, and Linda Hogan, among others.

1999   Publication of two works of nonfiction, *Some Horses: Essays* and *The Longest Silence*.

2000   In April, awarded the Evil Companions Literary Award for *The Longest Silence* (given annually by *the Colorado Review* writer living in or writing about the American West). Publication of *Upstream: Fly Fishing in the American West*.

2001   Selected to the Montana State University Spring Writers Series. In the summer, awarded the Roderick Haig-Brown Award for *The Longest Silence* by the National Federation of Fly Fishers. Accepts an academic appointment at the University of Wyoming.

2002   Publication of his novel *The Cadence of Grass*. In mid-November, participates in the Texas Book Festival.

2005   On his sixty-sixth birthday McGuane is inducted into the National Cutting Horse Hall of Fame. His story "Old Friends" is included in *The Best American Short Stories 2005*.

2006   Publication of *Gallatin Canyon: Stories*.

Conversations with Thomas McGuane

A Chat with a Novelist

Jim Harrison / 1971

From *Sumac* IV, no. 1 (Fall 1971), pp. 121–29. Reprinted with permission of Jim Harrison.

When I turned up Deep Creek Road the sheep bordered the cattle guard and their "ba ba ba bahhs" seemed to reflect the question: why would anyone live here? But I drove on through the Engleman spruce and withered sedge for a few miles then turned when I saw BUSHWACK PALACE branded into a rail fence with McGuane, Prop., below it. I drove another mile through a pasture of sudan grass noticing the flattened rattlers with their clouds of flies on the road, a few conical piles of bear doodoo with even more flies and prairie falcons hovering in abstract gyres above the trail. Why not live here? I queried myself. When I drew up to the ranch which closely resembled the movie set from *Shane* Mr. McGuane's huge dog jumped bristling onto the car hood but her master's voice called and we walked through the darkened house to a yet darker study. I noticed Mr. McGuane looked a trifle old for his age which hasn't been determined though I would guess between the mid-twenties and mid-thirties. Like the redoubtable Pynchon he makes an unfortunate fetish out of privacy. Pourquoi? Who knows. Perhaps no one cares but that's not what we're talking about, is it? There was a two gallon swiveled decanter of cheapish gin and some ice on his bare desk. Mrs. McGuane, nee Portia Crockett, brought in a pewter platter of braised leeks and sweetbreads which we nibbled at with a chilled off-year Chateau Margaux. Mr. McGuane glowered as if this intrusion for the sake of contemporary letters was unwelcome. He put on a Linda Rondstadt and a Dolly Parton album and sang along rather loudly with them, not well I might add. My questions punctuated this noise with some difficulty.

Interviewer: Is it true what you said about Bob?

McGuane: Nope.

Int: You seem to key off the Midwest in your work. You were born and raised there but you commute between Montana and Key West without a nod to Michigan and its rich literary milieu. Why?

McGuane: I have a genetic horror of the Midwest, a dark image of the past where Mortimer Snerd screwed three thousand times a day to build that heartland race.

Int: Oh.

McGuane: Yet I miss those piney woods, those beaver ponds and rivers, the feebs and dolts who run the bait shops and gas stations, the arc welders in the legislature, the ham with chicken gravy that poisoned me in Germfask when I fished the Driggs.

Int: You're not denying your roots?

McGuane: Cut that shit out.

Int: A.O.K. What do you think of the Drug Generation?

McGuane: The Driggs is a fine river for brook trout.

Int: Must I always be a wanderer between post and pillar, the virgin and the garrison, the noose and the cocktail lounge?

McGuane: That's your bizness.

Int: Who do you think is really good right now?

McGuane: Grass. Hawkes. Landolfi. Cela.

Int: Do you care to elaborate?

McGuane: Nope.

Int: Were it possible, how would you derive the novels you would like to write?

McGuane: Cervantes, De Rojas, Rabelais, Swift, Fielding, Machado de Assis, Melville, Gogol, Joyce, Flann O'Brien, Ilf and Petrov, Peacock, Dickens, Kafka, Chesterton, Byron of the letters.

Int: Do you think Nabokov excessively conumdramatic?

McGuane: Is that like hydramatic?

Int: You jest, mega-fop!

(A two day interruption was made here to attend a Crow Indian Pow Wow. The interviewer became very ill from semi-poisonous tequila which he mistook for white table wine. The Custer Battlefield of Thomas Berger fame was visited. How life imitates art!)

Int: Officially Montana is your residence, is it not?
McGuane: Yes, the bleak cordillera of the Absaroka consoles me.

Int: Why don't you live on one of America's marvel coasts?
McGuane: I'm glad you asked. I've been to those places. And the Left there to which I belong was developing an attitude toward the people of the interior and the unfashionably pigmented poor that is best described as racist. For example the Left implicitly considers any white born in the south to be congenitally evil.

Int: What about the whole "novel scene" now?
McGuane: Only that the serial preoccupations of fiction could be replaced by the looped, the circuited, and the Johnny Carson Show. Even something so ductile as an eclaire has an inner dynamism not inferior to a hard-on or a terrified Norway rat.

Int: I think most of our readers are unfamiliar with your interest in pastry.
McGuane: It ends with eclaires and their analogue reality (or not).

Int: I wonder how many of our readers realize that your aunt was the celebrated Irish novelist Flann O'Brien?
McGuane: Very few.

Int: What other things come to mind that our readers probably don't realize?
McGuane: What is the name of your magazine?

Int: *Sumac*, which unfortunately some think is French for stomach.
McGuane: Well one of the things that *Stomach* readers doubtless fail to realize is that D. H. Lawrence was Norman Douglas's wife. It was the first society function hazarded by the widely resented "surfboard aristocracy" of Tasmania, also I might add their first transvestite wedding.

Int: Oh. One critic describes your fictions as being "laced with canals of meaning and symbolism."
McGuane: Yes, yes . . .

Int: Is that true?
McGuane: O yes, yes yes . . . Why gee yes.

Int: What do you think of, I think it was either Granville Hicks's or George Steiner's contention, that fiction should be spelled "fickshun?"
McGuane: No.

Int: What of your fabled love of animals?
McGuane: I would handily commit 3,300 acts of artistic capitulation to keep my dog in Purina.

Int: Why have you never mentioned the Budweiser Clydesdales in your work?
McGuane: O god, hasn't that been done to death?

Int: May I ask for the first sentence of your new novel?
McGuane: Of course. "Upstairs, Mona bayed for dong."

Int: MMMMmmm. How ironical. Yesterday in the local tackle shop I was told you had invented a new fly for trout.
McGuane: Yes, I call it the Republican Indispensible. You tie it up out of pig bristles and carp feathers.

Int: Have you ever caught Gila trout in New Mexico?
McGuane: No.

Int: Arizona?
McGuane: O, not at all.

Int: Are you offended by calling a large trout "Larry Lunker" as do many of our sporting writers?
McGuane: Au contraire. The term frequently hangs on my lower lip like a figment of dawn.

Int: Are you stoned?
McGuane: No, intermittently never.

Int: What constitutes a horse's ass in our literature?
McGuane: A difficult question! I'd say 1. parsimony 2. sure fire Babbitry 3. snorkeling 4. New York 5. San Francisco 6. Irving Berlin 7. this is your life not theirs 8. pick up sticks 9. Mary Jane and Sniffles 10. U.S.A. Meatland Parcels 11. a million baby kisses 12. a bad cold 13. corasable bond.

(Mr. McGuane ran out in the rain to install a new starter solenoid in his Porsche 911T. We then left immediately for the Black Foot Reservation in Browning, Montana, to see the birthplace of James Welch. We were there for three days. Mr. McGuane unfortunately mistook tequila for a widely known ginger ale, hence spent much time yodeling in the thundermug as the Irish would put it.)

Int: I'm interested in what you think of Barton Midwood's contention that the modern novelist has lost his audience. They've all gone to the beach.
McGuane: Hopelessly true. We're lucky if they've gone no farther than the beach. If they were at the beach a year ago when Midwood made the statement they are surely in Tibet by now.

Int: What is the last book you didn't write?
McGuane: *The Possums of Everest.*

Int: I understand you were working on a contemporary western but have abandoned it?
McGuane: Yes, the book was centered in Big Pie Country or Big Fly Country, whatever you will. The title was *Ghost Riff-Raff in the Sky.*

Int: Why did you give up the title *Wandell's Opprobrium*?
McGuane: It would have sent everybody to Tibetan beach.

Int: Don't you think the title should have been *Walkie Talkie*?
McGuane: Not at all.

Int: Your politics, rather the lack of them, is a point of interest to some critics. Do you have a comment?
McGuane: I suppose I am a bit left of Left. America has become a dildo that has turned berserkly on its owner.

Int: Do you feel lionized?
McGuane: I feel vermiculized.

Int: Do you have any deeply felt interest in poetry?
McGuane: O, a great deal. So much in fact that I find myself overwhelmed. I would like to add this, for decades the Pruniers' restaurants have had the reputation of being the best seafood restaurants in the world.

Int: What of your college years?
McGuane: I graduated from Black Pumpkin in 1956. Since then, I might add, our Pumpkin group has dominated American letters.

Int: What about the underground?
McGuane: What about the underground?

Int: I mean what about the Underground?
McGuane: Oh. The Underground has become the Overground, in essence a parable of the Gay Cabellero.

Int: Is that in the same genre as the Spanish Cavalier?
McGuane: No. Only that every hamster is a hostage to fortune.

Int: Have we touched on organic gardening?
McGuane: We had one of those things out at the end of the lawn. A lot of work. Then a certain horse named Rex got loose in the night and ate the whole plot to ground level. Sad to say but the most organic thing in the world is pus. I read it yesterday.

Int: Are any of your friends living in domes?
McGuane: Yes. I have a close friend who has built a $100,000 home that looks precisely like a Spalding Dot.

Int: The golf ball, I presume?
McGuane: Yes. From time to time he and his family can be seen scuttling in and out one of its pores. It's a noble way of life. Also, they have a duck inside with them.

Int: Where has everyone gone?
McGuane: Bolinas.

Int: All of them?
McGuane: All of them.

Int: For the striped bass?
McGuane: For the pachouli.

Int: Why did you call your dog Biff?
McGuane: Sprat.

Int: Dink?
McGuane: Frab. . . . (snit).

(The interview terminated here. An inevitable tedium seized us.
Mr. McGuane attempted to sing from Jarry's *Ubu Roi* accompanying a
Merle Haggard record. Then he read to me from some aerosol cans he
gathered in the bathroom: "Never spray toward face or open flame, avoid
inhaling. If rash develops discontinue use. Contains riboflavin." etc. . . .)

Thomas McGuane: An Interview

Albert Howard Carter III / 1975

From *Fiction International* 4/5 (1975), pp. 50–62. Reprinted with permission of Harold Jaffe, editor-in-chief of *Fiction International*.

Thomas McGuane was born in Michigan in 1939 and was educated at Michigan State University, where he studied English, the Yale Drama School, and Stanford. At Stanford he held a Wallace Stegner Fellowship in creative writing. McGuane currently divides his time between Montana, where he has seven hundred acres, and Key West, where he has three boats. McGuane is a sun-tanned outdoorsman, an enthusiast of fishing—for trout in the woods, for bonefish in the Keys—boating (chiefly sailboats), and natural oddities from bats to dense, tropical hardwoods ("Don't strain yourself, but just lift this log to get an idea," he exhorted me). He is 6'3" tall, lean, with strong facial features; his brown hair used to flow to his shoulders. "Now I look like a redneck," he reports.

McGuane drives two veteran vehicles, each pushed into its second hundred thousand miles, a Cortina and a Dodge panel truck, which appears to be the prototype for Payne's truck in *The Bushwhacked Piano*. On the bumper of the Cortina, in careful symmetry, are two stickers: "Support Your Local Sheriff" and "Support Your Local Police State."

This interview took place in an outbuilding behind McGuane's Key West home. Two of the three rooms are given over to marine paraphernalia, parts, charts, repairs. The office is full of a desk, files, and loads of books ranging from Machado de Assis to Flaubert (he was rereading *The Sentimental Education*), from Bachelard, St. Teresa, Rabelais, and Woolf, to a two-volume study of rattlesnakes, a *Chronicle of the Yellowstone*, a monograph on bats, and Joao Guimaraes Rosa's *Devil to Pay in the Backlands*. The phone rang now and then as relatives, friends, editors called. (McGuane does some writing on boats and fishing for *Sports Illustrated*.) Cats, dogs, birds sported in the tropical growth lining the yard. McGuane fixed tea, added honey generously, and spoke in a deep, resonant voice that cracked occasionally. The interview was taped, transcribed, then edited by mail by both parties.

McGuane's first published novel, *The Sporting Club*, appeared in 1969 when he was twenty-eight. The second, *The Bushwhacked Piano* (1971), won the Richard and Hinda Rosenthal Award of the National Institute of Arts and Letters. His last, *Ninety-two in the Shade*, appeared in 1973 and was nominated for the National Book Award; parts of it appeared earlier in *Fiction* and *TriQuarterly*. Since then, McGuane has written three screenplays: *Rancho Deluxe* opened in New York in the spring of 1975; *The Missouri Breaks* was filmed the summer of 1975, directed by Arthur Penn and starring Jack Nicholson and Marlon Brando; and *Ninety-two in the Shade* with Peter Fonda, Margot Kidder, and Warren Oates, premiered the summer of 1975. McGuane directed *Ninety-two* himself.

Howard Carter: How did you find doing movies?
Thomas McGuane: Anyone can learn the technical end of it in ten minutes. After that, it's just like novels: you have to tell a story. With novels, though, you only have a beat-up typewriter. With films, as Orson Welles said, it's the best toy train set-up a kid ever had. Movies are a lot more fun to do. And, contrary to what a lot of people say, the cinema has enormously to do with language.

Carter: You've changed the ending of the screenplay for *Ninety-two* so that Nichol Dance does not kill Skelton. Surely that's not a Hollywood cop-out.
McGuane: Surely not. I thought about that ending for some five years and decided that another aesthetic might also work, that those characters might violate their principles in order to honor their affection for each other.

Carter: The novel continues to sell well?
McGuane: Yes, it keeps trickling along. I was quite apprehensive about the reception of *Ninety-two*. I thought my more popular sorts of readers would find it too elliptical, and that the sophisticates were going to abandon it when they discovered that the essential narrative system was as plain as it says it is.

Carter: But your instinct and the public's acceptance must also tell you that it's not simply the plot that makes the book, but how it is handled.
McGuane: Sure. Somebody once said that everybody in the world has better ideas for novels than do novelists, and that it's all in the execution—and that's too dear to be repeated, but I think anything will do, at one level of

narrative. I think that you can work any narrative effectively. Even in terms of putting people to work there's something to be said for traditional themes.

Carter: Would you want to put anyone to work, as a teacher?

McGuane: No, I don't think so. I've already had some offers to teach in university writing schools, but I've turned them down. I'd rather be free to write, to manage my own affairs, and I really have serious doubts about teaching anyone to write anyway. I don't even like to go out and do readings. And I reject the notion that the writer must be protected, that he's not capable of handling his own affairs. I enjoy that part of the business and don't plan to run away from it. But of course when great writers like John Hawkes seem to want to teach, you make such remarks with care.

Carter: So back to novels? Do you have one in mind?

McGuane: Yes, I've been easing into one. It's going to be three pages long and take over ten years. The results will be terrible. I will be hailed for o'erleaping my epoch and certain prizes will be delivered to me by hand. It will be a powerful instance of going for the gusto.

Carter: You've been doing a novel every two years quite regularly. Is that the shape of the future?

McGuane: No, it's just happened that way. Of course when my first novel came out, I had been writing ten years, and all that stuff was going in the closet. So *The Sporting Club* was really my fourth or fifth novel. I get the impression from reading reviews that people think having a novel every two years is really tossing them off, but it doesn't seem that way to me at all.

I work really long hours when I'm writing; I work six or seven days a week, nine or ten hours a day. At the end of six months there's a lot of work done. At the end of a year there's a lot of revision. At the end of a year and a half we're starting to get there.

Carter: How do you work, by hand, typewriter? Many drafts?

McGuane: I do four or five drafts of a novel—this all typed, chiefly because my handwriting's so bad. And these drafts keep shrinking. The first draft of *Ninety-two* was twice as long as the published novel. But the revision and cutting is so exciting to me, even more exciting than the original draft. William Burroughs almost makes sense with his talk of cut-ups and fold-ins, because you can make very strange things happen when you cut, pull things out, reverse orders, and so on.

Carter: Do you work from an outline or just power ahead?
McGuane: The latter. I'd like to work from an outline, but I can't. The kind of inner system of fiction—whatever it is—tends to be self-creating, and the kind of energies that end up being in it prolong each other.

Carter: Sort of a chain reaction?
McGuane: Exactly, and an outline tends to obviate that. I like to catch and follow a pitch—take that musically or altitudinally—and ride it into the ground, deciding later whether it will stay in and help create the whole work.

Carter: I have a feeling from your very style that words, for you, are a plastic and growing medium. Take Samuel Alexander's notion of the artistic medium as a creative force, itself. Your feelings?
McGuane: This doesn't answer your question, but Fitzgerald talks about writing as being like swimming underwater. You just go down and swim, and when you run out of air, you come back up, but you must go back down again and swim. This submergence is a level of mental operation that is not the same as outlining or revising, it's a base of operation. But although I can't outline, my respect for orderly work means that I resign myself to a lot of revision.

Carter: You leave the formats of three parts or numbered chapters of the first two books for a different texture in *Ninety-two*.
McGuane: Yes, that's quite self-conscious. I wanted a different texture, a pattern of lacunae through the book with certain assumptions about what will not be said, what doesn't need to be repeated, so that the narrative can be carried more tenderly through a larger world.

Carter: You assume a reader then.
McGuane: Yes, I feel some sort of presence, I don't know who, but you have to have a notion about who's actually reading what you're writing. I like to imagine that person, whoever he is, as getting a lot smarter, getting to be a better reader of mine so that we can enlarge the world that the book discusses and concentrate the size of the book. It's what racing-car people call

power-to-weight ratio: you try to make a faster car with a longer range between fueling stops, and a lighter machine.

Carter: This impetus gives a lot of fun to a reader of your corpus: even simple things, like the mention of the bat tower in the beginning of *Ninety-two*.
McGuane: One of the reasons I did that was because other writers have given me fun that way. I like that kind of inner reference; it's part of the game. But I like it done in a way so that it's not a vain remark. There are writers who put keys to tell you to read all the canon or none of it, and I don't mean to say that. For me it's pure fun.

Carter: Can you point to any essential quality in fiction?
McGuane: For me, it's a quality of energy. Books that are first of all energetic are already saved. Even something like Hunter Thompson's *Fear and Loathing in Las Vegas*, which to me has no morally redeeming features, deserves to survive because it has energy.

Carter: Do you admire Céline's work for this reason?
McGuane: At one point I read a lot of him, and liked his energy, but he's not central to me now.

Carter: Which, of older writers, do you hold in high esteem?
McGuane: It's an odd list, and it changes, but when I was at Yale, chiefly avoiding the draft, and not doing very much in the Drama School, I'd take a sandwich to Sterling Library in the morning and stay there all day reading. I did that for three years, daily. And the things I found I liked included Thomas Nashe's *The Unfortunate Traveler*, Turgenev, Flaubert, all of Cervantes, the Elizabethans over and over, Cervantes' *Exemplary Novels* in the great English of Mabbe's translation, and the beloved James Joyce, Burton's *Anatomy of Melancholy*, Gogol, Tolstoy, Sir Thomas Browne, the King James Bible, Urquhart's Rabelais; but especially, and I think rather thoroughly, twentieth-century fiction: Céline, Miller, Landolfi, Faulkner, Biely (*St. Petersburg*), Svevo, Hemingway, Fitzgerald, Nathaniel West. Oh God, and especially Knut Hamsun. But I've forgotten a lot of others—and this gives no credit to Jonathan Winters, Lenny Bruce, or Bob and Ray, nor to the thousands of hours of rock and roll that began for me with Buddy Holly and Richie Valens. Nor to all the movies and TV and hot rod magazines.

Carter: You seem comfortable in Key West. Do you feel the same way in Montana?

McGuane: I never want to leave one place for the other, but I don't feel like a real Key-Wester, or a real anything. Nabokov's been referring to himself lately as a "friendly outsider," and I find that a salubrious phrase. If I feel anything, it's a writer, a space man who's just landed. I'm pretty rootless, however sad that may sound.

Carter: You've lived on all four borders, plus stays in Ireland, Italy, and Spain.

McGuane: Yes, and I grew up during some years in Venice, Florida, but most of my relatives are from around Boston, and that's what the family usually takes to be home.

Carter: And high school?

McGuane: Most of my growing up was in Michigan, and, after fifteen, I went to boarding school.

Carter: Was that helpful to your growth as a writer?

McGuane: No. I didn't get any help with my writing—and I was serious about it that early. If anything, I was discouraged. The school was in the hands of obtuse assholes.

Carter: Did you show your work to anyone?

McGuane: Yes, I had friends. One is now a very strange and good writer, and in school he was sort of a guide. He had read all of Proust by the age of twelve. Anyway he gave me these extraordinary lists to read: Huysmans, Lautréamont, Wilde, and so on, and for a long time, that's what I thought literature was, that tradition. That's what serious literature appeared to be, until I started adding some comic writers like Ronald Firbank, and Evelyn Waugh.

Carter: That's interesting, since it seems to me that at least one of your roots is that dark side of romanticism, including decadent writers, or even, in some ways, the naturalists. Do you care at all for London, Norris, or even, in his own way, Lawrence?

McGuane: I think probably my biggest blind spot in twentieth-century literature is D. H. Lawrence. I've read him rather carefully, but I just don't like him at all. And it's a temperamental dislike, a truly primitive dislike. I don't like his voice, the way he acts. . . .

Carter: Too overbearing?

McGuane: Something like that. His tone, the way he expresses himself, his tyrannizing kind of personality, and I think he's also really full of shit, you know. I think his program's dumb. And also there's a kind of vanity I really can't bear. I will defer to better minds. But my reaction is that Lawrence is an awful writer. I'd rather watch paint dry than read that boob again.

Carter: And what about those other characters, Norris, London, Dreiser? At least they efface themselves as narrative voices.

McGuane: Yes, but as writers they're just too technically crude for me. Now writers like Stephen Crane and Mark Twain, I know, have had a lot of influence on my work.

Carter: I wanted to ask you about Twain in particular, your interest in humor and social criticism. I thought, for example, of his charlatans in relation to your C. J. Clovis in *The Bushwhacked Piano*.

McGuane: Yes, I've read all of Twain, very carefully, even that monstrous novel, *The Mysterious Stranger*.

Carter: What about the oral tradition in Twain. Many of your characters are gifted raconteurs, able to turn out a lovely anecdote in less than a page, for example, Quinn telling about his father's accident with the golf cart in *The Sporting Club*.

McGuane: I hate writers who describe themselves in some sort of ethnic way, but my family, especially my mother's family, are really heavy-duty Irish, and my mother had four or five brothers who were always fantastic storytellers. My maternal grandmother's house was kind of a through-the-looking-glass place for me; it was just full of people who really valued wise-cracks and uncanny stories—that was the structure of life in that house, and the really unforgivable sin was to go on too long.

Carter: A school for self-editing, then?

McGuane: Oh, listen—the kind of derision a story with just one extra sentence got, really. I suppose it sounds like I'm making this up, but if I was going on too long, as I tended to do, my mother would interrupt me with a question like "What do you think of cottage cheese?" And if I'd start to reply, she'd leave the room. And they were just as merciless about tedious storytelling.

Carter: And if a story was well-told?

McGuane: Then there was back-slapping and congratulations. One of my uncles was a judge in Fall River, Massachusetts, and he was an incredible storyteller, the kind that becomes a legend. You get to be a legend if you're a good storyteller in that society. I remember going to his court one time during the era when college boys would do panty raids. He had two young men up before him for a panty raid at a nearby girls college. He heard the case and gave them his charge card for Filene's Department store in Boston, telling them to go there and return to the court next week having exhausted their interest in ladies' underwear. They were then to describe their experience to the court. That was the fabric of his mental life, a precise kind of repartee. One-liner would be too cheap a word.

Carter: In that case, of course, he was instructional; what about the story for pure enjoyment. Your characters, Quinn in *The Sporting Club*, and Payne in *The Bushwhacked Piano*, insist that many of their wacky actions are sheerly for fun. Tell us about fun as part of your esthetic.

McGuane: The question is too tough. The answer has to do with the moral obligation one has to be happy that Samuel Butler is so eloquent about.

Carter: And what about clownishness, practical jokes. You said you acted up in school a lot. Do you like being able to "act up" within the safety of the literary experience? Is this an Edgar Allan Poe sort of perversity?

McGuane: I remember a review of *USA* in which the reviewer said it was like an explosion in a cesspool. I thought, "God, I'd love to have that review." And John Barth had a review in which his great *Sot-Weed Factor* was called "maniacal." I wanted that one too. I have from time to time gone to great lengths to personally deserve those descriptions. And if I can squeeze away some of the instinct for going too far into art, I shall win on a number of counts—including dancing my way past the entrance to the madhouse, raising a family, and going in the boat.

Carter: Do you feel an urge to shock as a biological drive?

McGuane: Something like that, but it's not the simple kind of *épater le bourgeois*—for one thing they aren't around that much any more. For another they're too stupid to know they've been shocked.

Carter: Is your function to be a clown "at large," to use your closing phrase in *The Bushwhacked Piano*?

McGuane: First of all, I'm not entirely owning up to being a clown. And secondly, a kind of work that until recently was done by loose and inspirational kinds of clowns or *picaros* is now headed by preciser compulsives. That's why I think so much about the illustrious Knut Hamsun. He was, I should say, a real fiend. So, to answer your question, let's simply substitute "fiend" for "clown."

Carter: Your books are often built on practical jokes, swindles, hoaxes, and the like. Do you feel this is a kind of vengeance a writer can take against the many forces that impinge on us?

McGuane: Well, of course, anything built upon a swindle is a step in the right direction. And in an essentially *nasty* society like ours certain disruptions present themselves to the lucid—writers or otherwise.

Carter: All three of your novels are built on protagonist-antagonist conflict, with a girl usually thrown in. Tell us something about your sense of nemesis.

McGuane: It is just that there is a kind of doubting that I believe in. I mean, just as I feel that marriages, say, are made in heaven, there are certain things that are made in hell. And they are not tollhouse cookies. They are a nuanced sequence of Eumenides—ranging from ants at the picnic all the way to that cast-eyed fucker who eases out of the palm shadows with a razor.

Carter: It's interesting that your heroines keep evolving to less and less satirical forms, from Janey and Mary Beth in *The Sporting Club* through the super-intellectual Ann in *The Bushwhacked Piano*, to the rather attractive and normal Miranda in *Ninety-two in the Shade*.

McGuane: I'm glad you think so; some people think my heroines are getting more simple-minded. There's a larger issue here though, how males in America view women, and I feel that I'm working through a problem that many of us are stuck with. There was an attitude when I was growing up that you weren't supposed to know anything about women, and that they were really kind of scary. Boys were supposed to go their own way and do sports, and especially at boys school there was a total ignorance of women. And in college we glided with alacrity to a kind of fraternity horsing around that did nothing to help us. It's a kind of pervasive joke in this country about young

men's ignorance about women. Just a half hour ago I was talking to a friend
here in Key West and he said, "God, I had this tremendous piece of ass last
night," and I said, "What was she like?" And he said, "Well, let's put it this
way: she had one." Well, *you* think it's funny in an odd kind of way, and so do
I, but isn't that our nervousness about the whole business, that a woman
should be some kind of post with a hole in it, a comic totem like Jeannie
Carter in *Ninety-two*, the ex-cheerleader, "a simple pink cake with a slot"?

Carter: Do you feel then that your novels are exorcising this sort of foolishness?
McGuane: Absolutely. I'm trying to work closer and closer to an authentic
vision of sexuality, using satire as a purgative.

Carter: And is that how you would answer a feminist critic, who might not,
after all, be pleased with some of your women characters?
McGuane: Sure. In fact, there was an article in the *Village Voice* about a film
in Greenwich Village that was being picketed by radical lesbians. The piece
was by Molly Haskell, I think, and she was wondering why they always picketed films and not television or even books: they should be picketing the
publishers of Thomas McGuane or James Dickey. I realized that maybe I was
part of a larger process than I realized and that maybe the trajectories in my
work were heading further than I knew. I also felt that I didn't deserve that
and maybe Jim didn't either but that as a writer you are always liable to
become a convenience of someone else's polemics.

Carter: Your satire can be pretty rough, especially on lower class folks. One
review suggested you were being a bit snobbish.
McGuane: Yes, I remember that, and it brought me up a bit short. And I have
regretted some of my portraits and shots against, let's say, "easy marks." But
there are other forays that I don't regret. I agree to being a snob—but I can
document that I'm harder on the rich than on the poor, by far.

Carter: How about some of your military folks; you're pretty merciless with
them. "Amo tell you one thing sumbitch," you have a retardate sailor say at
the end of *The Bushwhacked Piano*.
McGuane: Yes, and I don't regret that portrait at all. I remember one batch
that saw a black guy swimming in a canal, and they wouldn't swim there
themselves until the tide had changed three times. I understand their

problems and their background and so forth, but I don't think they're funny anymore. They're not even workers; they're not plumbers or carpenters or makers of anything. They've got a serial designation, E-4, or something. To me it's something that deserves to be called to accounts.

Carter: How do you square this judgmental side of your work with the notion of artistic freedom, *disponibilité?*
McGuane: I don't have a theory about life or even literature. But I do have a certain feeling about right and wrong and a sense of importance of, let's say, charity, all as kinds of armatures for what I'm trying to do. I feel them as a back wall against which I can work.

Carter: Your fiction seems to mark out clearly the limits of what you would ever want to consider philosophy, and that these limits are pretty tight. I'm thinking of the image of the gopher and the rattlesnake in *The Bushwhacked Piano* or the following passage from *The Sporting Club:* "Remember that help yourself is a novel of please, and if you try too hard you will be seen to the door, your mind belly up and your hat in your hand. Life is a greedy railroad and that's an end on it." This seems to come from Quinn's mind, but who knows. I don't suppose you have a gloss for that?
McGuane: No, I surely don't. I wonder what that could possibly mean.

Carter: Might the passage on the other hand signal your setting of limits on your fiction's pretensions to philosophy?
McGuane: Yes, that's a fair statement. What I find is that writing is a job, like any other, and the more you do it the more you have a sense of its center, its edges, and even the ragged edges, where you can set a foot outside, but you must pull back in. You're fabricating an experientially microcosmic situation by installing yourself in a job which theretofore didn't exist. So you're both in the job and in a satellite position to it, outside the initial boundaries. So you sense a point that lies too far out, where you might issue statements or tamper with the narrative in a way that would stretch the book too far, to where it fatigues.

Carter: And this fine-tuning shows up in a nervousness of style, mixed metaphors, and so forth, to mark the boundaries.
McGuane: That's it, because you get the feeling of the edge and that one false move will break up the orbit altogether and that you'll lose the author and

end up with an abandoned fragment which no one but an incunabulist would ever find.

Carter: Let me ask you, then, whether you feel more partial to either of the following views. Northrop Frye suggests that all literature is made out of literature and that the writer is little more than a medium to shape this inevitable flow of traditions. Some one like Henri Bergson, on the other hand, would see the creations of an artist as something absolutely new, fresh, virtually without precedent.

McGuane: Both views seem absolutely true to me, as one of those absolutely immutable paradoxes, a brilliant paradox.

Carter: You have a lot of technical information in your work, about boats, fish, cars, cameras, bats, bullfighting, and on and on. Do you collect this consciously?

McGuane: No, it just piles up. It's really just part of my life interests; I've always been fascinated by how things work. I've always been sort of a monomaniac, and whenever I got interested in something, I just immersed myself in it, and a lot stuck. Scott Fitzgerald said that the test of a good mind is to be able to carry two contradictory things at one time without going to pieces. Well, I can't do that.

Carter: Do you feel the same way about your writing, that total immersion is the best method?

McGuane: Very definitely. I have to do that, and not just for writing. Even around the house, when I'm trying to do something, I have to give myself to it totally, and if Becky says "When do you want dinner?" I become disoriented and lose my focus. So, getting loaded sets in.

Carter: Developmental psychologists speak of children as having "participation perception," meaning that they'll become totally involved in one thing, yet change their focus so rapidly that they'll drop the thing to the floor. Do you feel that, for your esthetic, childishness is a prerequisite for being an artist?

McGuane: I am only certain that there are no prerequisites for being an artist. I know a lot of them and they have nothing in common; though I would say that the survivors seem to be able to concentrate.

Carter: Let me ask you about a couple of particular passages in your work, to get a feel for more ideas and working methods. At the start of Chapter 11 in *The Bushwhacked Piano* you have a wonderful catalogue of Ann Fitzgerald's possessions. How did that get put together?

McGuane: I remember that distinctly; it came all at once. No rewriting.

Carter: How about, in the same novel, the hilarious scene in Chapter 12 of Codd peeking in at Payne and Ann making love?

McGuane: There is this: I myself am not above Codd's actions in that scene. Until recently, I had seen more people killed than fucked. So, you have your morbid curiosity. I would hang from a roof to watch people fucking. Any day. William Eastlake, the great, told me that sex is all that nature cares about.

Carter: The scene can be read as a brilliant parody of the fair scene in *Madame Bovary*; did that scene, or any other, serve as a model? Do you ever feel conscious of reworking a setting from another novel?

McGuane: Vanity would propel me away from such recognition. If you aim to get your rocks off as an artist or Messiah you have to feel fresh as a daisy morning, noon, and night. Moreover, there are so many glorious books already, that knowing repetition violates the deal an artist has with the dead.

Carter: You seem especially attuned to the sounds of words. I'm thinking of a piece of wit and sound in *Ninety-two in the Shade* (p. 124, first ed.): "The one-part 'mock' epoxies were 'just the thing,' a lady clerk volunteered, for simple household repairs, including china, furniture, butter churns, ice skates, and simple treadle assemblies." The last three words seem especially funny and euphonious.

McGuane: Yes, I'm aware of those sounds, and I spent some time tinkering with that sentence. It's basically a joke for the reader who is patient enough to make it through the whole series.

Carter: What *are* "simple treadle assemblies"?

McGuane: I have no idea.

Carter: What about all the comparisons people make between you and Hemingway?

McGuane: I admire him, of course, and share a lot of similar interests, but I don't really write like him.

Carter: It's easy enough to point to the interest in sports, Key West, maleness, even writing for *Sports Illustrated*. Where do you see differences?

McGuane: We have totally different styles. His world view was considerably more austere than mine. His insistence on his metaphysical closed system was fanatical. And he *was* a fanatic. But it gave him at his best moments a very beautiful prose style. And anyone who says otherwise is either stupid or is a lying sack of snake shit. We have few enough treasures in this twerp-ridden Republic to have to argue over Ernest Hemingway's greatness. But that is the price of his Byronic personal domination of his situation—before which I imagine him to have been helpless. Ernest Hemingway was a fanatic. For my generation of artists, schizophrenia is oxygen. We are scanners. We look for topography rather than veins. But the nostalgia for veins is, if not killing us, at least brutalizing us.

Carter: On the other hand, reviewers seem to shy away from any comparison to Vonnegut, who would be closer in tone, if not subject matter. Your feelings?

McGuane: In the recent past, so many writers had their film overexposed by the passage of Ernest Hemingway that comparing a writer to him amounts to a primary lumping kind of attack on that writer. Rudyard Kipling used to be employed similarly. And Dickens. It's a question of finding a blunt object. By his presence and actuality, it is harder to brain an artist by hitting him over the head with Kurt Vonnegut than with Ernest Hemingway. But we must remember that there is an as-yet-unborn novelist who will be brained by the dead Kurt Vonnegut. And so it goes.

Carter: How do you feel about the more philosophical sort of current American writers: Pynchon, Coover, Barth, Gass?

McGuane: The American Literature of the Academy, in short. This tradition is of course important. These writers recommend themselves to, or design themselves for, exegetes. They fit into teaching.

Carter: And you feel more comfortable with a non-academic esthetic of writers such as . . .

McGuane: Ken Kesey, Richard Brautigan, Larry McMurtry, Harry Crews, Jim Harrison, Donald Barthelme. I have a feeling about this sort of writer being *out there*. They're not back at the factory. Actually I like a lot of the first group of writers we named, but take the pattern of John Barth; it seems almost archetypal for them. He started off writing really delicious novels like *The Floating Opera*, but became increasingly cerebral to the point that the fiction died out from under him as the theory advanced.

Carter: Your dislike of theories—is that why the *Time* piece suggested you weren't a thinker?
McGuane: Yes, I think. Or, concomitantly, I am not a thinker.

Carter: And you find systems, theories, rational critiques as simplistic, as compromising of our organic life?
McGuane: Yes, and I'm not sufficiently romantic about the visionary quality of the human mind to believe that I or any other writer can arrogate a theory of, say, the decline of the West, or class warfare, or anything like that. First of all, I don't believe in historical eras; I see an enormous sequence of cultural islands. I don't think that there was a Roman empire or an age of the United States. These things didn't really happen.

Carter: And, rather, they're hypotheses?
McGuane: Yes, a kind of cybernetic shorthand.

Carter: So that history is really a form of literature?
McGuane: Yes, that's really what it is. And what I want to represent are numinous collusions of human life that are universal. That's a latinate way of putting it, but why couldn't the households of Tennessee Williams's plays exist in Imperial Rome, or why wasn't *Farewell to Arms* a Napoleonic episode? It really doesn't make any difference. If it does, then I am obligated to recognize that my esteemed friend Richard Brautigan wrote all of his works in 1911, even those he hasn't written yet. And everyone knows that Jim Harrison is a neolithic Polynesian. Then too, his tits aren't as big as they used to be.

Carter: "Collusions" are clear, since your characters constantly scheme, plot, figure, conspire. But "numinous"? There are a few privileged moments, in the last sentence of *The Sporting Club*, in Payne's speech about fun, his bronco ride, his memories about the Seminole girl, and even in Skelton's death, "the discovery of his life," but these all fleeting, all evanescent. Even the

bushwhacking of the piano and the violin playing of Skelton's father suggest
a dream denied. "Numinous"?
McGuane: *Oui, mon enfant.*

Carter: Is there any progression from the violent conflicts of the first two
books to the phrase that comes early (p. 5) in *Ninety-two in the Shade,* "the
epoch of uneasy alliances."
McGuane: You know, I thought of *The Sporting Club* as an experiment in
anarchy, a political paradigm. Of course it didn't work out that way, but I still
have those urges. I'd like to fly a long black banner from my boat, feeling that
no one would know what it was. As for any sense of resolution in the last
book, I hope I brought it down to some very clean paradoxes, an irreducible
handful. And that is what I am up to for the following very good reasons:

1. That's the best we're going to get.
2. We'll never get out of here alive.
3. You're only as pretty as you feel.

The Novelist in Hollywood:
An Interview with Thomas McGuane

Leonard Michaels / 1981

From the *Threepenny Review* 1, no. 4 (Winter 1981), pp. 4–5. Reprinted with permission of Katharine Michaels.

Before the interview, I suggested that Tom McGuane needn't answer my questions precisely, or even answer them at all. He could talk about whatever came to mind in regard to writing novels and movies. In the first exchange, McGuane did this. The effect is a little asymmetrical, but the spirit of the occasion survives in McGuane's humor and personal energy. The transcript is close to what he said: there are a few tiny deletions for the sake of clarity. McGuane was smart, funny, and candid.

The audience—about a hundred people at the Berkeley Writers' Conference—seemed to want to ask questions. Early in the interview, I surrendered that privilege to them.

Leonard Michaels: I'd like to begin by asking you to say something about the relations of movies and books, from a particular point of view. What I have in mind is this: I've noticed that when I'm in an airplane and reading a book, the person next to me will often start a conversation as if I were doing *nothing at all*. Do you think reading has ceased to *count* as a human activity—compared, say, to watching a movie?

Thomas McGuane: The relationship between novels and movies is very complicated, and it's different in every case, but it has to do with this process of *generation*, and the way we apply that word to replicating or attempting to replicate things. If you pass a word around the room, it deteriorates at each stage. There are more stages, from the writer's point of view, in the making of a movie than there are in the process by which we supply a printer with something to be published. Sometimes that works to the advantage of the writer, but it seldom happens in ways which he absolutely foresaw. Scripts are absolutely always changed. Sometimes they're much improved by the changes.

It's hard to answer your questions generally, because each case is different. I wrote a movie called *The Missouri Breaks* which was designed to be so cheaply and easily made that I would be asked to direct it. At that time a cheap movie was under two million dollars. And Marlon Brando was persuaded to show up for a million dollars for ten days, and at that point they were unwilling to use the kind of austere locations and simple approaches to the physicality of the film that I had designed, and they turned it into a kind of *Paint Your Wagon*, which is also partly the kind of theater background that Arthur Penn brought to it. And the co-star, who was a fairly minor character in the script, turned out to be Jack Nicholson, so he could no longer be a co-star. And everyone said, "You wasted Jack Nicholson in the movie," and I said, "I never wrote Jack Nicholson in the movie." We'll have to get back to that.

But anyway, there is a lot of pressure on the writer to change things, and if the writer doesn't cooperate, they either find another writer or the actors begin to wing it. Or in some cases the writer—usually by diligence, bad temper, Vietnam night-fighter drugs—manages to prevail and actually get his way. There are flashes of what was intended, there are flashes of actors' brilliance at the expense of the script and so on. And the whole stew, in the end—which is examined, I think comically, from an *auteur* point of view—is the thing that goes to the theaters. So pride of authorship is something that's not directly served by the movie industry. French film theoreticians have never had much of an impact over here.

Michaels: Do you think that a movie and a book are profoundly different sorts of things, and that there really is no way that they can be discussed as one?

McGuane: I don't feel the profound difference. On the other hand, ten or twelve years of moving back and forth between the two has perhaps evaporated the boundaries for me. They seem to be directed on very similar missions. And as I encounter younger and younger writers—which is an ominous phenomenon—I have to say that the amount of reading that's done these days on the part of younger writers makes the difference between books and movies. Because the old—not *old*—the references which still seemed to be holding up ten, fifteen years ago just don't seem to exist anymore. It's easier to talk to most younger novelists about movies than it is about books, even if those books are three hundred years old. Something's happened—the center didn't hold.

Michaels: Let's talk about some specific writing questions. A lot of writers seem to notice, after they've gotten started on something, and it's going fine, that all of a sudden something's going drastically wrong. Does that ever happen to you?

McGuane: All the time.

Michaels: Do you think that testifies to some psychological matter, some knot in your soul, or something?

McGuane: I suppose that's often possible. I think that most writers, if not egoists, are very romantic about themselves in the world, and they project themselves as certain kinds of writers or kinds of people and then they can't really deliver the goods. And I'm really liable to do that sort of thing. You know, I'll decide I want to write a book about a guy who is just immensely sensitive and intelligent, a real Errol Flynn type—and he's going to take a yacht to South America and he's going to, you know, take over the cocaine trade. And I find, twenty pages into it, the things that would test a real Errol Flynn make me chicken out as a writer.

Michaels: Would you care to talk about humor in your own writing, and its complicated ways of existing in writing? What I mean, very specifically, is that sometimes you're writing something that's pretty severe and yet it's got a sort of lambent humorous quality.

McGuane: Well, writers are to a certain degree always salesman, and there are certain ways of getting your foot in the door. And it's a well-known ploy to present that you're funny—it's a real good way to get in the door. In fact, I think from Cervantes and Lazarillo de Tormes and Fielding—you can take it up to the present—it's the way in which novelists argue for their admission. And I think it's been very close to the origins of what we've decided is the novel.

Michaels: Maybe this is a good time to see if the audience would care to ask some questions.

An Audience Voice: Could you perhaps talk about making a living as a writer?

McGuane: I think anybody who writes either makes a living as a writer or he's dead. In other words, you've got to find some way to do it, even if you're T. S. Eliot and working in a bank. I never really learned to do anything but write. The only jobs I ever had were working in gas stations and working on ranches and minor construction jobs, so I was impelled to find different ways of finding how applicable the one skill I had (which I thought was respectable) could be. I mean, I would love nothing better than to concentrate all my efforts on the literary novel and never do anything else. But, I have four children in the house and mortgage payments to make. What happens is that you have to be very, very careful about metering your own energies, because, frankly, it's easier to make money in some ways than in others. Let's say you go to Hollywood and you're kind of miserable and you stay sort of loaded at night and the time flies by, and suddenly you get this big paycheck, and this paycheck was intended to support two years of fiction-writing. And as you're about to leave town, somebody says, "You want to stay for another six weeks, you can make another hundred and fifty grand," or whatever they're paying you. So what happens you're not really sure when the invitations are going to work and when they're going to disappear. But it finally takes a certain amount of courage (that you don't always have) to say, "I'm just not coming back for a couple of years," knowing that probably when you come back they won't have anything for you. So you have to balance that off against doing journalism and other things that pay. I wrote a book called *The Bushwhacked Piano* that got reviewed pretty favorably in every report and paper in the country, it was on the front of the *New York Times*, it won a fiction prize in the American Academy—it took two years to write and earned me $3,700. I just can't live on that. So, it's very hard to earn a living on the kinds of things that one did when one was Stephen Dedalus.

I find it's less taxing—it takes less out of my desire to go on writing the kind of novels which will always be the main thing I want to do—to do some journalism or to go to Hollywood than it would be to go work for my uncle in Massachusetts as a secretary, or get a burger franchise in Anaheim. So I'd rather do that. But every now and then you overkill. You know, you just think, "Well, I'm going to break my neck this year, and I'm going to be free," and you find that after that year is up, you've been in scandals, and you need a psychiatrist, and you don't feel like writing novels. And then it's just a matter of character how you survive it—Faulkner survived it absolutely. You know, the body count of good writers in Hollywood is endless. That's what astonishes you when you go down there—screenwriters—who've read everything in the world, are more fun to talk with, are more familiar with what you've done than any other novelist—who are doomed in a very unspectacular way. They're just sort of washed up. And I don't know whether I've solved it, but I've been able to keep writing fiction kind of on a weekly basis. Not that I have an absolutely cynical attitude toward working in the movies—I like writing screenplays. I wanted to be a playwright, but the situation in the American theater became very discouraging, as far as I was concerned, because, unlike novels, there was really no place to send a play, even if they were going to reject it. You couldn't mail one in—it's just not there, or at least it wasn't when I last gave up. Also, I think that we don't necessarily have to reflexively take the view that just because people go to movies, just because people go to rock-and-roll, just because people watch television, there's something wrong with it. Maybe there's something right.

Another Audience Voice: How did you start writing?
McGuane: I've written all my life—I've been writing since I was ten—and I wanted to be a writer long before I wanted to write. I know this is supposed to be the wrong approach to it, but to be perfectly honest, I thought writers were extremely romantic. Also, it looked like a great way of getting out of a lot of things. I was not very good about authority—I was in trouble and in jail when I was young, and I couldn't imagine working for anybody. So it was a way of not having a boss. Then I noticed that literature was also interesting.

Audience: I thought *Rancho Deluxe* was one of the wittiest films I've ever seen, and it seemed to me the humor has sort of an eastern quality to it. I wonder if you agree, and if so, why?
McGuane: I agree with that, and I think (and I hope this won't be misunderstood), but I think that language—both written language and spoken language—belongs more to an eastern sensibility (that is, we're talking about North America). And I've lived in the West more than I've lived in any other place in my life. But I still feel that writing and reading and a sense of language are probably more there in the East than in any other place. Certainly the kind of blabbermouths that populate *Rancho Deluxe* are very, very far from the monosyllabic surf-baboons of Southern California, who could never be characters in a witty movie or a witty novel.

Audience: Is it technically difficult to write a script?
McGuane: They are real easy to write—for a novelist. I think because they're very close to novels, really—novels of a certain kind. I don't think John Hawkes could write a screenplay that could get made—and he's one of my favorite writers, a very powerful, good writer—but it's just that he doesn't

think in those terms. But generally it's not hard for literary people to go to Hollywood. The only thing I notice is that film students and film buffs are unable to make the change—they seem to know less about the practice of filmmaking than anybody in the world. I think—and I'm not being facetious, but I think a good construction straw boss would be the ideal candidate for a movie director. But certainly not some film nut from UCLA who just did his thesis on Carl Dreyer—he wouldn't know the sound cables from the cameras.

Audience: Where do you see the film and the television industry heading?

McGuane: I don't know where television is heading. I think that the people who predict things about that very seldom have much success with their pre-dictions. I've just been reading a piece, I think it was in *Esquire*, about— remember the video revolution that we were supposed to have had five years ago? It never happened. These things just very often don't occur. There's a phrase in the rock-and-roll and movie industries, "Nobody knows what makes a hit." This finally is what keeps everything honest—you know, it's always some Lulu from Dubuque who comes in and gets it all done.

But I don't know where they're heading. I think that movies are on a kind of gloomy course right now—and strangely enough it's been in the hands of some of the most intelligent moviemakers. I mean the selection of this course. By that I mean that people like Francis Coppola and George Lucas have institu-tionalized, from the critical level on down to the bottom line, the blockbuster as being the only thing that somebody ought to spend their money on. And that's had a very, very tough effect on new ideas. You remember—I guess it was in the middle sixties—when there were all those off-center little movies coming out of Hollywood, twenty or thirty of them a year, and you kind of wanted to go see them? You can't do it. It's much easier now, for example, if you're trying to persuade a studio to back you in a film, to tell them that you're going to need thirty million dollars to do it, than to tell them you can do all of it—the editing and everything—for $750,000. You don't have a chance. They just feel very insecure when you're actually talking about a modest budget now.

Audience: Did *Rancho Deluxe* survive relatively intact from the screenplay stage to the finished product?

McGuane: Yes, in fact, I had that in the back of my mind in the early remarks I made about films and novels, and films and screenplays. *Rancho Deluxe* kind of had the wrong director. The director was an extremely literate fellow who felt that the screenplay—which was written in about fourteen of fifteen days—must *not* be changed, under any circumstances. Nothing—no commas could be moved; it had to come down from the mountain on tablets of stone. And all these rather innocent monosyllabic surf-baboons that were in the movie would hand him this stuff—and they had great ideas, you know, things that they could add and subtract, just kind of grace notes that actors and directors and cameramen bring to the parts—and this guy would say, "No. The pause is where the comma is." So when I see the movie, while I think that some of it is still funny, I feel that there's a kind of stiffness about it which could have been helped, really, if the actors had just felt they could move things around a little bit.

But that was a very odd instance, and I'm sure quite an isolated one. When we did *Missouri Breaks*, I had written the bad guy in the cowboy movie as the equivalent of a nineteenth-century contract killer, and my friend Warren Oates was going to play him, and he was going to play him right from his Kentucky roots. And when they cast Marlon Brando they came back and told me that he wanted to be an Indian. Moreover, he had a pet wolf, and he wanted the wolf in the movie. And they said, "Marlon doesn't like the character of the girl's father," and I said, "Meaning what?" and they said: "Well, he wants the wolf to kill the girl's father." Anyway, they sent me out there to talk him into being something other than an Indian, because it didn't make any sense—the Indian kills everybody in the movie and *he* said he wanted to do something for the Indian people. I persuaded him that was not in the best interests of the Indian people. So, finally the costume lady came to fit Marlon for his outfit, and he says, "Well," he says "it's going to be all white calf-skin, and it's going to have fringes," and he describes this whole outfit. And she says, "Well, I've been on location in Montana, and you should know"—this is a lovely line—"you should know that out there anything that weights 250 pounds and is covered in white calf-skin, they throw on the ground and brand." But he's a good-humored fellow, and he said, "Well, I guess we got to get another outfit." Anyway, then he ran amuck, and the last thing I saw of him he was in a dress, burning down somebody's barn—I had no idea what that was for—You really get the sense of having created a monster.

After the Storm

Jim Fergus / 1981

From *Rocky Mountain Magazine*, December 1981, pp. 46–49, 87–90. Reprinted with permission of Jim Fergus.

We're bouncing down a particularly bad stretch of road in Paradise Valley, outside Livingston, Montana. Thomas McGuane is at the wheel of his truck and he's showing me his new wristwatch, an anniversary gift from his wife, Laurie. It's an expensive watch, a Patek Phillippe, "the greatest watch in the world," McGuane boasts.

"Better than a Rolex?" I ask, skeptical.

"Oh, a hundred times better than a Rolex," he says.

"I've never heard of that watch."

"It's been the best watch for three hundred years," he says. "They have this registration card that comes with the guarantee; it says if you want to list your name with the great names of the eighteenth, nineteenth, and twentieth centuries, fill out this card!" He laughs and shakes his head in appreciation and amazement.

"This is the year," he continues, "when we shouldn't have had any extravagance because we're trying to buy this new ranch. But Laurie's been having these garage sales and selling little odds and ends of furniture. This is the one luxury item I've always wanted, but I never would have bought it myself."

McGuane's father always wanted a Patek Phillippe watch, too. "That's one of the things that used to piss me off about him. He was a prosperous guy and he could have afforded one, but he just couldn't face how expensive this watch was. Getting one is for me kind of a wedge between his way of looking at things and my way of looking at things. To me it's an indication that life is not absolutely that bitter work ethic."

"Say, you want to meet my little boy?" McGuane asks. "We'll stop over there first. I want you to meet him. Then I desperately want to show you the new ranch."

Thomas McGuane is proud of a lot of things. He's proud of his wife, Laurie; his fourteen-year-old son, Thomas (by his first wife, Becky); his

twelve-year-old stepdaughter, Heather (Laurie's daughter by a previous marriage); his six-year-old daughter, Maggie (by actress Margot Kidder); and his
twenty-one-month-old baby girl, Anne (by Laurie). He's proud of the horses
he and Laurie raise and ride, and of his bird dogs. He's proud of his new
ranch and his new novel. He's generally proud of his whole life right now.

But it wasn't always quite like that. Much has been written about McGuane,
about his art, about his life and hard times. Much of it has been idle gossip,
and McGuane has done plenty of things to gossip about. He's been married
three times and has indulged in every other excess for which writers are
infamous. He's been accused of being a macho chauvinist, a phony cowboy,
a snotty Hollywood type, even of being burned out as a serious writer of
fiction. He's had troubles.

But later, as I sit in Thomas McGuane's kitchen while he's preparing a wok
dish for his family and baby Anne is tugging on my pant leg, I hear that his
wife's nickname for him is "Ozzie."

"Why Ozzie?" I ask.

Laurie smiles and says, "Well, you know, after Ozzie Nelson."

Ninety-two in the Shade is a story of the late 1960s and early seventies.
Thomas Skelton—blown away by drugs and despair, looking for his home
in Key West, Florida—returns to his family and his true love, Miranda. But,
as we all found out in that era, those things had changed, or at least our perceptions of them had changed. Suddenly, family and old lover were seen as
if through a fish-eye lens, and home was more terrifying than anything on
the outside. Young writer Thomas McGuane had knocked around a good
bit—from Michigan to California, to Montana, and finally, as if he could
go no farther, to the southernmost tip of the United States. He was looking
for home, something that in this country in those times perhaps no longer
existed.

"*Ninety-two in the Shade* was written from a pretty druggy consciousness,"
McGuane says. "It's more in the language than the events. It reflects the fact
that I felt I was in some sweeping cultural change in this country. I wasn't
really a hippie—I didn't want to make a journey to India or get stoned all
day—but at the same time I was somehow or other one of the dissident
elements in the society and I knew something drastic had changed. It was
in the tone of things, the voice of things, the kind of disconnectedness of
lives against a background of connected lives—the lives of our parents and
grandparents." For Thomas Skelton, as for his creator, Thomas McGuane,

connection could not be found in a family whose undercurrents of insanity became an inherited short circuit. Nor could it be found in the love of a woman, because experiencing and accepting infidelity had become the rule rather than the exception. Like McGuane, who was an avid fisherman and part-time fishing guide in Florida for several years, Skelton sought a purchase on sanity on the tidal flats of the Florida Keys by developing what McGuane calls "high specific skills" in a world where natural science and purity might provide respite from an age that had itself lost its hold. "I hated mellowness," says McGuane. "Mellowness is still my red flag."

With *Ninety-two in the Shade* Thomas McGuane seemed to suggest that there was an alternative to mellowness. Threatened with death if he went through with his plans to guide, Thomas Skelton applied the force of what McGuane calls "his metallic extremist view of the world," a kind of personal gallantry in an era of broad moral generalizations. He guided and was killed for it, "and the question of his courage and conviction was answered."

But life does not always imitate art, and for Thomas McGuane the path out of the quicksand would not be so well defined. He would have to reconcile the hallucinatory times, a family he could not come to terms with, and his own extreme metallic views.

"When my father drank he would get very nasty about my work," McGuane says. "He would ask me, 'Who do you think you are, Ernest Hemingway?' And I would answer, 'Ah, no, I'm a little better than *that*.' Well, then he'd really go through the ceiling."

Thomas McGuane's first novel, *The Sporting Club*, published in 1969 when he was twenty-nine years old, established him as an important young writer. The *Nation* called him "original and interesting." His second novel, *The Bushwhacked Piano*, published in 1971, won the Richard and Hinda Rosenthal Foundation Award of the American Academy and Institute of Arts and Letters. *Ninety-two in the Shade*, published in 1973, was nominated for the National Book Award, and because of the book McGuane was hailed as "brilliant" and "a genius." He was compared to Camus, Hemingway, Faulkner. But critical literary acclaim is an especially tenuous star in a country where stars burn out as quickly as they rise. From the brilliance of *Ninety-two in the Shade* McGuane would reenter the movie industry (*The Sporting Club* had been made into what he calls a "very bad" movie), and a succession of personal crises would test his hold on survival.

The dedication to McGuane's new novel, *Nobody's Angel*, which will be published by Random House in February, reads: "This book is for my beloved wife Laurie, still there when the storm passed." Laurie, thirty-three, is his third wife and the sister of singer Jimmy Buffett. She is a dark-haired, tawny-skinned beauty with a compact, athletic figure and a rich southern laugh. "She's been the solidest thing in my life," says McGuane. "I hate to use those other folks for comparison, but you know actresses are always announcing how personally strong they are. Laurie never makes that announcement, but for absolute on-the-ground strength I mean she *is* strong. She's strong to the point where sometimes it scares me. She can face and handle anything. She can handle *me*, and I have proven in the past to be quite unhandleable. As the cutting horse people say, 'The others would need to pack a lantern to light her way.' "

They met six years ago at a time when he was known locally, in Key West, as "Captain Berserko." It was one of those off-center scenes that might appear in a McGuane novel. He was lying on the floor of a bar in Key West. He had no idea who she was when they were introduced, but when he heard her melodic southern drawl he had a drunken fantasy of being whisked away and cared for in her stately mansion. His first words to her were: "Please marry me." When he learned she did not have a mansion, McGuane looked up from the floor, only mildly disappointed. "Well, that's okay," he said. "Will you marry me anyway?"

"Keep her away from that person. Keep her away from Captain Berserko," became a standard refrain among Laurie's Key West friends, and she and McGuane were chaperoned with a kind of chastity-belt invincibility. But, as he says, "One night about three o'clock in the morning the last chaperone just couldn't keep up anymore. We finally wore 'em out, and then we made our deal. It was the best deal I ever made in my life."

They were married two years later, and their "deal" together in Montana has provided McGuane with the handhold he has always sought in his life and in his literature, a handhold a generation seeks with him. Like all survivors McGuane has learned to live by certain codes and within a certain structure. He and Laurie have immersed themselves in their family, in the horses they raise, and in the cutting horse pen where they compete, not as a hobby but with what has been described as McGuane's "quantum energy level." A consummate sportsman, he believes proficiency is not enough—one must be the best. He has applied this conviction to all his pursuits—from fishing to hunting to steer roping, all of which are chronicled in a collection of McGuane's sporting essays, *An Outside Chance*, published in 1980.

"The reason I'm passionate about developing specific skills is that it's quite natural for me to get lost in my thoughts and become just a goofy, babbling daydreamer, which I will spend half my life doing anyway. It's a little like backing away from the mirror. You can't get all wrapped up in your fantasies with the idea that whatever trickles out is all you're going to bring to the world. You can't get on a cutting horse with that attitude. I faced the fact some time ago that I am a complete nut and it wouldn't be enough for me to amuse myself, to entertain myself. I have to go out and get extra good at things to counter effect the fact that there are a lot of real whirling fragments of chaos and regrets in my mind. It's an almost pharmaceutical approach to staying sane."

It was five years between the publication of *Ninety-two in the Shade* and the publication of *Panama* in 1978. "I just didn't feel anything happening for a long time," McGuane says. "I just didn't have a point of view, except I felt things were going downhill like lava that's just ten degrees short of solidifying. It's moving all right, but what is it?"

If the times were vague and seemed to be creeping downhill, McGuane's personal life was in a free fall. It was during this five-year period that he went to Hollywood. He wrote the screenplay for the film *Rancho Deluxe* and during the filming embarked upon a widely publicized romance with actress Elizabeth Ashley. Then he wrote and directed the film version of *Ninety-two in the Shade*, which was shot on location in Key West. "I looked at it and I said, 'I think I'll just go ahead and go through the whole thing. I'll see what the whole deal is, and I'll direct a movie, and I'll screw up, and I'll go to the premieres. I'll do the interviews and I'll show up for the press parties. I'll do it all instead of being this meek guy on the back burner who says, "Here's the script; I hope you like it." ' Well, of course, that got me in all kinds of trouble, some of which I brought on myself. I have some pretty good friends who were around when I was making *Ninety-two* and they said I was insufferable; I'm sure they're right. The only excuse I can make is I think when you live in that world, you get a little remote, a little arrogant, and a little crazy. I was very happily and stably married the first time, and I don't think it's absolutely coincidental that my marriage ended that year."

The physical, mental, and chemical abuses of Hollywood, the disintegration of a fourteen-year marriage to his first wife, Becky, and a stormy one-year marriage to actress Margot Kidder (whom he had met during the making of *Ninety-two*)—from it all came *Panama,* McGuane's most personal novel. It is the story of a man who hit bottom but was resilient enough to take a slight bounce.

McGuane says, "I'm so proud of *Panama,* which was far and away my most unsuccessful book. It almost ruined my ability to make a deal, a good deal. But there's a Castro line I'm always quoting: 'History will absolve me.' I hate to get into that my-baby-orphan syndrome about my books, but I know that compared to others I busted a gut on *Panama;* I know that it's written in blood."

The bloody creative process expended on *Panama* was met with an equally bloody reception by the critics. Hollywood has never been considered a dignified destination for a serious writer, and those who go rarely survive the trip. "It has to do with the idea that I had sold out," McGuane says, "that I was this glittery show-biz type who was going back to literature to show the po' folk I could still do it. I had just been in one too many gossip column situations. But I think it was a little implausible that people got so *enraged* that I went off and worked in the movies for a while. Quite a bit of it is material envy on the part of the reviewers. I'd be in great shape in terms of my reputation if, instead of going to Hollywood, I'd just stayed home and gotten strung out on heroin. They'll accept that—murder, heroin—just fine, but they will not put up with this Hollywood business; the reason is they know you're getting some dough to go, and they can't stand that."

Chester Hunnicutt Pomeroy, the hero of *Panama,* burned out by overnight fame and fortune, is unable to acknowledge the existence of his father and doomed to lose his love, Catherine, forever—situations mirrored by McGuane's own life. "In many ways Catherine became Laurie," he says, "and I know that there is a specific emotional power in the ending because I went through the hero's loss imaginatively as I wrote the book. I thought I was going to lose her. I was choking and typing with one finger as I closed in on what I thought was the inevitable." Just as *Panama* reflected McGuane's personal collapse, it also reflected the final death throes of the sixties and seventies, what he calls "the dark side of the moon of *Ninety-two in the Shade.*"

"The feeling behind *Panama* is that there is something very harmful, very sick, very diseased and injured about living on a totally exacerbated, narcissistic, egotistical performance basis. In a funny way it's rock-and-roll book. What started out as entertainment, which is all rock and roll ever was—not civilization, not culture, just entertainment—gradually became the idea that we've got to run around and act as if our statements and point of view are quite final instead of just reciprocity, which had been sufficient for centuries. You have your point of view, but you *wait* for a reply. You're in the world with a lot of other people. The end product of putting on a T-shirt that has Zig Zag or Free Huey on it and turning yourself into a road sign is that your mind, which has a natural forward motion, ends up being this gear with all the teeth worn out of it, just spinning. That was the idea behind *Panama*—that people were absolutely mashed up against the mirror, to the point where you were either going to go through it and the broken glass would kill you, or you were going to back off and look around the room."

At the end of *Panama* Chester Pomeroy stepped back and "took a look around the room" by acknowledging the father he had denied: " 'You know who I am,' [his father] said quietly. 'Can't you say hello?'. . . He just watched me say the word, and after that either of us could go, knowing there was more to be said and time to say it." For McGuane it was a step toward survival as well. "In a way I see it as an optimistic novel. He started by laying down one little brick, and he had the rest of his life to build on it."

It is 5:30 A.M. sharp, and dark, cold, and drizzling outside when I arrive at the McGuanes' door to ride with them to a cutting horse contest in Billings. When Tom McGuane lets me in the house he is dressed only in boxer shorts. He moves into the kitchen in his long, loping, slightly pigeon-toed stride, chattering away in that odd early-morning twilight-zone consciousness. "I woke up thinking about theme parks," he says. "I was thinking that Hugh Hefner or Bob Guccione or one of those guys should open a theme park, you know, something along the lines of Disneyland. They could call it Land o' Wee Wee!" He giggles and pops a beer. The horses are loaded into the trailer in the dark with a good deal of confusion. By the time we get on the road the sun is trying hard to create a dawn in the rainy gloom. Another car hugs our rear bumper, a situation that causes McGuane to discourse frequently and vituperatively. "I will *never* understand these Montana drivers," he says. "There can be two cars on a hundred-mile stretch of road, and one just *has* to ride the bumper of the other. They're not interested in passing. It's like their car wants to screw our car!"

"Ozzie, stop it!" Laurie says with a burst of laughter, slapping his shoulder.

"Remember in the fifties we always used to talk about pet peeves," McGuane says. "Well, I'll tell you my *real* pet peeve: Erma Bombeck. You know, she has her own television show now? I can be lying in bed in the morning and I'll hear her voice and I will surge out of bed and dive across the room, clawing for the off button."

In Billings, with the horses unloaded and saddled, Tom and Laurie are clearly in their element. They warm the horses up, chatting with their cutting friends in an indecipherable technical jargon.

Cutting is a superbly refined sport, as much an art form as a sport. Put simply, the rider chooses a cow from a herd of perhaps fifteen, cuts it out, and then must control it, preventing it from returning to the herd. It requires intense concentration, perfect control, and subtle nuances—a "marriage" between horse and rider.

"It takes you out of your mind and makes you healthy," says McGuane. Watching him perform on his roan gelding, Lucky Bottom 79 ("Roany" to McGuane), one sees all his artistic and physical talents focused in a two-and-a-half-minute time span that gives no quarter to frivolous thoughts. Horse and rider move slowly and with the utmost gentleness into the herd to avoid scattering the cattle. They choose their cow and ease it away from the others. The herd closes in behind as the isolated cow faces them, its natural impulse to find a way back to the throng. McGuane's horse lowers his head and locks on the cow, his front feet forward and slightly splayed. His attitude is more like that of a bird dog than a horse, and when the cow suddenly darts to the left, wheels, and then moves back to the right, Roany tracks him with short precise dance steps and dime-tight turns, his eyes never leaving the cow. McGuane's shoulders are slightly bowed and his lanky frame shifts in perfect sync with his horse. Together they control the cow in motion as fine as crafted prose.

"This new novel," McGuane says, "combines my acquired and hopefully worked-for sense of having a place I want in terms of home with a view of someone who's born to it in shattered circumstances and can't stay." *Nobody's Angel*, set in contemporary Montana where McGuane has lived for fourteen years, is the story of Patrick Fitzpatrick, an ex-army tank driver who has been stationed in Germany and has returned to take his place on his family's ranch. "It is a book I thought had to be written with real solid familial feeling for the place the character's living in. It couldn't just be cobbled together with

observed realities and study. I had to have that feeling, and it took that long
to get it. I had to put a couple kids through school before I could write this."

The book was three years in the writing; in many ways it is his most
complex and ambitious novel to date—and in many ways his most romantic.
"I wrote it," he says, "when I was under the spell of a lot of nineteenth-
century English novelists—Brontë and Jane Austen. I wanted to get into a
more romantic frame of mind than male novelists are usually able to do."

It's a tragic, ghostly story that develops a theme prominent in McGuane's
life and fiction—a family fractured by missed connections, death, and insanity. For Patrick Fitzpatrick this fracture is an unrelenting curse that stalks and
destroys even the redeeming hope of love.

Many people who have read the manuscript believe *Nobody's Angel* may be
McGuane's breakthrough book. "With *Ninety-two*," he says, "I tried to invent
a style, which I think I did. With *Nobody's Angel* I tried to improve it and give
it the benefit of my age and increased experience, carefully comb it free of
cheap effects and leave something which had some real dignity. It is meant,"
he adds with a smile, "to bring gallantry back to my work"—and, one
suspects, to his life.

"My family's a wreck," McGuane says. "My father's been dead for six years.
My mother died this fall in Key West. My sister had problems with drugs and
died in her twenties. My brother's been under psychiatric care for fifteen
years. So I don't have that western family view of the world. I'd like to have
one. I'm trying to make one." He and Laurie have recently moved to a new
ranch, a splendid place abutting the Absaroka Range. McGuane says proudly
that from his place he "can get on a horse and ride all the way to Wyoming
without cutting a road.

"I'm in a real happy era of my life. I got my first pair of reading glasses
last week with a tremendous sigh of relief that I had survived into my forties.
My kids like me, and now I still want to make money, but I want to do it a little more circumspectly. One of the delightful things about hitting forty is
that there are a certain number of windmills you quit fighting. Once you
learn your trade it's nice to start concentrating on your family and friends
and the things you truly like to do. You don't have to be in an *in extremis*
posture all the time."

McGuane was in Hollywood recently to write rock-and-roll music with his
friend Warren Zevon, whom he considers a fine musician as well as a fine
songwriter. Although the life style of rock-and-roll artists seems to recall the

dark sinkholes of *Panama* days, McGuane now has the overview of a man who has been there and memorized the way back. He and Zevon, who is renowned for excesses of his own, have performed small, mutual rescue missions for each other; they are both fond of Ernest Hemingway's admonition to F. Scott Fitzgerald: "Of course you're a rummy . . . most good writers are. But good writers always come back. Always."

Robert Redford was recently in Montana to discuss with McGuane a film version of *Nobody's Angel*. McGuane has kept a hand in the movies. He wrote the screenplays for *The Missouri Breaks* and *Tom Horn*. "Strictly speaking, the book business has never supported me and my family," he says. "This idea of having sold out is preposterous. It's an essentially negative point of view of what a writer is to begin with. It implies that he is somebody who is continually ready to go kiss ass and fall to his knees in the face of these sort of charismatic business people who dominate the movies."

Yet McGuane will approach the carrot Hollywood dangles before its writers with a certain acquired wariness. "I know now what the movies can do for you and what they can't do," he says. "It's pretty irresistible for a while. You babble away on your Olympia portable, and everything you write they say, 'Great, fabulous, we don't even have to look at it.' And they pay you these enormous sums of money, and you buy your ranch and you fix the kids' teeth. The price *you* pay is not the weeks it took or months, the price is a psychic price and a physical price because you end up being strung out somehow or other. We didn't learn from Fitzgerald. You have to fight the fight yourself, and if I seem cocky now it's because I've been through it."

Literature will always be "the most important thing" for McGuane. "I've just decided I love it. I'm so happy when I'm writing, and everything else goes better. The kids like me, Laurie likes me, my drinking drops by about two-thirds. It's a beautiful, beautiful, beautiful trade. I just feel so lucky to be a novelist. I don't want to wake up ten years from now saying, 'You got to be one and then you pissed it away.' I do not want to be a victim of that particular regret."

With *Panama* McGuane learned a lesson the critics eventually teach to all novelists. "They really blew all my gaskets," he says. "I don't think they can get to me anymore. Someone once said to Faulkner, 'I understand you don't read your reviews anymore.' He said, 'That's right.' 'Well, why don't you?' He replied, 'Because I read them when I was young and they hurt my feelings so much I just didn't want to do it anymore.' Well, they really hurt my feelings that last time out. They hurt 'em bad." McGuane is cautiously optimistic about the reception he can expect for *Nobody's Angel*. "I think they got their rocks off on *Panama*," he says with a laugh.

McGuane is even cautiously optimistic about an age he once described as going from "bad to worse." He says, "The thing that was perpetrated in the sixties was, Don't trust anyone over thirty, the pigs, the man—these mass executionerlike judgments about whole halves of the country. I don't think people think that way anymore. I think an eighteen-year-old might really like his mailman now. He's not simply the uniformed pig from the government who delivers letters. I'm optimistic in the sense that people are beginning to remember the traditions and the myths and the heroes of this country. It's great when popular culture comes up with a character like Indiana Jones."

If a peace has followed the storm in Thomas McGuane's life, he remains realistic about living with an artistic consciousness that has always been volatile and must always harbor its share of demons. "Basically, as a writer you're going to be a substantive abuser and an economically screwed-up character one way or another," he says. "One of the things I'm starting to get out of the Hemingway letters is that you don't become a born-again Christian over it, you don't join a monastery or quit drinking forever. You fight your fight like you would a brush fire. Don't rush in and say, 'I've had enough of brush fires! Cancel that brush fire!' It doesn't go away that easily.

"I still have storms. But they're more residual storms now. I have teenagers, and that's a storm. I have to watch my drinking—that can be a storm. But none of it's crazy. It's not where you don't know where the steering wheel or brake is. I see it now as a basic struggle, struggling *for* something. I'm struggling to buy this ranch. I'm struggling to have a family seat, a place that this fragmented family of mine will call home even when they're all grown up and gone."

A Conversation with
Thomas McGuane

Liz Lear / 1984

From *Shenandoah: The Washington and Lee University Review* 36/2 (1986),
pp. 12–21. Reprinted with permission of Lynn Leech, managing editor of
Shenandoah, and Liz Lear.

Thomas McGuane was born in Wyandotte, Michigan, on December 11, 1939.
He received a B.A. degree from Michigan State in 1962, and his M.F.A. from
Yale University in 1965. A Stegner Fellowship in writing followed at Stanford.

McGuane's books include: *The Sporting Club*, 1969; *The Bushwhacked Piano*,
1971; *Ninety-two in the Shade*, 1973; *Panama*, 1978; *An Outside Chance*, 1980;
Nobody's Angel, 1982; *Something to Be Desired*, 1984. His screenplays are:
Rancho Deluxe, 1973; *The Missouri Breaks*, 1976; *Tom Horn*, 1979.

McGuane lives mostly on a ranch in Montana with his wife Laurie, and
various children: his, hers, and theirs. In prosperous years he spends some of
the winter in Key West, where he keeps a sailboat. He is an accomplished and
avid sportsman, with a preference for hunting, fishing, sailing, and riding
cutting horses, which he also raises. Looking every inch the rancher/sports-
man, he is tall, dark, and ruggedly handsome.

This conversation took place in a house in Key West that McGuane had
rented from fellow writer Bill Wright. It was a warm tropical night in March
of 1984. We sat around a dining room table piled with books and the just
completed manuscript of *Something to Be Desired*. Through the open French
doors a lighted pool glimmered and the soft breeze carried the floral scent of
something nameless but sweet. From an adjacent room, the clear young
inquiring voice of McGuane's daughter Anne occasionally interrupted the
story being read to her.

LL: I have always been intrigued with what attracts creative people to certain
places. I wonder what or who brought them here and what makes them stay.
Why are you in Key West?

TM: I first came to Key West as a boy with my father to go fishing. When I decided to come back here as an adult, it was because I associated the island with writers, reading, and writing.

American writers love exotic atmospheres, and yet really don't want to live outside of the country. Key West is one of those places that allow them to have it both ways. It's a southerly town without the burden of southern history. It's intrinsically a nice place. I enjoy the ambience of a place where Spanish is spoken. I like that fecund smell that the island has. I love to be out on the ocean: for better or worse, I'm still a sportsman and the ocean is one of the last frontiers where we can live in a civilized way next to that great wilderness.

LL: Did you always want to be a writer? When did you start?
TM: Yes. I always wanted to be a writer and I began when I was ten—at least to try.

LL: Did you ever do any other work?
TM: I never really made a living, of course. I worked as a boy and young man at odd jobs, the same kind of things other kids did. I worked at a gas station. I worked as a cowboy—cowboy is too big a word for it: I worked on a ranch in an unskilled way. Then I went off to school and was just hell-bent to write, to read and write, and that's it.

LL: I have just finished an intense McGuane re-read. I found your books just as fresh and vital now as they were at the time of publication. Most first books are supposedly heavily autobiographical. Is this true of your first book, *The Sporting Club*, and in reality did such a place exist?
TM: Absolutely not to the first part of your question. There was a club that was loosely the physical model, but in reality it was a very innocent little club: hunting and fishing. Quite a few Michigan people belonged to it, as did my family. I had very happy times there. I invented a "ship of fools" type environment—of course, the real thing never was that.

The Sporting Club reflected a lot of literary preoccupations of those times: the interest in comic writing and black humor. There was a great wish for serious comic literature in those years. I know I craved it tremendously. I read people like Evelyn Waugh, Kingsley Amis, J. P. Donleavy, and Terry Southern. My book reflected that atmosphere, plus my own interest in rivalry and my morbid but comic fascination with violence.

I was intrigued with the Stanton-type character, a person who has cut the moorings and is really going too far; the madman fool so wonderfully portrayed by Marlowe, Cervantes, Gogol, and Melville, who have turned their world upside-down and tried to reassemble themselves. The only way I could see to handle it without getting a long face was to see its comic possibilities. I don't think the truth is diminished because one finds it funny.

LL: *Panama,* I feel, was actually about six years ahead of its time. I found it even more disturbing the second time around, possibly because I came to it with more understanding. Reading the book I felt made me privy to the dark recesses of someone else's mind. It was both exciting and frightening. I was glad I had the experience but I was relieved when it was over. Are you relieved that those times are over, and in writing the book did you release yourself from a lot of psychological burdens, guilts, and hurts?
TM: Yes, in both instances. I'm glad that era is over for me. One transmutes some of that into fiction and gets a form of release from doing so. It's funny, Bill Wright has a copy of *Panama* here, and I was reading in it today. I haven't done that in a long time.

For a couple of reasons I still have pride in that book. The personal era, which may or may not have been shared by others, was announced in *Ninety-two in the Shade* and drew its final curtain in *Panama*: the hope of certain things as announced in *Ninety-two* and the despair for its accomplishment as announced in *Panama*. I'm excited that in two thirds of a decade one could examine the rise and fall of a dream, and that's what those two books do. Even if that's only known to me, I'm completely happy that I got it down.

I find it interesting that you think the book was ahead of its time. It was roundly attacked when it came out. It also received two of the best reviews I ever got, one in the *Village Voice* and the other in the *New Yorker,* so it had people who felt strongly and positively about it. You know, it's never been out of print and it seems to gain momentum and a wider readership all the time. I would say that with the almost epidemic spread of cocaine throughout American society, that book is going to seem scriptural to more and more people.

LL: I also saw a lesson in the book which I hope some will heed: don't go down that road too far because it only leads to despair.
TM: It doesn't really turn on drugs, it turns on egotism, stardom, or cocaine, whatever it is that keeps you from looking out and seeing the world and the

people around you. That's the thing that will get them in the end, just as it got Chester.

LL: You mention a writer friend in the book who provides a little sanity and good advice. At one point he says, "I'm getting off the rock. I love the rock but it's a bad rock." In real life you apparently shared his sentiments. In fact you sold your house and left town. Was this character based on Jim Harrison, to whom you dedicated the book?
TM: No. The burnt-out writer with little skeletal hands sitting watching the hotel burn, that's me. Pomeroy is another part of me, it was one part of me talking to another.

LL: What about Don, the guardian angel. Was he another alter ego?
TM: Yes, this was my shadow.

LL: Why did you dedicate the book to Jim Harrison?
TM: Because Jim, as you know, is one of my oldest friends.

LL: You know, I really can hear him saying "get off the rock, I love it, but you've got to get off it."
TM: Peculiarly, I think Jim is one of the people who didn't "get" the book. I dedicated it to him, and do you know he never acknowledged that. It was years before I even knew whether he had read it or not.

LL: We all worry about the threat of nuclear war and the possible annihilation of the human race. In one of your books, I think *Ninety-two,* your hero says, "God, if they will only leave the ocean alone I can handle anything," and, "who on earth, slipping it to a truly desirable woman, can seriously interest himself in the notion that the race is doomed." As a real survivor, Tom, do you honestly believe that?
TM: The language is comic of course, but within that, I acknowledge that in human questions there are orders of magnitude. On one hand it seems mathematically predictable that we are going to blow ourselves up and yet part of us insists that we will wriggle out of it somehow.

LL: So you see a glimmer of hope?
TM: There is ample evidence for continuance. In some perverse way we don't buy the doom bit, maybe that in itself becomes a self-fulfilling prophecy and we will survive.

LL: Do you revise as you go along?
TM: I revise as I go along. Sometimes I think I write so that I can revise. Revision is two-thirds of the effort.

LL: Do you write every day on a set schedule?
TM: No. When the project has come to life for me, then I write every day. Then there are long unhappy periods when I don't write every day, these are unquestionably times to be avoided. Nothing goes well for me if I'm not writing.

LL: Do you keep a notebook or diary?
TM: Yes. I scribble things down, notions, things I think will be of great utility. They never are.

LL: Do you ever suffer from writer's block and if so how do you overcome it?
TM: Yes. I think all writers do. I overcome it by forcing myself to adhere to regular work practices. Showing up to work at the same place and time every day, sooner or later this works for me; but for a time there it is painful.

LL: Some writers find starting the day confronted with an empty page very disconcerting; they will always try to leave half a page with which to start the new day. How do you handle this?
TM: I try to leave off on a good note with the feeling that I've left something living there that will still be alive the next day. I try not to leave on a note of discouragement.

LL: Who are your favorite writers?
TM: I'm such an eclectic reader that I can't give a fast answer to that. In the past, my heros have been Twain, Stendhal, Aristophanes, and Stephen Crane. Among the contemporaries, of course, I read my friends, Jim Harrison, an Indian writer named Jim Welch—I'm talking about my favorites now— Robert Stone, and Phil Caputo. I don't want to leave anyone out, but when I'm writing a book I forget everything . . . Walker Percy, Norman Mailer, Styron, and Raymond Carver.

LL: What about new ones, the young ones coming up, any that give you hope for the future of literature?
TM: It's funny, the ones that seem young and coming up, like Raymond Carver, are close to my age. Barry Hannah, Raymond Carver, and Jayne Ann

Phillips, they seem to me to be the newer voices coming up that I'm most excited about.

LL: Do you enjoy the company of other writers?
TM: Immensely.

LL: Have other writers been supportive of your work or do you sense any feelings of competitiveness?
TM: Yes, they have been supportive *and* competitive—yes, but mostly in an invigorating way, not in an abrasive one.

LL: Flaubert said that we must love each other in our art the way mystics love each other in God. Do you think this sentiment exists today, or indeed do you think it ever has?
TM: I don't think it exists today and I suspect that it never did. I think that writers, in so far as they feel beleaguered within society, have a sort of comradeship that disappears when they are in a situation where they are entirely within their own world. For example, when we are in Montana we are all madly in love with each other because there a writer isn't a highly esteemed individual. When we are in a place that is writer-dense, like Key West or New York, we tend to have our fangs out for each other to a degree, like any other competitive group. Every one wants to be acknowledged in that strange kind of writer's pecking order. Maybe this statement is a bit strong; I think it's both true and not true.

LL: Do you think it's possible for a person to write like an angel and yet on every other level be a despicable person?
TM: It's highly possible and in many instances a fact.

LL: If you had the opportunity to sit down with any writer either living or dead and discuss his or her writing and yours, who would that be?
TM: Socrates.

LL: Are you a social creature?
TM: It's kind of a moth and candle thing. I have spells when I feel quite social, then I'm overwhelmed and exasperated very suddenly and unpredictably, and want to get away from people entirely and think. I find that

I can't get much thinking done in an intense social situation. I get almost hunger jitters to get off and figure things out. I don't think I'm unusual in that way. As I become more focused on absolutely what I want, in terms of my friends, my family, and my work, I've become more impatient with things that don't fall into that category. I have figured out that life is short and I have a lot of work to do, and things that I want to do with my family. I often get maddened when I'm derailed unnecessarily by a not particularly interesting social situation.

LL: Someone once said that we go through life with a diminishing portfolio of enthusiasms.
TM: F. Scott Fitzgerald. I'm not sure, but I think it's either from that nauseating thing he wrote called *The Crack-Up* or his letters. Scott Fitzgerald went through life with a diminishing portfolio of enthusiasms. As an Irishman I recognize that as a sort of racial failure of the Irish, which is the horrible disappointment that youth passes and one's dreams have not been fulfilled. I think the Irish are very prone to that, and the drinking Irish, the absolute worst. I don't think there's a more pusillanimous document in American literature than Fitzgerald's *The Crack-Up*. The gist of it is, "you all let me down and I'm going to be pathetic because you did this to me and I'll do it on cue."
   I think it's impossible not to go through life without some diminished enthusiasms, in the sense that they are diminished in their quality. Obviously, one discovers things you don't want to do any more, so you stop doing them; presumably, the ones that remain, you do with greater skill, concentration, and ability.

LL: In one of your books, I forget which one, you used that Fitzgerald quote.
TM: I might once have thought of that line with approval. I probably did. I now think we are supposed to rise above that. I mean a forty-four year old man can't wander around among his friends and family and tell everyone how disappointed in life he is. I think that's terrible.

LL: I get the distinct impression from your books that they are more than a little autobiographical. Are they?
TM: No. I'm using myself insofar as I think I'm good material, things that have happened to me or things I've seen, but I really use those as points of departure. We all start out with an image, something always catches the eye,

the mind, it's usually something that has happened to us, something out of our own lives and it might sustain us for half a book, but the art is there to be served and we go where that's supposed to go, not where the paltry details of one's life might dictate. I often use things that I've seen, that are true of me, a place to sort of lift the edge of the material so that I can enter.

LL: You are then always aware of the art?
TM: That's part of the job.

LL: Someone said that you share a genius with Celine for seeing the disparate materials of everyday life as a highly organized nightmare. Is this true and do you continue to see things that way?
TM: I think that's a polite way of saying "paranoia." Yes, I think that's true. In the book I'm working on how the narrator reflects that the natural state of the universe isn't heat, but cold. I think we all exist on a very fragile tissue of life and vitality. I've seen a lot of death close up; it can happen instantaneously. Remember last year when Annie was so ill. She was only four years old. The doctors said that one end of the spectrum of what she had was death. She was in perfect health when I left and a week later Laurie telephoned to say, hurry home, Annie's in an oxygen tent. One realizes that you can walk out of a door—or that people you love can disappear like a puff of smoke. We are surrounded with that realization. I believe that very strongly. The other day a group of writers assembled for a photograph; this time next year probably some of them will have gone on to the next world. That's not really paranoia, but at the same time I feel the pressure of it as a day to day reality. I remember the dates when people close to me died as if they were only a few hours ago. A favorite aunt died, then a week later her namesake, my sister, died; ten months later my father died and a short time ago my mother died. In the meantime several friends have died. I don't really feel threatened by a sense of my own mortality, though I suppose we all are to a certain extent. I'm forty-four years old and I'm at the middle or end of my life. I don't know which. I've experienced much and had a lot of years to feel full about. What really bothers me is that the people who haven't had much chance to do things are just as subject to the arbitrary fall of the ax as I am. The sense of all that is a continuing force for me, the idea that we are all on the brink of eternity.

LL: Re-reading your books in quick succession brought to my attention something I might otherwise have missed. There's a rather frightening image that develops from book to book. It starts very subtly in *Bushwhacked Piano*, suddenly it's there and then it's gone, like something seen out of the corner of the eye. You speak of hearing the pad of feet in the darkness downstairs and the sound of dogs or wolves or coyotes drinking out of the toilet bowl. In successive books, there is reference to unseen dogs barking or coyotes howling like some kind of death knell. The climax comes in *Nobody's Angel* with that hideous scene of a house littered with slaughtered and skinned coyotes.

TM: How marvelous! That's very perceptive of you. That was something that crept up on me. I hadn't realized that the man and wolf thing ran so deep in me. I love dogs and I know that they belong to humans, and yet they also belong to the wild, to the jackal side of the world that preys on humans when things fall apart. We have a very deep bond with dogs, but I know that if the bomb drops there will be packs of dogs feeding on our dead, charred bodies. I see this as a powerful image of what happens to our basic hard-won deals when the rest of the planet is falling apart.

LL: It doesn't have any personal psychological significance that culminated in *Nobody's Angel*; something you had finally worked out?

TM: I think it's one of those things one never works out, either it's there or it isn't. Average people like Tio and his coyote hunting friends in *Nobody's Angel* turned on the dogs of the world before disaster struck. They anticipated Armageddon.

LL: I have never thought of dogs in that context, pigs maybe. I remember reading that pigs were a common sight, rooting among the dead on the battlefields of the Civil War.

TM: I read a wonderful book last year by Franklin Russell called *The Hunting Animal*. There are some passages in it about hyenas that are just unbelievable; you recognize the dog family. Packs of hyenas will pull down an antelope on the plains; they are complete feeding machines. The minute they have slowed the creature to anything like a stop, they begin to feed; they don't kill. The antelope just stands there gazing around at this mob of ravenous creatures who are literally eating it before it has had time to die.

People love dogs and dogs love people. Until people absolutely drop the ball; when dogs realize people have lost civilization, then they will become wild again and feed on people.

An Interview with Tom McGuane

Kay Bonetti / 1985

From *Missouri Review* 9.1 (1985–86), pp. 75–99. Reprinted with permission of American Audio Prose Library, Inc. All rights reserved.

Interviewer: Can you tell us a little about your life and upbringing?

McGuane: I was raised in the middle West, in Michigan, but my parents were both Boston-area Irish. Except when we were in school, we were always back there in Massachusetts in the big kind of noisy, Irish households of the forties and fifties. My parents were upward-striving, lower middle class people who had a facility for English. They both were English majors in college. My father was a scholarship student at Harvard; my mother went to a little school called Regis. Books and talk and language in general were a big part of growing up for me. My family was not excited about me wanting to be a writer; they thought that was very unrealistic.

Interviewer: It is difficult to support yourself as a serious writer.

McGuane: I think any writer, even an unserious writer, has a bad time of it; a pulp writer or a sold-out writer or a hack has a hard time making a living. To understand the economics of writing is to know that writing and publishing and acquiring some kind of esteem in your community of peers is merely a key to your finances. For example, prestigious writers whose reputations are confined to the literary all live pretty well. They are getting grants, and teaching jobs. I would say the people I've seen who teach writing are underworked. Other writers, like me, have been able to find work in film or journalism. There's always a way to get along. I think it's inevitable for writers to sort of feel sorry for themselves and to feel sorrier the more serious they perceive themselves to be.

Interviewer: In the introduction to last year's summer fiction edition of *Esquire,* Rust Hills claimed that the academy has become the patronage

53

system for writers . . . and was defending it, moreover. What did you think of that?

McGuane: I thought it was silly. I think patronage, especially homogenous patronage of the kind that academic writers receive, is exceedingly dangerous and leads to trafficking in reputations.

Interviewer: What do you mean by homogenous?

McGuane: The colleges are, to a great degree, alike in their form of protection. I think it's good for writers to be in the world, not talking to the converted in English departments day after day—scrambling for survival, having to talk to illiterate neighbors. Obviously mine is a minority voice; this point of view is going to lose. The camp that Rust Hills describes is obviously the camp of sweeping victory.

Interviewer: Because the writers who teach are living pretty well . . . financially?

McGuane: When I've been on campus I notice that everybody seems to be getting along better than ranchers in Montana are. There is great security there, the kind of security that the civil service or the post office provides, and it goes hand in hand with complacency.

Interviewer: I take it you feel that this situation has a measurable impact on the kind of writing that is being done.

McGuane: Well, you get these books like the latest Alison Lurie book that is built around sabbaticals. I think John Barth has suffered from being around colleges. To me the most interesting work that Barth did was the earliest work, before he knew what was going to happen to him—the *Floating Opera* and *The End of the Road*—books which I think he now kind of repudiates. His stuff lately has been less lifelike, less exciting.

Interviewer: So you disagree with Hills's notion.

McGuane: I think Rust Hills needed to make a case for the situation now and I think that he felt he needed to overstate it. I think Rust and *Esquire* are excited about making categories, the new realism or the revival of fantasy, the kind of categories they come up with for the purposes of pigeonholing writers.

Interviewer: So you feel that it's the type of writing that working within the academy encourages that has the negative effect; you aren't saying that because somebody teaches he is going to end up just writing about other teachers . . .

McGuane: No . . . no . . . I'm not saying that, but I do think that kind of life, that kind of support, is going to limit the access to information and material writers might otherwise have, obviously. I think maybe the best writer we have had in a long time is Saul Bellow and being a chronic teacher hasn't hurt him at all.

Interviewer: So there are obviously exceptions to the rule.

McGuane: There are, yes, but there is also a kind of academic writer who meters out his publications, who measures himself and politicizes against other academic writers, and that writer is of no use to readers. I think the kind of thing Hills describes in that article represents a severing of the connection between writers and readers.

Interviewer: To be fair, we should think of some notable exceptions; one thinks of Stanley Elkin.

McGuane: He scarcely seems like an academic writer in any way. There are writers in the outside world who are vastly more academic than Elkin. But when I think of Norman Mailer in the outside world, or of Walker Percy, I think of more adventurous spirits reporting to us from the whole world rather than one of its hyper-specific laminates. This is a purely personal reaction, but I am just more interested in people who have not gone to campuses.

Interviewer: Your books are full of work, aren't they? And skills? Useful information?

McGuane: Little odds and ends of that sort. Jim Harrison used to needle me because I would hang around the repair bay of a gas station—it really wasn't research. I like to watch people do their thing and I don't care what it is. I like to watch ladies sew, I like to watch people cook, I like to watch people fix cars, I like to watch people commercially fish. I would have to suppress that by some fiat to keep it out of my writing.

Interviewer: At what point did you start thinking of yourself as a writer?

McGuane: Very early, it was really all I have ever wanted to do.

Interviewer: Did your parents ultimately support you?

McGuane: Well, my father had a nice rule—and it's the same ruling I take with my children, to the degree I can afford to do it—he basically took the position he didn't want to argue with me about what I wanted to do. He would support me educationally. I was a premed major, I was a prelaw major, I went to the Yale Drama School. I was finally an English major, but I waffled around knowing that I was free to do that. Going to school kept me writing. Then I got a grant at Stanford and that extended another year and in fact when I finished there, I was publishing.

Interviewer: Do you value the Stegner experience?

McGuane: Not really, no. I value having had the time. I didn't get much out of the Stegner thing; I didn't think he was a good teacher. It was the middle sixties—most of the other writers were thinking that writing was dead and they wanted to march on the electrical engineering building or war contractors; they just weren't interested in literature. I remember Allen Ginsberg coming up in those years and talking to people and finding they hadn't read Ezra Pound and hadn't read Whitman, didn't care, didn't want to know the names. It was an illiterate age and Stanford was just a place to get out of the weather and work on a book.

Interviewer: Is there some particular break that enabled you to start supporting yourself by writing?

McGuane: Well, yes. I had a book on submission to *Dial* for six or eight months and was working pretty closely with them. I was encouraged to think that we were close to being able to publish the book. Then, suddenly from overhead the book was killed by the then editor-in-chief, E. L. Doctorow. It was just completely out of the blue and it was the most complete devastation I ever received. I remember thinking that I was going to snap. I had been writing daily for ten years and I didn't really think I could go on. And then . . . And then I suddenly realized, God, I didn't know how to do anything else. I had had minor menial jobs, but I just didn't really know what else to do. So I kind of holed up and wrote *The Sporting Club* in about six weeks and sent it to Jim Harrison. Then I lit out for Mexico thinking that I would figure out my life down there. While I was down there a cable came to this little town where I was camped out on the beach in a sleeping bag. This Mexican came out—he had a gun strapped on his waist and he came walking down to my camp and he strode right up and I thought, My God, this guy is going to shoot me. I thought I was going to be placed under arrest or something. I was pretty paranoid. He walked up and thrust out his hand and said in bad English, "Congratulations, your book is accepted." We went hooting and drank beer and had a big celebration. So I came back up and even though the book was accepted there was still work to be done on it. I moved to Montana and worked on the book, and when it came out it did pretty well. Then it was sold to the movies and was made into the worst movie in history.

Interviewer: What was the name of it?
McGuane: *The Sporting Club.*

Interviewer: Never saw it.
McGuane: If you blinked, it was gone. But I was paid for it. I had been accustomed to living on two to four thousand dollars a year and to suddenly get a movie check, man, I was looking at a decade's writing. All of a sudden I realized that if I did nothing but fill up scraps of paper I was gonna be a writer for a while.

Interviewer: The only real money in fiction now seems to be movie money. I know several writers who have managed to buy their first house because of their movie options.
McGuane: Well, I'm one of those writers for sure. . . . I came out and bought a little ranch here and then it quadrupled in value. I resold it and bought another ranch out east of town and resold it. That turned into my land base and that's what my security derives from now. But when I look around I see these kind of writers—I won't name names—who published one exquisite book of short stories twenty years ago, and have had pretty remunerative academic jobs for twenty years on the basis of that one tiny volume. I would say those writers have made a lot of money off their books.

Interviewer: I hadn't really thought about it that way.
McGuane: Look what you have to do to get a comparable teaching job on the straight and narrow road: get a doctorate, fight your way through the MLA conventions, hope to get the nod from some backwater school, fight your way for tenure. I think writers have it very easy in colleges. Don't you think so?

Interviewer: In a way, you could say that. And it is unfortunate, because being a good teacher is one skill, being a writer is another. They are not necessarily the same thing at all.

McGuane: I spoke to that issue at a writers' conference. I said, teaching ideally requires considerable pedagogical abilities and just because you're not making a living entirely by your writing does not mean you have to become a teacher. I've had some miserable writer teachers; they thought they were purely totemic value sitting at the head of a class monosyllabically reacting to students' questions.

Interviewer: Yet some writers feel that it was extremely beneficial to have that community of other writers. . . .

McGuane: Oh, I give you that . . . and the Stanford thing was quite interesting that way, the drama school was great that way, but where that was truest for me was as an undergraduate at Michigan State. I had three or four chums there who were really driven to write. Chief among them was Jim Harrison, of course. But there were others of us there, some of whom were very good and didn't make it. We had a really passionate literary situation. It was really beyond anything that I saw thereafter.

Interviewer: I don't think I have ever talked to a writer who didn't agree that writing is a very lonely profession.

McGuane: I don't think loneliness is the word. John Graves said writing is "antilife." I'm forty-five years old, I've been writing full-time since I was sixteen, I've been writing almost every day for thirty years; and as I look back with a degree of resentment, I realize that I literally lifted chunks of my life out for drafts of things, some of which got published and some didn't. And there is no experience to show for it, there is nothing but sitting in front of a legal pad for what now must amount to a third of my life. It's as though that was a hole in my life.

Interviewer: But you have had this friendship with another writer, Jim Harrison, all these years. Has it had an impact on your work?

McGuane: I'm sure we've had an impact on each other's lives and thinking. We've managed to bolster one another in a fairly high view of the mission of writing, so that in lean years and blocked times it still felt that it was kind of a religious commitment. I don't know what writing is seen to be now, but I know that I continue to believe sort of what I believed then; I'm like someone who is intensely and successfully raised as a Catholic or a Lutheran; it just didn't go away from me. And now as I look on a future of freedom from the kinds of worries I used to have, my only vision of excitement is to be able to read and write harder and do what I wanted to do in 1955 or 1956. I am sure that the fact that Harrison and I have been writing back and forth for a quarter of a century almost entirely about writing has been one of the things that keeps that thread intact. Having a handful of writers around the country whose reality is there for you, knowing they are out there, knowing they might get what you are doing, makes you independent a little bit.

Interviewer: Are they the people you write for in a sense of an ideal reader?
McGuane: There are some writers whose opinion really matters to me—who could really hurt my feelings if they said the book was terrible, who could make me excited by liking it. The three or four people whom you respect thinking that you're not a complete fool can really keep you going.

Interviewer: Who else do you want your books to be accessible to? In the sense of Virginia Woolf's "common reader"?
McGuane: Let me wind back a little bit by saying I think that the sort of burnt-earth successes of modernism have left prestigious writing quite inaccessible to normal readers. There used to be a perennial *New Yorker* cartoon where some yahoo from Iowa was standing in front of a painting at the Museum of Modern Art saying, "All I can say is I know what I like" and I think it was meant to show how stupid the average guy is. I actually think that the average guy is right in saying I know what I like. I'm a little bit dour now when it comes to books which are terribly brilliant by some sort of smart-set consensus, but which nobody I know can read.

Interviewer: How important is the language of a novel to you, the joy of words?
McGuane: There is a thrill to be had in language viewed as music, but I think for that tail to wag the dog is a mistake. Obviously there's an infinite mix and there is no right and wrong about it. At this point in my life the writing that I really like has clarity and earned and rendered feeling as its center. Writers who have done that most successfully leave you feeling experientially enlarged, rather than awed or intimidated—those things which have been the basis of the modernist response in writing.

Interviewer: It seems to me that *Nobody's Angel* and *Something to Be Desired* are moving towards a simpler and cleaner style than your earlier work. Do you think anything in the earlier work prepared you for this?

McGuane: I think there has inevitably been some kind of an evolution for me in the rise of emotional content. It's also been a moving away from comedy. I set out to be a comic novelist and that's become not clear to me as time has gone on. Things have happened—you can't live forty-five years without things happening to jar and change you. The biggest change for me was a tremendous uproar in my life during the seventies. My mother, father, and sister died in about thirty months flat. I remember very specifically feeling that it was a watershed, that I would never be the same again after that happened. When you have attended that many funerals that fast, it's very hard to go back to a typewriter and say, "What is my next comic novel?" You simply don't do that. But reviewers think you do. Reviewers say, "Why isn't he still as funny as he was before all those deaths?" Reviewers are endlessly obtuse. And that makes you shrink away from what they represent; it makes you shrink away from publication in a funny way, because you realize there's this dreadful stupor that you are going to have to march through with your latest infant in your arms.

Interviewer: I'm gathering from what you're saying that the "word drunk" style in your earlier work was tied in with the fact that it was comic.

McGuane: Well, yes. I wanted then and will want again to write comic novels. I love comic fiction.

Interviewer: Do you see comic fiction as a tradition and if so, what are some of the elements of it?

McGuane: Good comic writing comes from a very nearly irrational center that stays viable because it is unexplainable. It often disports itself in a kind of charged language. That is to say it is not appropriate to use exactly the same prose style for writing an all-out comedy as it is for writing a rural tragedy. Each book demands its own stylistic answers. At the same time, one has the right to expect a writer to have a style. I don't think a writer has to be as transparent as the phone book. I don't want to be that. I think, though, as you perfect your style you should hit the target on the first shot rather than on the fourth, and a good writer should get a little bit cleaner and probably a little bit plainer as life and the *oeuvre* go on.

Interviewer: But it seems to me that there is a *charged* plainness in your last two books. The simplicity has under it all the skills that went into the others.
McGuane: Oh, I sure hope so. You want something that is drawn like a bow and a bow is a simple instrument.

Interviewer: There is a lot of wit in *Something to Be Desired.* It's sad in some ways but it's also got a satirical edge. Was that intended?
McGuane: It wasn't intended to be satirical, but it was intended to be comic. I wanted to take a piece of crazy venture capitalism and show how desperate a private business really is. For some people getting their backs to the walls and starting a successful business can be as desperate an action as taking drugs. The guy says, "My God, I don't know what I'm going to do, I think I'll open a pizza parlor. My life is at an end, I'm going to start a dry cleaners." That seems to be a wholly American approach to desperation.

Interviewer: It also is pretty funny.
McGuane: It's hilarious. But once you spot it, you can go into a town and all you see is desperation. You see some sad lady with a fashion outlet in downtown Livingston, Montana. You know, the wind is blowing through the town and the town is filled with snow as she is standing behind the plate glass, with a lot of imitation French clothes. What could be more frantic?

Interviewer: Critics talk about you as a comic novelist but always with the implication that this is heavy social comment, social satire and that sort of thing.
McGuane: Well, there was an old Broadway producer who said, "Satire is what closes on Saturday night" and I think he is exactly right. I think satire has as its fatal component an element of meanness. It more or less says, look at what those awful people are doing. I'd never do anything like that, but by pointing them out I hope that you people will change them. Comedy, on the other hand, says, look at the awful things those people are doing. I could be doing the same thing, but for this moment I'm just going to describe it.

Interviewer: It strikes me that you have a lot in common with Mark Twain.
McGuane: I find that hugely flattering. Nothing could please me more. I see him as immersed in a well-loved American milieu, schizophrenically rural

and urban, inclined to bursts of self-pity as the autobiography would suggest and also inclined . . .

Interviewer: In wild and hairy business schemes . . .
McGuane: Wild business schemes which I have been guilty of.

Interviewer: That always failed.
McGuane: I'm a better businessman than he was.

Interviewer: His always failed.
McGuane: And also an element of anger and rage disguised as comedy as in "The Man Who Corrupted Hadleyburg." Some of them are more bitter than anything else and the bad side of Twain is something I identify with, too.

Interviewer: One subject that seems to unify all your books is what happens to people who get hung up on an untested idea.
McGuane: One of the great themes of Irish-American literature, if I can pretend to be Irish-American professionally for a moment, is spoiled romance. Scott Fitzgerald was the master of this and while the elements were in balance he was marvelous. But when it became something as ugly and pusillanimous as *The Crack-Up*, which to me is one of the most loathsome pieces of writing in the language, you see the Irish-American stance fall apart. What frustrates me when I think about Fitzgerald is it seems, from the evidence of *The Last Tycoon*, that he was about to go into a thrilling middle phase; having survived drunkenness and shattered romance, he was now going on to be a grown-up writer. We never get to find out about that.

I remember one time meeting Gore Vidal and he sort of stared at me and said, "Funny thing about all you Irish writers, you're all social climbers." And I think that is kind of true, the ease with which the Irish could move in American society once they got going. True of John O'Hara and Scott Fitzgerald for sure.

Interviewer: In many ways, especially in their endings, your last two novels, *Something to Be Desired* and *Nobody's Angel*, remind me of Henry James. They're similar in the sense of the psychological violence, the cross currents of violence that leave people wiped out. They come to the place where they see too much, they see too clearly.

McGuane: I, of course, come to it from a sort of cruder perspective. Partly from being in the horse business, I've spent a lot of time in the oil belt and I've gotten to know a lot of petro-chemical zillionaires who breed horses and do things like that. I have also gotten to see a lot of people on what was recently the American frontier who are now living in the world of answered prayers. They go down to the 7-Eleven store in helicopters; they go to Scotland and buy the winner of the dog trials to bring back to keep around the house; they jet around the world and things get very, very accelerated for them. All of a sudden they are up against the accumulated values of the civilization to that point, but they have to deal with them because money, drugs, speed, and air-planes have brought them to a point of exhaustion. Sooner than it ever did before. They are up against the American dream as it's expressed in western America in a way that makes it something that can't really be survived.

Interviewer: But, when you think of the material James dealt with—nouveau riche Americans. The pattern of *Something to Be Desired* reminded me so much of the pattern of John Marcher in *The Beast in the Jungle,* who at the end replaces obsession with obsession on top of obsession.
McGuane: It really is a case of a man discovering that a narcissistic crisis is going to bear penalties which are permanent. I think that the nature of the age, say the sixties, the seventies, and the eighties, has been the indulgence of the "me" figure without suitable precautions. People should understand that, yes, it might be marvelous for you to go on a mission of self-discovery, but understand that people will not necessarily be here when you get back. I don't think Timothy Leary ever told anybody that; I don't even think Ken Kesey told anybody that. I think they more or less said that you paint your bus psychedelic colors and you take off, and when you come back the things that you wanted to be there will still be there. That turns out not to be the case. My book is about that. Its implications are not tragic because the narcis-sist is not a good tragic figure.

Interviewer: You've said a couple of interesting things about your earlier books; I wonder if you would care to comment about them.
McGuane: I see the progress of those first three books as technological jumps from each other. The first, *The Sporting Club,* was meant to be a really con-trolled acid comic novel of the kind that I was then appreciating. Henry Green and Evelyn Waugh . . . Your first two or three books represent all that

you wanted to do during the previous twenty-eight years . . . you come out and want to write *Hamlet,* and then you want to write *Don Quixote* and then you want to write *The Divine Comedy.* Then you begin to simmer down a little bit. My second, *The Bushwhacked Piano,* reflected my fascination with picaresque novels. The third book really derives from my interest in surrealism, juxtaposition. *Ninety-two in the Shade* has more jagged layering of voices and situations than any book I wrote before or since. When I was writing it I was trying to not write a protagonist-centered novel. I was trying to take a different whack from a different angle and not write a Jamesian novel and not confine the information to what could be seen from a single point of view. And when I look back I realize that I must have gotten so aloft in this project I wonder how I could find the bathroom at the end of the day's work.

Interviewer: That book has been called a giant pun on Hemingway, and your earlier books were compared to Faulkner. Were you in any sense conscious of that element?

McGuane: That is just absurd. Hemingway is a figure that casts a tremendous shadow for better or for worse. In the United States, it's a cottage industry to produce books about how terrible Ernest Hemingway was. So when Harry Crews or Jim Harrison or I are called Hemingwayesque, it's merely a way of saying, "We don't like this writer."

Interviewer: The criticism that I've read implied that you were writing the anti-Hemingway novel, turning the Hemingway mystique or code of behavior upside down.

McGuane: I would say that the gist of the Hemingway comparison over the years has been by way of belittling my work. But I don't feel singled out. When I talked with Gore Vidal, he said, "I've been rereading Ernest Hemingway, and he is so scriptural and dull," and I said, "Well, I don't know what it is, Gore, but the people of the world go on wanting to read Ernest Hemingway." He said, "Not this people of the world." I think that is a kind of *stance.* There is a deep, deep hatred of Ernest Hemingway in the American literary community. And they should just admit it.

Interviewer: But you do admire his work?

McGuane: I don't like all of his work. Actually, in fact, I don't like maybe more than half of it. But, the thing that is obviously interesting is that

Hemingway can acquit himself in prose. Nothing needs to be said in defense of him; his influence will continue to erode his enemies' bastions.

Interviewer: How does a novel come together for you?

McGuane: There are two ways a novel can come together for anybody. One is answering to a plan. I've found over the years that that doesn't work very well for me. I'll outline everything and then the outline becomes irrelevant. The writing I like the best is when I don't know what I'm doing. This is another way of saying, if I can foresee the shape of a book and if I can foresee the outcome of things I've set in motion, then that is almost a guarantee of its being too limited. I would rather be a sort of privileged reader in that I get to write what I get to read, and chance having to write six or seven hundred pages to produce a two hundred page book. Then there is an element of real, deepdown excitement about the process. It is the harder way to write a book, the wilder way. It's the Indian way to write a book.

Interviewer: Can you identify the place where an identifiable voice, a narrator or protagonist, takes over?

McGuane: Yeah, but that comes up from within. It's like metal. You heat it and you heat it and then light comes out of the metal. You can't just go right up to the thing and say, "happen." It has to arise from some level of your *self* that you don't control.

Interviewer: I'm thinking of what Stanley Elkin has often said, that the first thing he hears is a voice and then the next thing that comes to him is an occupation.

McGuane: Sherwood Anderson, who is by way of being my favorite writer these days, always used to try to get the pitch right. He would keep writing and writing on his first sentence until the pitch was right and then he could write it. That sounds very familiar to me. On the other hand, Peter Taylor, who is a superb writer, said one of the wiliest things that I've heard in a long time. He said that when he begins to hear the voices in a story and the story begins to write itself, he tears it up and throws it away. So there you have it. These things are highly personal. I know lots of fine horse trainers who use systems that are diametrically opposite to one another; they would seem to cancel each other, but they all end up making really fine horses.

Interviewer: Do you think people reading your books tend to confuse you with your characters?

McGuane: Oh, yes, I'm sure they do, and I'm sure that's partly my doing. I don't think I would have much luck writing a book from a stance or a point of view which I didn't share at all. But you want to separate yourself from your narrow focus in order to broaden the geometry of the book. I used to think in terms of these utterly perverse plans for books. I was once going to write a detective novel in the form of a cookbook. I was hell-bent just to shake up the kaleidoscope. I don't feel that way any more. I find it hard enough to write interestingly and to write well, giving myself all the tools I can handle. I no longer think it is necessary to make it crazy or write a six-hundred page novel that takes place in two minutes.

Interviewer: A lot of critics and a lot of readers seemed to think *Panama* was autobiographical. When the narrator says, "I'm working without a net, for the first time," is that you giving away yourself?

McGuane: First of all, that's a strategy to draw the reader into my web. There is nothing more handy to an author's purposes than to have a reader say, "Ah ha, now I'm going to find out." Then you can take him anywhere. In fact, it was tonally very much autobiographical; in specific incident, it was partly autobiographical. At the same time I wanted the reader to believe what I was saying, because sometimes one could make up something that would better illustrate an emotional point than the actual thing that happened. All of us have gone into a store and looked at a plastic doll or something that doesn't mean a thing and suddenly been overwhelmingly depressed by it. I can remember when the McDonald people brought out Egg McMuffins and there were Egg McMuffin signs all over Key West. I looked at it and I thought life was not worthwhile anymore if I had to share the planet with Egg McMuffin. Well, that doesn't translate, it's not usable.

Interviewer: But does the experience described in *Panama*, this narrator who's been in the fast lane and gotten totally burned out, at all reflect what happened to you after *Ninety-two in the Shade* and the film?

McGuane: Yes, I think I got pretty burned out. . . .

Interviewer: You got in big trouble?

McGuane: Yes, I did. It was big trouble, but it was good trouble, in some ways, because I often revert to being a control freak, as they say. And you know, I really had been such a little monk trying to be a writer for so long that I was sick of that. I saw all of these wonderful social revolutions going on around me and I wasn't part of them. Everybody was having such a wonderful time and I was always in the damn library and I was getting tired of it. And so, in 1973 when suddenly I was on the front page of the *New York Times* and movie producers wanted to give me money and people wanted me, I just said, "Yes." I said, "I'm going to go do this for a while," and I did and at the end of it, I was pretty played out. It was a bad time to be at the end of it because that was when my family started dying off. That was not a happy time. At the same time, I could hardly repudiate it; you know I wanted, as the girls used to say in the romantic dramas, to live a little. I wanted to go out and do a lot of things and I certainly did. I got out and I saw just about everything that was going on.

Interviewer: And did a little of it, too?
McGuane: I did *all* of it.

Interviewer: And you did it in the seventies instead of the sixties. You were a late bloomer.
McGuane: I still am.

Interviewer: You seem to be a person for whom a rich family life and your work out here on the ranch is very important.
McGuane: Yes. I'll stick to my guns on that one. You'll find me doing this twenty-five years from now if I'm lucky enough to be alive. I have eliminated a lot of things now, and I really like my family life. I'm married to a wonderful, tough girl who knows what she wants to do. I don't have to prop her up, she's just fine, she fights back. It's great. My kids like me.

Interviewer: How many times have you been married?
McGuane: I've been married three times really, but I was married very, very briefly the second time. I was married for fourteen or fifteen years in my first marriage. Then I was married for eight months or something like that. I've been married for eight or nine years now.

Interviewer: Did the burnout you went through in the seventies have anything to do with the breakup of your first marriage?
McGuane: I think so . . . I think so. But it also had sort of run its course. It was not an acrimonious conclusion to a first marriage. I very much admire

my first wife. She and I continue to be friends. In fact, she and my present wife are great friends.

Interviewer: Your second wife was an actress, wasn't she?
McGuane: Margot Kidder. It was just an arbitrary event, has nothing to do any. . . . The record speaks otherwise so I can't say this, but I'm really kind of a monogamist.

Interviewer: What do you do here on the ranch? Can you tell us a little bit about the cutting horses?
McGuane: Well, we have a band of broodmares, twenty or twenty-five mares that we use for breeding purposes. Then we run anywhere from seventy-five to 125 yearling cattle. We raise and sell and break and train cutting horses. Which is actually a bit of a monster; it takes up more time than I want it to.

Interviewer: What is a cutting horse?
McGuane: In the West, cattle are sorted horseback, at least they always were. Horses are getting replaced by motorcycles and feedlots and weird things, but still a cutting horse has always been a valuable tool to a cowman for sorting cattle. They take diseased cattle out, or nonproductive cows or injured cattle. To go into a herd and bring a single individual out requires an incredibly smart, skillful, highly trained horse and a very knowledgeable rider. That situation has produced a contest animal, just as range roping has produced rodeo roping, and horse breaking has produced bronc riding. That's what we raise here. We have probably one of the better small breeding programs in the nation. We work hard at it. It's not a hobby. We raised the Reserve Champion of the Pacific Coast in the Cutting Horse Futurity, we raised the National Futurity Reserve Champion, and I've been Montana Champion three years in a row, and we've had the Open Champion up here.

Interviewer: What relationship does it bear to your writing life?
McGuane: It keeps me thrown among non-literary people a big part of my life. I spend a lot of time with cattle feeders and horse trainers and breeders and ranchers, and I like that. It also has made me sort of the village freak in their world. When I rode at the national finals at the Astrodome, it was horrifying. As I rode toward the herd, I could hear these blaring loudspeakers: "Novelist, screenwriter," quack, quack, quack. It is as though this geek has

come in to ride, you know. That is kind of disturbing. I'm really not one of the boys in that sense. On the other hand, I can compete against them and beat them and they respect our breeding program.

Interviewer: Does it keep you sane?

McGuane: Well, it's the outer world. You know you can't go out there and mope around and be narcissistic and artistic in a band of broodmares with colts on their sides who all need shots and worming and trimming and vaccinating.

Interviewer: How do you schedule the two different things?

McGuane: It goes up and down seasonally. For example, there's not a lot to do in the winter. All we can do is feed. And then about now, as soon as things really get going in the spring, it gets to be too much and sometimes I kind of resent it, because I'm working on a book, and I don't want to be out there doing that all day long.

Interviewer: One thing we haven't talked about is the father-son and son-father element in your work.

McGuane: Yes, I would like to say something about that. It seems funny. My father's been dead for almost a decade and I'm forty-five; it seems I should stop thinking about that. But it has never really seemed to quite go away. When I was a little boy, my father and I were very close and as I got older and he got more obsessed with his business and became more of an alcoholic, he kind of drifted away from me. I think I've been inconsolable about that for a big part of my life. Inconsolable. I mean when I look at a blank piece of paper, all of a sudden Dad comes out. It's there and all I've been able to do is write about it. Try to get it down. I think maybe I got it clear in *Panama* and I'm not obsessed with it anymore. I'm more obsessed with my relationship to my children and trying to feel that I've made some progress. If I could write as long as I want to, and I can think of maybe ten books that I want to write right now, I think it will be seen that this is sort of the end of that father-son era in my writing.

Interviewer: What about the business of games people play as an organizing principle in your work?

McGuane: Once you leave subsistence, you enter the world of games, whether you move from subsistence to warfare or you move from subsistence to art. They can all be viewed as a situation where people say, "I'll tell you what, you take that position and I'll take this one . . ."

Interviewer: And we'll see what happens. . . .
McGuane: And we'll see how it turns out. For some reason it is quite automatic for me to see that interpretation of what's going on. I don't mean it in a reductive way. When I see games in life I don't say that life is just a game, that's not what I mean at all.

Interviewer: You do tend to write about people who aren't necessarily against the wall economically. They have the means by which to enter the realm of games.
McGuane: In fact, even ranchers, like the people next door here who just barely make it financially every year, have time to do anything they want to do. You talk to people in Livingston, which is kind of a blue-collar town, and they'll often say, "You've got time to ride horses and do all the things you want to; we're really up against it." Yet they'll pay $5,000 for a snowmobile and they'll go buy these campers, but they see that as their necessity material. As opposed to silly stuff like horses, they've got serious stuff like campers and snowmobiles.

It's not a valid point, but one of Reagan's henchmen said, "How can we as a government address the problem of poverty when the number one nutritional problem in the United States is overeating?" And it was a real snarky remark, but at the same time I see a lot of people who say "I have a dishwashing job, and you get to be a writer." They don't have to have that job. And it makes it boring for me to write about dishwashers, because I don't see why they do it or why they want to do it.

Interviewer: I take it at some point you've got a character and you say, let's see what happens to him if we put him in this situation. That's in a sense sort of . . .
McGuane: . . . a game. In fact it seems to me that life is like that. I mean, that makes the Lewis and Clark expedition a game.

Interviewer: Yes.
McGuane: That makes democracy a game. Maybe even first strike capability is a game. I don't know, I mean I think this game idea gradually moves into meaning nothing. It just means life, charged life versus passive life.

Interviewer: But you do see it as an organizing principle and it certainly shows up in your work.
McGuane: I love play. Playfulness is probably the thing that marks our household.

Interviewer: You said something earlier about this Irish family you came from.
McGuane: My grandmother was orphaned at thirteen. She was the oldest of the family and she raised all these children, her brothers and sisters. My father came from a small town, and had very little means. He was so astonished he went to Harvard that, to him, life became "before" and "after" Harvard, so we never revisited his origins. But I looked into the stuff. My grandfather's mother died of tuberculosis and malnutrition at twenty-nine with five children. They really didn't have much of a chance. All the girls in the family listed occupation: weaver, address: boarding house. You know, all the way down through these records. I just realize how terribly hard they really had it. And then, by the time I knew any of those people, I realized that's why life seemed so exciting to them. They were very optimistic people, and they had had it as tough and as mean as you can have it.

You remember the thing that Galbraith said years ago, "There is a vast difference between not having enough and having enough, but there is very little difference between having enough and having too much." I think that there are a few sectors of this country that really have too much. Certainly the country has too much. That makes me believe that our burning our candle at both ends, while much of the world has no candle, must represent at least the prospects for decline. I sometimes think I see signs of that, though my view of life is not entirely that dour.

Interviewer: Why not? How do you accommodate the discrepancies?
McGuane: Well, for example, I have a five-year-old daughter who is very excited about the orchard and the horses, the new colts. I don't really think I need to beleaguer her with information right now about Biafra, nor do I think that the activities of a Bernard Goetz undermine the reality of her pleasure in new colts. All those things aren't necessarily connected. Some people feel they are, and maybe they're right, you know. It's a sort of religious loftiness that I don't have. I think, though, that the people who do have that sensibility don't seem to ever see anything in the foreground.

Interviewer: Do your books stand, in and of themselves, as a defense against what you see around you that's subject for despair?

McGuane: Everybody has a responsibility to develop some sort of island theory. I think that life kind of hurtles forward in a massive way for the world, but within it, people invent islands—islands of sanity, islands of family continuity, islands of professional skills and powers, islands of craft, art, and knowledge. Those islands basically are contributors toward a cure for despair, in ways that we probably cannot quite understand.

The Art of Fiction LXXXIX: Thomas Mcguane

Sinda Gregory and Larry McCaffery / 1985

First appeared in *Paris Review* 27, no. 97 (Fall 1985), pp. 35–71. © 1985 by The Paris Review. Reprinted with the permission of the Wylie Agency.

Thomas McGuane's fiction projects a volatile, highly personalized mixture of power, vulnerability, and humor. His first three novels—*The Sporting Club* (1969), *The Bushwhacked Piano* (1971), and *Ninety-two in the Shade* (1973)—while never achieving mass-market appeal, earned McGuane considerable critical attention: *Bushwhacked* won the Rosenthal Award, *Ninety-two* was nominated for the National Book Award, and all three works were widely and favorably reviewed. In addition to his novels, McGuane was also writing screenplays: *The Missouri Breaks, Rancho Deluxe, Ninety-two in the Shade, Tom Horn.* During the mid-seventies, McGuane's tempestuous personal life—drinking, some drugs, two divorces—won him the nickname of "Captain Berserko." From this tempest, McGuane produced his fourth novel, *Panama* (1978), his most surreal and nakedly autobiographical work to date. *Panama's* Chester Pomeroy is an exhausted, artistically depleted, emotionally wrecked rock musician who resolves to come clean with himself and the world, to work, for the first time, "without a net." The critical response to *Panama* was overwhelmingly negative, not merely lacerating the novel, but also attacking the promising young novelist for having "gone Hollywood." Although McGuane continued to believe *Panama* his best work, he was troubled by the vehemence of the criticism and his next novel did not appear for five years. Both *Nobody's Angel* (1983) and his latest novel, *Something to Be Desired* (1984), reveal changes in McGuane's craft; less rambunctious in their humor, with more subtle textures of characterization and a tighter control of language, these last two works indicate an attempt at a quieter, more evocative kind of verbal power.

Since the mid-seventies, McGuane and his wife, Laurie, have lived just outside Livingston, Montana, where their ranch has been a focal point for a

burgeoning artistic community—people like William Hjorstberg, Peter
Fonda, and the late Richard Brautigan have made this western town into an
enclave of diverse talents. The McGuanes' is a working ranch, and they are
justifiably proud of their spread, where they raise and train cutting horses,
some to be sold for ranch work, the best to be used in rodeo competition.
Tall, muscular, rugged, McGuane has been the Montana cutting horse champion three years in a row, and, at forty-six, exudes a powerful physical presence. He is the kind of man who knows how to do things, who studies how
things work, who can talk with equal assurance and knowledge about guns,
horses, books, boats, and hot peppers from Sonora. As he took us on a tour
of his ranch and we talked about water problems, fishing, and his fiction, we
got a sense of McGuane's approach to things: when you find something you
want to do, whether it's learning to tie casting flies or writing a novel, you
work at it systematically. That you'd want to do it well, that you'd be willing
to make whatever sacrifices are necessary to that end, goes without saying. As
we sat together over coffee with the busy, cheerful household buzzing around
us, McGuane seemed a man at peace, emerged hale and whole from a difficult time of personal and professional upheaval. It was to this period of turmoil that we addressed our first question.

Interviewer: Has the personal storm really passed?
Thomas McGuane: The storm has passed in the sense that my steering link-
age has been restored. A storm system is still in effect, though, and in fact if it
weren't, I'd want to change my life because you can get to a point where the
risk factor has been overregulated. That's an alarming condition for me,
a ghastly thing.

Interviewer: Without going into all the particulars, could you talk a bit about
what you feel, in retrospect, was going on in the mid-seventies—the period
of stumbling down the yellow line, when you were known as "Captain
Berserko"?
McGuane: During the early part of that time I had been successful in creating for myself a sheltered situation in which to function in this very narrow
way I felt I wanted to function, which was to be a literary person who was not
bothered very much by the outside world. My twenties were entirely taken up
with literature. Entirely. My nickname during that period was "The White
Knight," which suggests a certain level of overkill in my judgment of those
around me.

Interviewer: What sorts of things had led you to develop this White Knight image?

McGuane: Fear of failure. I was afflicted with whatever it takes to get people fanatically devoted to what they're doing. I was a pain in the ass. But I desperately wanted to be a good writer. My friends seem to think that an hour and a half effort a day is all they need to bring to the altar to make things work for them. I couldn't do that. I thought that if you didn't work at least as hard as the guy who runs a gas station then you had no right to hope for achievement. You certainly had to work all day, every day. I thought that was the deal. I *still* think that's the deal.

Interviewer: I've heard that you had a brush with death in a car accident that shook you up pretty badly. The usual, maybe simpleminded, explanation is that you suddenly realized that you could have died there without ever having given yourself a chance to live.

McGuane: That explanation is not so simpleminded. I still don't know exactly what it meant to me at the time. I do know that I lost the power of speech for a while. And I had something like that realization going through my mind. It was outside Dalhart, Texas. I was driving fast, one hundred and forty miles an hour, and there was this freezing rain on the road that you couldn't see, so when I pulled out to pass, suddenly life was either over or it wasn't. I thought it was over. The guy I was driving with said, "This is it," and all of a sudden it did appear that it was the end: there were collisions and fence posts flying and pieces of car body going by my ears. It would have been as arbitrary an end as what's happening to a friend of ours who's now dying in a hospital of cancer, or our friend who has an awful neurological disease, or a kid who chases the baseball out in the street. You believe all this stuff, but then suddenly you're standing in the middle of it with the chance to choose and it seems like a miracle or a warning that you've been spared this time but you'd better get your life together. I remember thinking along these lines, but my thoughts were so overpowering that I couldn't speak for a week, even to ask for something to eat.

Interviewer: Pomeroy says at the beginning of *Panama* that he's going to be "working without a net." It's tempting to read that novel as *your* attempt to work through some of your own turmoils from that period. If you were up there, taking the risk to expose yourself, the highly negative, even personally vicious, reviews of *Panama* must have hurt a lot.

McGuane: The whole *Panama* episode really jarred me in terms of my writing because that was one time I had consciously decided to reveal certain things about myself. I was stunned by the bad reception of *Panama*; it was a painful and punishing experience. The lesson that I got from the reviewers was, Don't ever try to do that again. And it was odd to watch reviewers incorrectly summarize the story, then attack their own summaries. It was like watching blind men being attacked by their seeing-eye dogs. But then, I look back at when John Cheever published *Bullet Park*, which was the advent of the good Cheever as far as I'm concerned, and the critics and public crucified him over that book. Afterwards he went into an alcoholic spiral. People don't understand how much influence they can actually have on a writer, how much a writer's feelings can be hurt, how much they can deflect his course when they raise their voices like they did over highly personal books like *Panama* or *Bullet Park*.

Interviewer: If it's any consolation, I feel *Panama* is your best book.
McGuane: I think it may be my best too. In the middle of all this outcry, I'd get the book out and read stuff to myself and say, "I can't *do* any better than this!" I really do love *Panama*. But I'd also have to admit that right now, if I were driven to write another novel like that I wouldn't even try to find a publisher for it. It simply wouldn't be published. I'd be writing it to put in my closet upstairs.

Interviewer: So what effect did the *Panama* experience have on your work?
McGuane: Its first effect was to confirm my desire to write a book that was, in a traditional way, more shapely than anything I had done before. Actually, I'd been wanting to do that for a long time. That at least partially explains the architecture of *Nobody's Angel*. The novel I'm working on now picks up from *Panama* more than from any other point. Importantly it's not a book in the first person, which made *Panama* completely different from anything else I've ever done, so it doesn't sound and look like *Panama*. But *Panama* is still the last piece of growing tissue that I've been grafting from.

Interviewer: In terms of its flights of poetic language, its surrealism, and other formal features, *Panama* is probably your most extreme novel to date. And yet these features seem entirely appropriate in capturing the sensibility of its crazed narrator, Pomeroy. Was creating this voice and perspective especially difficult for you or did your identification with him make things easier, in a way?

McGuane: It was very difficult. I invented a word once a long time ago and I was always going to write a book that could be described with this word. The word was "joco-splenetic." *Panama* was to be my first joco-splenetic novel. What was especially difficult about that book was that I knew that in certain parts I wanted Pomeroy to be absolutely lugubrious. I saw him as somebody who would live quite happily in a Gogol novel, a laughter-through-tears guy. I knew that his emotions are frequently "unearned," that the kind of hangover quality in which he lives produces fits of uncontrolled weeping. I'm not saying that the book isn't sentimental in that technical sense, but I also felt that this tissue of distance that I created between myself and Chester was adequate for people to understand this and to see the book for what it is. For people who don't like the book, when poor Pomeroy goes off into one of his spirals, they think, "What right does he have to this?" The point is that he *has* no right—that's what's interesting about him.

Interviewer: This sounds like the same sense of moral indignation that seemed to be directed at you during the mid-seventies—the sense that here's this talented person who has everything going for him and yet here he is taking all these drugs and doing all these bizarre, self-destructive things.

McGuane: There are those who question the right of a wealthy person to commit suicide. A person who doesn't have enough to eat has the right to commit suicide but not a person whose income is over fifty thousand dollars a year. It's as if wealthy or talented people have no right to be miserable. So in this age of cocaine we just expand this principle and say, "My God, look at all that Chester's got" (half of which is made up: his automobile, his house, they don't even exist). The idea that he's so miserable that he can't name his dog and can't get his true love back, that doesn't count in this strangely economic-based view that only certain people are entitled to their unhappiness.

Interviewer: I gather that in some ways you transformed some of your real-life feelings for your wife Laurie into the figure of Catherine.

McGuane: Yes, in many ways Catherine became Laurie. I saw Pomeroy going downhill in various ways and, being madly in love with Laurie at the time, the most miserable thing I could imagine for him (or me) was to lose this person he loved so much. That's one of the reasons I think there's a specific emotional power in that ending, because I was going through Pomeroy's loss, imaginatively, as I wrote it. I felt that the coda to all the pain in that book had to be that loss, but it was so absolutely agonizing that, unlaminated to something better, it was nihilistic. And I'm not a nihilist and didn't want this book to be nihilistic.

Interviewer: Is that why you have that last scene with the father, where Chester finally seems to acknowledge him and you write, "There was more to be said and time to say it"?
McGuane: Partly, although this business about what he's going to do about his father is present throughout the book. At that point in the end, when he's hit absolute rock bottom, the question becomes, does he bounce or does he flatten out and lie there. In my opinion he bounced. Slightly.

Interviewer: All five of your books seem to have distinctive stylistic features. *Nobody's Angel* seems to be almost understated in comparison with your earlier books. Could you talk about the specific evolutions your prose has undergone?
McGuane: I started my career distinctly and single-mindedly with the idea that I wanted to be a comic novelist. I had studied comic literature from *Lazarillo de Tormes* to the present. The twentieth century history of comic writing had prepared me to write in the arch, fascist style that I used in *The Sporting Club*. Then the picaresque approach was something I tried to express in *The Bushwhacked Piano*, although I've now come to feel that the picaresque form is no longer that appropriate for writing; writers are looking for structures other than that episodic, not particularly accumulative form; at least I am. *Ninety-two in the Shade* was the first of the books in which I felt I brought my personal sense of epochal crisis to my interest in literature. It's there that you find this crackpot cross between traditional male literature and 'The Sid Caesar Show" and the preoccupation with process and mechanics and "doingness" that has been a part of American literature from the beginning—it's part of *Moby Dick*. The best version of it, for my money, is *Life on the Mississippi*, which is probably the book I most wish I'd written in American literature. When I got to *Ninety-two* I was tired of being amusing; I like my first two books a lot, but I tried to put something like a personal philosophy in *Ninety-two in the Shade*. That book also marked the downward progress of my instincts as a comic novelist. Starting with *Ninety-two* I felt

that to go on writing with as much flash as I had tried to do previously was to betray some of the serious things I had been trying to say. That conflict became one that I tried to work out in different ways subsequently. The most drastic attempt was in *Panama*, which I wrote in the first person in this sort of blazing confessional style. In terms of feeling my shoulder to the wheel and my mouth to the reader's ear, I have never been so satisfied as I was when I was writing that book. I didn't feel that schizophrenia that most writers have when they're at work. That schizophrenia was *in* the book instead of between me and the book.

Interviewer: You don't seem to have lost your comic instincts, but I sensed in *Panama* a change in the *kind* of humor you were creating: a move away from satire, which characterized your earlier books, towards something deeper, more painful. There's a line in *Panama* that seems relevant here, where Chester describes "the sense of humor that is the mirror of pain, the perfect mirror, not the mirror of satirists."
McGuane: I now agree with that Broadway producer who said that satire is what closes on Saturday night.

Interviewer: Patrick in *Nobody's Angel* and Pomeroy both lose the woman in the end, but that loss somehow seemed more inevitable in *Panama* than in *Nobody's Angel*, where you appeared to give Patrick the chance to learn and change. I was a bit surprised you didn't devise a happy ending for Patrick.
McGuane: There's a difference in those two losses. In Pomeroy's case, it is a little bit as though there has simply been too much water under the bridge for him to ever get Catherine back. There is a momentum that has become so black that current conduct can't turn things around. With Patrick the ending has more to do with this notion of the outsider or stranger, which has fascinated me for a long time and is reflected in the book. Patrick's situation is the modern situation: the adhesion of people to place has been lost. This can be just ruinous. The result can truly be, as in *Wuthering Heights*, the ill wind that blows across the heath, a thing you can't beat—you either get out and do something else or the conditions will destroy you. I didn't think Patrick could win his war because his basics are fouled up, so he had to accept himself as an *isolato*. This isn't a very happy ending, certainly not one I would wish upon a dog, but it was the one I felt had inevitability.

Interviewer: Does this fascination with the figure of the outsider and the adhesion of family identity to place derive from your own family background, which like Patrick's is Irish?

McGuane: The outsider-stranger-bystander has always intrigued me in regard to my own family history. My family were all Irish immigrants originally and so I became interested in Irish history and traveled a lot in Ireland, which brought things even closer to home. People in Ireland feel like outsiders in their own country because the English have owned things for so long that the Irish consider themselves as living in a massive servants' quarters for the British Isles. When they immigrated to the East Coast (my family went to Massachusetts), they saw themselves as an enclave of outsiders in a Yankee, Protestant world. My parents moved to the Midwest, and I can assure you that, whatever we thought we were, we did not consider ourselves to be midwesterners. We saw ourselves as Catholics surrounded by Protestant midwesterners, and when we wanted to feel close to something, we went back to our old world in Massachusetts. When I moved to Montana in my twenties, I felt myself to be an outsider in still another world. The only thing that seems reassuring is that most Montanans feel the same way—they're mostly from somewhere else and their history is so recent that to be one of the migrants is really to be one of the boys. You can see this same feeling developing in F. Scott Fitzgerald. I'm sure that no one in his family felt like they were "from" Minnesota, which is one reason he was drawn to the East Coast and why so much of the magic of his fiction is his famous method of "looking through the window." And yet that mental quality, the glassy distance, is behind his craziness and his alcoholism. The vantage point of most authentic modern fiction is dislocation.

Interviewer: Your first three novels are all extraordinarily ambitious works in that each of them links the heroes and action with a vision of America at large. But in both *Panama* and *Nobody's Angel*, the move seems to be more inward, more personal. Was this a conscious shift?

McGuane: *The Sporting Club* was really the last genuinely political book I've ever done, at least political in an overt way. It was meant to be a kind of anarchist tract. I was reading a lot of political writers at the time, especially Kropotkin, and I was very self-conscious about using the situation of the novel as a political paradigm.

Interviewer: Isn't *Ninety-two in the Shade* overtly political? You seem to be using Skelton there to suggest a deeper crisis in America that is signaled in the very opening line of the book: "Nobody knows, from sea to shining sea . . ."
McGuane: ". . . why we are having all this trouble with our republic." Yes, I was using Skelton very deliberately in the way you're suggesting, but I was more interested in the inner, personal dynamics than in the larger, political implications. There's another line from the book that seems very appropriate to the political issue you're raising: "It was the age of uneasy alliances." But we're not in that age any more, which is one reason my fiction has shifted its focus. We're currently in the age of *no* alliances. We're in the age of, shake hands with the Lebanese and give their neighbors a bomber so they can blow their asses off the planet. We're in the age of the most sordid possible political cynicism. We're in the age of foreign aid to death squads.

Interviewer: I would assume that these sorts of attitudes make moving inward, away from the larger political arena, more attractive.
McGuane: Right, and that's one of the reasons that *Ninety-two in the Shade* is such a strangely public book compared to my last two. It was a kind of New Age book that reflected my sense that I was caught up in some huge cultural change that was taking place in this country. It was a book about private survival. You have your skills and your mate and your place, and you're aloof from an obviously suicidal society. The chief metaphor for the book should have been bomb shelters, with people storing water and tinned food. My father and I had very much of an adversarial relationship which is unresolved to this very day. I remember going to see a bomb shelter with him back in the fifties; one of our neighbors had built one of them. It was a very elegant bomb shelter and we walked around and looked at it; my father was a very direct guy, so when we came up he was filled with thoughts about this thing—the main thought being, Should I build one for my family?—and he pondered this, and I was very interested in what he was going to say. Finally he said, "I think we'll just stay up on the ground and take our lumps." Boy oh boy, did *that* ever become a model for future reflections on my part! It was a key point in our dialogue.

Interviewer: Skelton obviously doesn't follow your father's advice—he wants to find a shelter, a personal survival module.
McGuane: Right, which made *Ninety-two in the Shade* a rebellious book for me to write because I'd built this novel about a guy who obviously wasn't

thinking in terms of staying above ground and taking his lumps. He's at the fork in the road and he chooses to construct a place where he can be safe. Right now, though, the progress of my fiction is towards my father's point of view, to *not* build a shelter, to just stay up here and fight it out.

Interviewer: The father-son relationship is constantly a major issue in your fiction. Is some of the tension of these fictional relationships autobiographically based?

McGuane: This is plainly so. If you'd been around me while I was growing up you'd have clearly seen that my relationship with my father was going to be a major issue in my life. My father was a kid who grew up rather poor (his father had worked for the railroad) and who had a gift for English; he wound up being a scholar-athlete who went to Harvard, where he learned some of the skills that would enable him to go on and become a prosperous business-man, but where he also learned to hate wealth. My father hated people with money and yet he became one of those people. And he was not only an alco-holic but a workaholic, a man who never missed a day of work in his life. He was a passionate man who wanted a close relationship with his family, but he was a child of the Depression and was severely scarred by that, to the point where he really drove himself and didn't have much time for us. So while he prepared us to believe that parents and children were very important, he just never delivered. And we were all shattered by that: my sister died of a drug overdose in her middle twenties; my brother has been a custodial case since he was thirty; as soon as my mother was given the full reins of her own life, after my dad died, she drank herself to death in thirty-six months. I'm really the only one still walking around, and I came pretty close to being not still walking around. It all goes back to that situation where people are very tradi-tional in their attitudes about the family, a family which was very close (we had this wonderful warm place in Massachusetts where my grandfather umpired baseball games and played checkers at the fire station), but then they move off to the bloody Midwest where they all go crazy. I've tried to work some of this out in my writing, and my younger sister tried to work it out in mental institutions. She was the smartest one of us all, an absolute beauty. She died in her twenties.

Interviewer: There's an interesting structural relationship between *Nobody's Angel* and *Ninety-two in the Shade* that seems relevant here. In *Angel*, Patrick's father is dead, preserved within that Montana ice floe. In *Ninety-two*, Skelton lives in a fuselage, and the father figure is preserved, offstage, as part of his internal life. Was this a consciously designed motif?

McGuane: Let me answer that one as candidly as I can. When I started *Nobody's Angel* I was so tired of the pain of the father-and-son issue that I didn't want it to infuse yet another book. But for it not to be present at all would have falsified it. So I did what religion does: I simply canonized one of the characters and got him the hell out of the book.

Interviewer: Your characters at times seem to be trying to build a better model of society within their families than they find out in the society at large.

McGuane: The way I see it now is that you either make a little nation and solve its historical and personnel problems within the format of your own household—accepting all the mistakes that you've made, all the ones your parents have made, all that your children make, and all the mistakes your country has made—and you win that one, or you lose the only war worth fighting. That's what I'm trying to do; I'm trying to study this problem in my writing, intensifying it for the purposes of art, and in my own life. Moreover, as soon as you step out of this personally constructed world and, say, drive into town or stand out on I-90 and watch our nation cycle through these placeless arteries, it's there that you confront the true horror of the other option. The America you see in public is the monster who crawls up to the door in the middle of the night and must be driven back to the end of the driveway. That's the thing that scares me to death. We've all seen these nameless, faceless people out there, and when we track one of them back to wherever they came from we sometimes find that this is the one person who can pull a breech birth calf without ever killing the mother cow, or the guy who goes over the hill and does beautiful fencing even though nobody is watching, the valued neighbor who will get up in the middle of the night to help you get your water turned back on. But for some reason in this country, at a certain point this man turns into this absolute human flotsam whom we make fun of when we see him standing in front of Old Faithful. This syndrome is scary to me because I'm not sure which team is going to win. Are we really just going to rinse, like the third cycle in a washing machine, from the Atlantic to the Pacific? If so, why don't we get into *The Whole Earth Catalogue* mentality, really save some energy, and just shoot ourselves? I had that sense of family security with my grandparents, and then I saw the results in my own family of deciding that all that was worthless.

My dad had no use for it, felt that people who valued it were just dragging their heels.

Interviewer: You've talked a lot about your father and his family. What about your mother's side of the family?
McGuane: Actually, I derive myself matrilineally, and all the photographs you see around here are of my mother's family. There are two kinds of Irish people—one is the kind that doesn't say anything and the other is the kind that talks all the time. Well, my mother's family were talkers and my father's were the silent types. My father's father was a fine old railroad Irishman, and my father couldn't wait to get away from him. So we saw very little of my father's father. In fact—this is something I've slowly been reconstructing—my grandmother died fairly young and then my grandfather remarried a woman from Prince Edward's Island; she just loved the old man, and when he died she more or less didn't invite my family to the funeral. My feeling is that she went back up to Prince Edward's Island and turned down my father's offer to buy her a house or something. Firmly. She felt that the way my father did things and the way he had treated his own father was pretty shabby. So he died, she buried him, and she split.

Interviewer: Did you derive some of your own instincts for storytelling from your mother's fast-talking Irish relatives?
McGuane: Very much so. My maternal grandmother's house was always full of people who valued wisecracks and uncanny stories. And we had a real history there. I'm more homesick for that than for anything that ever happened to us in Michigan. My mother was so attached to her family that the moment we got out of school she'd pack us off back to Massachusetts until school started in the fall, and my father resented that tremendously.

Interviewer: Was it your father who got you interested in hunting and fishing?
McGuane: He set those out as great ideals, but generally when it came time to go out and do them, he never showed up. We went out enough so that I wished we'd do it more, but then there'd be some other grown-up who *really* wanted to go, and my father wouldn't like that because he felt he should be doing that but didn't have time. So he'd say, "Well, if he had his nose to the grindstone, like he should have, he wouldn't have time to take off and go fishing on Lake Erie with you." But one way or another, I was tremendously

involved in hunting and fishing all the time. I had a .22 and I was gone every chance I could get, out in the woods or on the lake or, if the lake froze over, I'd be out on the ice miles from shore. That *was* my childhood.

Interviewer: What is there about developing sporting skills that seems so satisfying to you?

McGuane: I'm not sure I fully know. When I'm involved in these things myself, I feel like I'm being asked a lot of questions. Tools of elegance and order, developed and proven in the sporting life, are everywhere useful. Right now, for the first time in my life, I feel like there's something wrong about doing sports just for recreation—if it's just that, I don't want to do them. Their purpose is more than getting away from the pressures of work. Also, part of my interest in developing specific skills is surely to counter the sense of fragmentation and regret that crops up. With horses, I feel I've discovered some ancient connection, as though in some earlier life horses were something that mattered to me. The close study of all animals teaches us that we're not the solitary owners of this planet. As my horses procreate, and as they search for food and companionship and try to grow up and face one another's death, we see these things and it's very moving. You can't be around it to the degree that Laurie and I are and just say, 'We'll synthesize our food and we'll get rid of these other species because they take up a lot of land." I don't know what that has to do with how we own the earth and own the universe, but in a way I feel religious about it. It's not an accident that there are these sentient creatures other than human beings out there. And we're not supposed to populate the universe without them. We're seriously and dangerously deprived every time we lose one of these animals.

Interviewer: Nicholas Payne in *The Bushwhacked Piano* says, "I've made silliness a way of life." Was "pranksterism" part of your own life as a kid?

McGuane: Yes, it was, but there's more to it than that. We have chances for turning the kaleidoscope in a very arbitrary way. I wanted to be a military pilot at one time and came that close to joining the Naval Air Corps until I got into Yale, which I didn't expect to happen. One of the practical things they teach combat fliers is that you can only reason through so much, and therefore in a combat situation if at a certain point you feel you can't reason through a situation, then the thing you must do is *anything*, so long as you do something. Even in the Navy, with its expensive equipment and its highly predicated forms of action, you are told to just splash something off and do it! Doing something arbitrary or unexpected is probably the only way you're going to survive in a combat situation. Game theoreticians have made this an important factor. The first strike is really very close to pranksterism. Pranks, the inexplicability of comedy, and lateral moves at the line of scrimmage can sometimes be the only way you can move forward. In silliness and pranks, there is something very great. It's in that scene I created in *Panama*—the decision to jump off the diving board not knowing if there's water in the pool. Sometimes that's not a dopey thing to do but a very smart thing. It's the first strike.

Interviewer: In your more recent books, your central characters are more likely to avoid confrontation.

McGuane: I hope it's a maturity on the author's part. The growing awareness of consequences is something *Nobody's Angel* reflects and it also reflects what is appropriate to Patrick's stage in life. There were things that Billy the Kid was able to do by the age of twenty-one that would not have been appropriate to Pat Garrett at the age of forty-one. And as we will our way through the world, we begin by laying about ourselves with a heavy sword. It's one thing to jump off a diving board into a possibly empty pool at a certain stage in your life, but that same person with three children is not doing something good. A man with three young children who dives into a pool not knowing if there's water in it is someone to be despised. Patrick has moved into another part of his life, and he's dealt with some inadequacies in his life—maybe he shouldn't have been diving into pools when his sister was falling apart, for example, and maybe he's reviewing that. I wanted to suggest that there's remorse in him.

Interviewer: You said just a minute ago that you wanted to be a Navy pilot. Hadn't you decided that you wanted to be a writer by the time you were in college?

McGuane: I knew from very early on that I wanted to be a writer, but I also knew that that was not a very practical idea. So I was constantly trying to think of a profession I could pursue and still write. As a kid I had always associated being a writer with leading an adventurous life. I used to read William Beebe, Ernest Thompson Seton, W. H. Hudson, writers like that. That's really a key thing for me: I associated a life of action and a life of thought as being the writer's life. But I didn't do much writing when I was a kid. I wanted to *be* a writer before I wanted to do any writing. Then when I went away to boarding school there was a good friend of mine who was very strange and marvelous, and who became a kind of literary guide for me—Edmund White, a fine writer actually beyond category. Interestingly enough, back in school we all knew he was gay, and remember, this was the benighted fifties. A lot of his friends were athletes and I was this macho punk, but we were all friends and nobody cared. Ed was not only a good writer at that time but he was also a scholar. He had read Proust by the age of twelve, and he used to give me reading lists. A lot of my early readings were things he had me read, mainly the decadent works: Baudelaire, Rimbaud, Huysmans, Lautréamont, Wilde, Proust. When I got to college, I kept reading but I was also trying to figure out what I could do. I tried everything: I was a premed student at one time, and a prelaw student, though I was mostly an English major. But I didn't really know *what* I was going to do to survive.

Interviewer: As a graduate student, you studied playwriting at Yale Drama School. How did this contribute to your ear for dialogue?

McGuane: That's when off Broadway was very wild, interesting, exciting. There were all those good young playwrights and the theater-of-the-absurd was a true force. Reading those European and American playwrights and seeing their stuff, to the extent that it was possible, had a lot of effect on the way I eventually wrote fiction. Dialogue is very important to me because I've always loved it in novels. Lots of people read novels racing from dialogue to dialogue. In fact, I would like to really compress the prose in a novel, without getting too arch about it. Some people, like Manuel Puig, have written novels almost entirely in dialogue, but it gets to be a little too much sometimes since readers need to know where they are a bit. At any rate, writing dialogue is probably the best thing I do, and I'm always trying to work up an aesthetic for my fiction that will acknowledge that fact. Of course, Hemingway was really a great dialogue writer, it's one of the reasons we read him. Dialogue is a very useful tool to reveal things about people, and novels are about people and about what they do to each other. That's what novels are for. They're not pure text for deconstructionists. One day, that will be clear again.

Interviewer: Could you talk a bit about the background of your first two books?

McGuane: I went from Yale to Europe to live in Spain, and while I was over there I worked on an early version of *The Bushwhacked Piano*, which was really my apprentice work. I was always working on novels at Yale and there were parts of that book that I had worked on for years. I sent it off to Stanford, on the basis of which I won a Stegner fellowship. *The Sporting Club* was really my fourth or fifth novel. By the time it came out I had actually been writing for ten years, with most of my material going right into the waste basket, where it belonged.

Interviewer: In addition to the playwrights, who were the writers you were reading during that period who had some influence on the direction your work was taking?

McGuane: I remember that Malcolm Lowry's *Under the Volcano* just floored me. Incidentally, I consider that to be quite a funny book; a lot of it isn't funny, of course, but its perverted energy is obviously akin to comedy. Fielding, Sterne, Joyce, Gogol, and Twain were heroes. So were Machado de Assis, Thomas Love Peacock, George Borrow. There has never been a period when I was not reading Shakespeare. I loved Paul Bowles when I was just starting to write, and I loved Walter van Tilburg Clark. Stephen Crane seemed to me a fabulous writer, especially the stories. Knut Hamsun, Evelyn Waugh, Anthony Powell, Muriel Spark, Henry Green, William Eastlake, Walker Percy. You know, Barry Hannah and I were talking, and we agreed that *The Moviegoer* is one of those books that, for a lot of writers, was looked at like *The Sun Also Rises* was by writers back in the twenties.

Interviewer: In what sense?

McGuane: Percy's insouciance. He seemed to retain passion, gentlemanliness, and this cheerfully remote quality about the things going on. It was exciting, like brand-new life. I still think just as much of that book today as when I first read it. It seems like one of the real ground-breaking books of the last thirty years. *Huck Finn* continues to be a book whose range of sadness and funniness, whose pure narrative momentum, is hard to get around. Unfortunately, it's become canonized and emasculated. Hemingway's stories. I don't know anyone who can honestly read *In Our Time* and say that there's not something wonderful in it or not be tremendously moved by that incantatory style. *A Farewell to Arms* is a tremendous novel. And I remember that *Henderson the Rain King* was another book that floored me when I first read it. The same for the Snopes trilogy.

Interviewer: Writers like Pynchon and Barth are conspicuously absent from your list . . .

McGuane: Actually I like their work, but if you compare them to Bellow or Mailer you start discovering their deficiencies. Barth and Pynchon are clearly *brilliant* writers, but that quality of what the Spanish would call "caste"—I'm not sure it's in those two guys. I guess I'm basically simpleminded as a reader. For example, I have no interest whatsoever in Borges. He just doesn't do anything for me, even though I would concur with the most positive statements that people make about his writing. He's just not for me. Neither is Cortázar.

Interviewer: What about Márquez?

McGuane: Márquez is unbelievably good. I just read *The Autumn of the Patriarch* and, God, it's fabulous stuff—I almost prefer it to *One Hundred Years of Solitude.* Márquez is breathtaking because you feel that down to the little harsh details, he's right on. Márquez and Günter Grass both present this tremendous congestion of life as well as more abstract issues. Márquez and Grass are two of the few writers who can engage their whole monstrous personalities in the projected world of their novels. Faulkner could do it. Melville did it. Mark Twain did it. They make the New England Renaissance look like an aviary. I am fascinated by this ability, and in fact I hope to get some of it into my own work. My biggest problem with the novel is whether or not I'm producing a sturdy enough tissue for that tension, since it's so miserably low in its lows and in its highs it approaches goofiness. I'm trying to find a way to avoid trivializing the serious stuff without undermining the comedy of it.

Interviewer: Are there any contemporary American writers you especially admire or feel affinities with?

McGuane: Nobody very surprising, I suspect: I like Barry Hannah, Raymond Carver, Harry Crews, Don Carpenter, Don DeLillo, Jim Harrison, Joan Didion. DeLillo has categorized a certain kind of fiction in a way that seems absolutely definitive: "around-the-house-and-in-the-yard fiction." There are a lot of good writers who belong to that group—a lot of recent women writers are in that school, for example, and many of them are tremendously good. At the same time, writers with broad streaks of fancifulness or writers who have trained themselves on Joyce or Gogol, as I did, may feel a little reproached when we compare ourselves to these writers who write about the bitter, grim, domestic aspects of living. You feel, gee, I'm pretty frivolous compared to these serious people. Sometimes this can be a misleading reproach because you may decide that you need to change your subject matter if you're going to be a serious writer.

Interviewer: Have comparisons to Hemingway been an albatross for you?
McGuane: There's a lot I like about Hemingway's writing, so when people say there are Hemingwayesque aspects to my writing, what am I supposed to say? Within the last year, writers as disparate as Cheever, Malamud, and Carver have been accused of Hemingwayism. When people say that, they're attacking you. Hemingway lived a kind of life that I would like to have lived, although I've never identified with him closely. I see Hemingway as being a real American Tory, the sort of guy I couldn't have gotten along with, and I see a cruelty and heaviness in his personality. When I was growing up, I was very much in rebellion against the midwestern, Protestant values he represents to me, so a lot of these Hemingway comparisons have seemed a mile off. His world view was much more bleak than mine, more austere, and his insistence on his metaphysical closed system was very deterministic, fanatically expressed. Still I have to say that there was a time when I would read his stuff and it seemed wonderful. I read books of his today that I still love. But when I look at a lot of his writing now I come across that clipped Hemingway rhythm, and it can have an appalling, scriptural feeling to it. At his best he was a fabulous writer. I just read an interview with Heinrich Böll and he acknowledged that Hemingway's surface was a carpentry that you just couldn't walk by without acknowledging. Any writer who says he has walked by without noticing it is a liar.

Interviewer: Your presentation of female characters seems to have changed distinctly for the better over the years.
McGuane: First of all, I would like to concur with Malcolm Lowry in saying that a writer is under no obligation to create great characters. Nevertheless, part of the explanation for my portrayal of women in my earlier works has to do with my trying to find my way through a problem that a lot of men from my generation have: the attitude that you weren't even *supposed* to know anything about women, that they were frightening or something to be made fun of. When I went back to my high school's twenty-fifth reunion recently, I noticed that the men immediately went right back into the adversarial

business that we had shared back in the fifties. When I was growing up men and women were raised in the atmosphere of what used to be called "the war of the sexes." One of the macho-comic aspects of *The Bushwhacked Piano* was to deal ruthlessly with the women in the novel, using satire as a purgative. I hope, though, that I'm coming closer to an authentic presentation of women in my recent books, a vision that maybe has something to do with me casting off some of my own ignorance about women. I'd say that a big part of my education about women has come from having three daughters. I wonder what type of place I'm helping to prepare for them, what societal vices I'm perpetuating for them. These are the kind of moral issues I want to deal with in my writing. I don't sit around worrying about what nations are invading other nations; I don't understand those issues.

Interviewer: Working here at the ranch must make your writing habits a lot different than those of most writers. What kind of routine do you have?

McGuane: Let me give you what my dream day would be, if I could stick to it. It would be to get up early, get all the horses and cattle fed so that wouldn't be hanging over our heads, eat a bowl of cereal and make some coffee, and then go to some really comfortable place and just read for three or four hours. Most of my morning reading for the past ten years has been some form of remedial reading, my personal list of things I feel I should have read, all those books that make me feel less than prepared when I sit down as a writer. For example, this last year during the winter—a season when I have lots of time to read here—I read the King James Old Testament. I'd never read it. I've known for thirty years that I was supposed to have read it, but I never did. All this type of reading is a steady scrubbing away of the possibilities of guilt, of the fear of pulling my punches when I sit down to write because I feel inadequate in my education. I think you should expect a writer to be a true man of literature—he should know what the hell he's talking about, he should be a professional. So this kind of preparation is one thing I'm trying to get covered, knowing, of course, it's a lifetime project. Anyway, after I read I spend three or four hours in the afternoon writing, and then I go back working on the horses until dinnertime comes, eat dinner, and then spend the evening reading things I just want to read until it's time to go to sleep. Of course, lots of things go wrong with that schedule. Part of it depends on the season, and there's days you've promised to do things with the children, or days you'd rather go fishing or hunting, or days when there's a problem with a horse and it takes four hours to get it straightened out. But that's the pattern I strive for.

Interviewer: What comes first when you begin new work?

McGuane: I hate to keep speaking in analogies—Charles Olson said that the Sumerian word for "like" meant both "like" and "corpse," and that the death of a good sentence is an analogue—but with some things you just have to use them. When I start something it's like being a bird dog getting a smell; it's a matter of running it down in prose and then trying to figure out what the thing is that's out there. Sometimes it might be a picture. This morning when I was writing I was chasing down one of those images. It was just a minute thing that happened to me while I was recently down in Alabama. We had rented a little cottage on the edge of Mobile Bay and at one point there was stormy weather out on the bay; I wandered out to see what kind of weather it was and the door blew closed and locked me out of the cottage. I thought about getting back inside and I sat down and there was one of those semi-tropical warm summer rains starting to come down like buckshot. Somehow the image of stepping outside to see what's going on and having the wind blow the door shut has stuck in my head. I don't know what that image *is* exactly, or what it means, but I know that ever since I came home I've been trying to pursue that image in language, find out what it is. That image begins to ionize the prose and narrative particles around it so that words are drawn in, people and language begin to appear. That's when things are going well. When that's happening, any reader will recognize that flame-edge of discovery, that excitement of proceeding on the page that is shared between the reader, the writer, and the page. You're feeling that gathering energy as it burns through the page. And it's not a made-up thing that you've laid on the page, it's an edge that you feel going through it. To me, it has always come in narrative form. Sometimes the process draws in these adversarial relationships, as with these rivalries, which are not a conscious thing on my part.

Interviewer: Once this "ionization process" begins to occur, do you know in advance where these relationships are going to be taking you? Or is it a process of discovery for you?

McGuane: The latter. I begin to feel where the fiction is going on its own and then I begin to guess at what the consequences of certain things would be. Let's say that you're riding your bicycle on a warm October day down the old road in front of the ranch here, and you're three miles from the house and you begin to think, what if it starts to snow? That's the kind of question I begin to ask while I'm writing. I may only have written about the bicycle ride and then I start thinking about the snow, positing the things that could happen. It's a cloud chamber: you have these clouds first and then you drive electrical charges through it and things begin to take shape. That's how I write—with a lot of "what if's?" Procedurally what I do before I start is to make a deal with myself that I am willing to revise to any degree that is necessary. I have to make that deal in a very sincere way: I assume I have all the time in the world to finish a book because I know it may take many revisions before I get it right. *Ninety-two in the Shade* took six or seven complete drafts. Once I've made that deal with myself, I'm free because as I'm writing I can try any kind of expansion of the armature of the novel as it goes, knowing that if it doesn't work, that's okay, I can try something else. I'm not going to say, "God, there's fifty pages I've just wasted." I don't let myself think in those terms. I'll also admit that I've outlined every book I've ever written before I've started it. Then I've thrown out every outline relatively early on. It continues to seem important to make those outlines because their wrongness energizes what I finally find, whereas that doesn't seem to happen if I simply start and roll on. But if I begin by trying to live up to the outline and then find forceful reasons not to use it, then I'm getting somewhere.

Interviewer: Could you talk about how you decide to leave things *out* of a book? In *Nobody's Angel*, for example, you chose to leave out the scene where Patrick discovers that his sister is dead.

McGuane: Whether or not that was a good idea I can't comment on, but here's the way I arrived at it: I decided that the situation had been prepared for to the degree that the reader's version of it would be better than the writer's. I also thought there was a grave danger of having almost *anything* that was said seem to be a trivialization of it. So I decided to say nothing. That was a tough choice and it wasn't a choice where I did it and immediately knew it was exactly the right thing; it was just my best judgment under the circumstances. I'm very interested in what's left out in fiction and in the stops a writer imposes on his material. Montaigne said that there's no better way that the power of a horse can be seen as in a neat and clean *stop*. There are great cutting horses who can run and run continuously, making all kinds of moves back and forth, but they're limited horses because they don't know when and where to stop. A *great* horse, though, like that roan out in back, will make a tremendous move and then *stop*: he knows that the cow is held, even though the cow is in a complete state of confusion, and he'll hold that position until he is threatened again by a cow trying to return to the herd, and then *crack*, he'll start again and then *stop*. This is so much more powerful a thing for an animal to do than simply roaring back and forth in front of the herd to prevent that cow from returning by sheer athletics.

Interviewer: You lay your plots out for readers differently in each of your books.
McGuane: Sure. Imagine a good gambler who is playing an important poker hand: the way he lays his cards down makes all the difference. With a certain number of cards, a certain number of the enemy are falling off their chairs, so the sequence of the cards can often determine who wins the hands. A writer needs to play his hand very carefully; he doesn't need to play fifty-two card pickup with the reader and throw the whole deck in his face just because he's got control of the deck. That's not playing cards at all.

Interviewer: One suspects that you've probably identified with all your main characters fairly strongly. Is that identification essential to your creative processes, or could you write a book from a perspective that is utterly foreign to you?
McGuane: Writing a book from that kind of a perspective is one of the things I love to plan to do, but I wonder if I could ever do it. I was trained on protagonist-centered fiction, and the first way I learned to write was to view the world from a single perspective—the protagonist's. I often wonder, given how much work it is, whether or not I could go the distance in a full-length novel in a point of view which is utterly alien to my own. I wonder how inventive I would be with that form. Nabokov obviously could do it, but he's so detached. And he is far more boring than it is proper to admit. The game-level is much higher in his kind of work, just as it is with Robert Coover, or Borges, or any of those other systems writers. But for some reason I've never been drawn to that kind of fiction.

Interviewer: You've said that you've never been very interested in the movies and don't really know much about it. Didn't that make the move from writing fiction to writing screenplays seem especially difficult?
McGuane: No, it didn't seem difficult. It's a bit harder if you've been writing screenplays to go back to writing fiction. Especially after you've seen some

movies made from screenplays, you know there's no sense in your doing a lot of interior decorating because somebody else is going to be building the sets. So you just write "Interior, the First Security Bank," in your script and that's all the evocation of atmosphere that you need to supply. Then you write the dialogue. Once you've written screenplays and you go back to writing fiction, you realize the weight of being the full production company for the novel.

Interviewer: Has your involvement with screenplays affected your notion of fiction writing?

McGuane: It's made me rethink the role of a lot of the mnemonic things that most novelists leave in their books. The worst about these things is probably Faulkner, who frequently had his shit detector dialed down to zero. We all read Faulkner in a similar way: we move through these muddy bogs until we hit these wonderful streaks, and then we're back in the bogs again, right? Everyone agrees that Faulkner produced the greatest streaks in American literature from 1929 until 1935 but, depending on how you feel about this, you either admit that there's a lot of dead air in his works or you don't. After you've written screenplays for a while, you're not as willing to leave these warm-ups in there, those pencil sharpenings and refillings of the whiskey glasses and those sorts of trivialities. You're more conscious of dead time. Playwrights are even tougher on themselves in this regard. Twenty mediocre pages hardly hurt even a short novel but ten dead minutes will insure that a play won't get out of New Haven. Movies are like that: people just can't sit there, elbow-to-elbow with each other and stand ten boring minutes in a movie. Oh, they will to a degree if they're prepared enough about the historical moment, if they're watching *Gandhi* or something, but not usually. At any rate, I think I go more for blood now, scene by scene in my writing, than maybe I would if I had never had that movie training. But basically it would be more appropriate to ask me if having to do my own grocery shopping has affected my writing. According to reviewers, I've spent the last ten years of my life in Hollywood, but to tell the truth I have logged less than thirty days in Los Angeles. Total. I do have one level of interest in movies, and that's that I like to read screenplays. They're little books. If I hear there's a wonderful new movie out and I can get my hands on the screenplay, I'll read that rather than go to see the movie itself. I enjoy shooting the movie in my mind. I love to read plays for the same reason.

Interviewer: You once said, "Contrary to what people think, the cinema has enormously to do with language." Do you mean that the cinema relies on dialogue?

McGuane: There's only one thing that you can't be without when you set about putting together a movie deal: you can't do without a script, the "material." This material is always some kind of bundle of language, it's a book or a screenplay. You can't take any director in the world and go to a financing entity (like a studio or a bank) and make a deal without that bundle of language. Producers always come back to the same point: who's got the book or who's got the best hundred and twenty pages of writing? Yet that point is often disguised. Screenwriters are not particularly prized members of the moviemaking community, and as soon as things get rolling suddenly it's the director who's the star, or an actor. But when that movie is over and they're ready to go back and make another one, suddenly they're desperate for a writer or a book. That's the irreducible element in the moviemaking business. And in most movies you go to, the characters are continually talking. You get the impression in reading from the *auteur*-theory days of cinematic criticism that there's no conversation in films, that they're all silent movies. And yet if a Martian were to come down and analyze what's happening in films, he'd say, "These humans never shut up. They have pictures of humans and they're talking all the time. They get in machines and they talk in the machines and then they lean out of the window of one machine and talk into the window of another machine."

Interviewer: One of the legends that grew out of your work on *The Missouri Breaks* was that you wrote the script and then Marlon Brando showed up wanting to change everything. Supposedly you two holed up for a week in a motel to thrash things out. Any truth to that story?

McGuane: None. The closest thing there was to that story is that Brando did have ways he wanted to do that film: he wanted to be an Indian and he had two pet wolves that he wanted to be in the movie; moreover, he wanted these wolves to kill the girl's father, wanted them to jump up on the girl's father's horse and eat him. So I was told to go out to Los Angeles and see Brando and get the wolf stuff stopped. I went out there and Brando was at home and I spent a couple of days with him. I had a wonderful time but we never talked about the movie at all. We just talked about literature. You know, he's a very erudite guy and really smart, a kind of crazy-connections smart. At the time he was reading a history of the Jesuits in Minnesota and a book about Louis Leakey's skulls and the prehominids in Africa. He'd get up in the morning and dress, gather all of his books together, and then get back in bed with his clothes on and read all day. He's on the verge of being downright scholarly. So that's what we did there, and when he eventually went off and did the movie he wasn't an Indian. I still don't know *what* he was. He was this kind of tubby Irish killer. I know many people hated that goofy, wild humor he injected into the movie but I appreciated it.

Interviewer: What about your involvement with movie directing? I would imagine that directing *Ninety-two in the Shade* must have been a difficult task for various reasons: it was your first film, it was based on your own novel, you were unfamiliar with the technical aspects of moviemaking . . .
McGuane: The technical aspects of moviemaking aren't that complex, and anyone who's ever directed would say that. There are technical components of the movies that are very complicated but no director knows them. Maybe Hal Ashby or Nick Roeg and a few other guys know the editing process, which is impossibly difficult to figure out, but I don't know of any director who really understands what the state-of-the-art sound or camera equipment is. For that kind of technical know-how you have to rely on your cameraman or sound man to give you what you want to see and hear, or on your editor to give you the narrative sequentiality you want. A director has to rely on the people around him. I had never directed before, and I'm not particularly delighted with the job I did, but at the same time it became clear pretty fast that this was just another typewriter and I had to sit there and write as good a tale as I could.

Interviewer: Instead of having Skelton killed at the end, you changed the conclusion of the movie and gave it a kind of wacky, funny ending. Given the kind of relationship that was developing between Skelton and Nichol, I could believe the new ending, but I wondered what your own thoughts were in making that change.
McGuane: First of all, unless you have a lot of money in your budget, you're forced to shoot out of sequence. So as I started doing the film I began wondering about the relationships of all the different parts, and I wound up shooting the ending both ways. You just happened to see a version of the movie with the happy ending; other people see it and it has the other ending.

It was released with both endings and they tried to find the one that would play best. That's called not having the final cut.

Interviewer: Which ending do you think works best?
McGuane: The ending as it was in the book is probably the better of the two, but the happy ending was fun and I thought it was amusing with Warren Oates reading that crazy letter and his angler going off into that surrealist Zululand, wading ashore with his trophy.

Interviewer: Are you interested in directing other movies?
McGuane: I don't think so. Strangely enough I was offered the directorship of *A Star Is Born*. Cute, huh? But while I was making *Ninety-two in the Shade*, I remember thinking what a pale experience it was compared to writing fiction. At first it was rather frightening, with all these people around and a lot of equipment and a lot of power-tripping going on, but then soon it had become as if I were trying to say something with this extremely ungainly typewriter. I kept thinking over and over, this is so much less good than writing fiction, because I'd get an idea and then I'd have to move all this junk around to shoot it, and then by the time I did that, inertia had set in again. That's why movies have to be so well planned, because that's the last chance you have to be really inventive; there's not much room for invention at the process level. At any rate, I don't think I'd want to direct again.

Interviewer: Does writing about Montana, or about the West in general, present some special challenges for a writer?
McGuane: Part of the difficulty for me has to do with the lack of attachment between people and place that I was talking about earlier. So an aspect of this crisis lode that I'm trying to mine as a fiction writer is that I have to make some kind of ligature of connection between people and place. That has to happen, but it doesn't happen here in the West, as has often been thought, by simply stationing human beings in this grand landscape. There's actually something much stronger than that going on between people and places out here. It's more numinous in the sense that "place" for my little daughter Annie is that tree which keeps the heat off her while she's on the swing set. That's what place is for her much of the day and that's what place is for anybody else, even though the *nature* of that place is different for someone from Montana than it is for someone from New Jersey, somehow. It's not different

simply in the calendaresque way, but it's hard to pin down how place really affects people. Somebody said that nobody is born a southern writer—Poe is not a "southern writer"—it's something you elect to be; you let place influence you or you decide it doesn't. I know people from Texas or Montana who are absolutely urbane. Do we think of Donald Barthelme as being a southern writer? Or Tom Wolfe? But I know people from Cairo, Illinois, who consider themselves to be deeply southern.

Interviewer: You're obviously one of those writers who has chosen to be influenced by place.

McGuane: I want to find a way to profit from having spent half my life out here, particularly the half of my life that has been superimposed on a really fragmented upbringing. I've struggled to have a sense of place; as a kid I was always saying, "When I grow up I'm going to go and live at Uncle Bill's house in Sakonnet and work on a lobster boat." But very early on I decided that as soon as I could I was going to go out West. I did, at fifteen, when I went out and worked on a ranch, so my fantasy life became my real life. Today, even though that fantasy is one of the most banal elements of my life, I'm still excited about it. I certainly don't want to become one of those regional writers who collect funny phrases, but I do think you can use nature to charge a fictional landscape with powerful results. I have no interest in replicating Montana or rendering landscapes in a recognizable way, but I do know there is something forceful about these landscapes that should turn up in language.

Interviewer: Is the myth about men and women being freer out here in the West really true?

McGuane: The air of the fresh start is alive here. People are willing to accept the idea that you can pull your life out of the fire and turn it around completely. It's an echo of gold mining days.

Interviewer: Or the story of some midwestern kid who comes out here, becomes a famous writer, and winds up being Montana's cutting horse champion for three straight years.

McGuane: Sounds improbable, doesn't it? As time goes by, I feel closer to Ring Lardner, Sherwood Anderson, Scott Fitzgerald—drifters from the Midwest. You fetch up somewhere. It just happens.

Contemporary Authors
Interview
Jean W. Ross / 1988

From *Contemporary Authors: A Bio-Bibliographical Guide to Current Writers in Fiction*, vol. 24, pp. 310–13. © 1988, Gale Group. Reprinted by permission of the Gale Group.

CA interviewed Thomas McGuane by telephone on July 16, 1987, at his ranch in McLeod, Montana.

CA: You've said that you grew up among storytellers. Who were the early ones, the ones who made you want to tell stories too?

McGuane: They were my mother and my uncle and my maternal grandfather, all Irish Catholics from the Boston area, where storytelling was a cultivated art.

CA: You were already writing seriously at Michigan State University, and after graduation went on to the Yale School of Drama, where you continued to write and graduated with a Masters in Fine Arts. How did your work at Yale fit into your writing plans?

McGuane: I was at that time interested in all fictional writing, including dramatic writing. I remember in the late 1950s and early sixties there was a wonderful creative turbulence Off-Broadway, and I was excited about that. I just wanted to write; I wanted to write plays, novels, short stories—whatever I could do. It seemed that starting in one place was as good as starting in another. But I was and am very interested in plays. At Yale I was a playwriting major, which meant that I was substantially an English major. I did a lot of work in Elizabethan literature and eighteenth-century English drama.

CA: Two novels were rejected before *The Sporting Club* was bought by Simon & Schuster. What were the lessons in the writing of those first two books?

McGuane: As in making anything, you get a better and better feel towards the material that you're working in, whether it's wood or words, through sheer gross exposure. I learned in the course of those two books that it was not enough just to blacken pages, that you must sense a curve in the material, a tendency towards closure and fruition. I found after a certain point that I could bring those things to it. I'm sure that writing novels that didn't work out had a lot to do with that education.

CA: Reviewers have made the inevitable comparison of your work with Hemingway's—based in large part on your mutual locales and themes—and compared you to a lesser degree with other writers. Are there influences or inspirations you can name among other writers?

McGuane: I only know who my favorites have been. It's always hard to say whether or not your favorites have had very much to do with your own practice. I never could see the conflict between liking Hemingway and liking Faulkner. I guess that's now an official conflict, just as the conundrum Tolstoy-or-Dostoevski is an obligatory one. I always liked Hemingway *and* Faulkner; I liked Fitzgerald; I liked Tolstoy, Dostoevski, Turgenev. Probably my biggest influences were Sherwood Anderson, Scott Fitzgerald, Ivan Turgenev, Anton Chekhov, Henry Fielding, Mark Twain, Stephen Crane. I once said to Peter Taylor, "You know, I'd really rather be a reader than a writer." He said, "Me too!" I kind of feel that way, but there's a point in reading at which a sort of frustration develops and you want to do it yourself. That's the interest for me.

CA: Writers who've read voraciously probably have many influences they aren't even aware of.

McGuane: I really like to read, and I've read some pretty unprepossessing stuff, too. I love to read semi-anthropological memoirs, diaries, and chronicles of old cowboys or Aran Islanders or Indians. Sometimes you can read stuff that's really not literary in nature but has the same sort of magic that you wish you could put into your own work. The surface of literature that we try to control is one thing, but there's this mercurial, living thing down at the center that's a mystery.

CA: From the beginning, your characters have spoken and thought in a very hip, wise-cracking kind of way that gives your stories a special snap. In a favorite example of mine, Chester Hunnicutt Pomeroy, in *Panama*, considers at one point that his life is "the best omelet you could make with a chain saw." How hard is it to achieve in the writing?

McGuane: Again, it probably goes back to the Celtic ambience that I grew up in. You look, for example, at Malcolm Lowry's *Under the Volcano.* It's a wonderful book, and it's always maldescribed by critics and reviewers as an altogether tragic book. One of the things that I think is at the core of its power is its wittiness. It's a sort of extreme gallows humor. If you just allow yourself to see that when you look back at the book, though its topics are dire in the extreme, it's on the verge of hilarious. I've always been fascinated by the tension of trench humor or gallows humor—inappropriate humor, a kind of intensification using a comic form of language in the presence of danger or mortality or sadness. I've found those situations more approachable for my particular abilities in that way rather than trying to write something that's really on the nose. I couldn't write morosely about death, for example; I wouldn't know how to do it.

CA: *Ninety-two in the Shade* was the book that got you into screenwriting (and, for that film, directing). Also among your screenwriting credits are *Rancho Deluxe, The Missouri Breaks,* and *Tom Horn.* Do you feel the movie work has strengthened the fiction, or the process of writing it, in any way?

McGuane: I think all writing strengthens the process of writing fiction. A genuine fictional talent should be a robust thing capable of taking on challenges from journalism, screenwriting, or any place that it finds itself. I remember reading an interview with Howard Hawks in which he talked about what a rapid, solid, resourceful screenwriter William Faulkner was. In fact, Faulkner was Hawks's favorite screenwriter because if you were out on the set in an emergency and you could find a folding chair for Faulkner, you could get a new scene. It's good to know those things. Young writers especially are encouraged to think that their talents are these ineffably delicate things that can be damaged and destroyed by a light breeze from the wrong quarter. I think that's not true. I don't think screenwriting ever destroyed the talent of anybody who was meant to survive.

But there's something behind what I'm talking about. After hearing for years about how I'd gone to Hollywood and therefore sold out, I came to think that at bottom journalists and reviewers are frequently envious people, and while they would rarely say that you had injured yourself or your talent through, say, heroin addiction, one trip to Hollywood and you're destroyed beyond recovery. The only thing that explains that is envy because you were highly paid, you were in the company of people in places where *they* weren't welcome. It makes them mad, and it's kind of like class warfare. They write with a certain kind of respect and reverence about someone who's been acquitted for crimes of violence and been in clinics for narcotics addiction. They'll all say what a wonderful thing it is for the book at hand. But about somebody else they'll say, This man was in Hollywood last year, and his present book shows it.

CA: Could you be lured back to movies, or to writing for television?
McGuane: I could be. I remember when I was young seeing great television programs—"Playhouse 90," for example; they did original screenplays. It would be fun to be invited to do something like that. I'd love Stanley Kubrick to say that he wanted me to do an edgy contemporary western. But these are very unlikely things. And I'm now in a situation where I don't have to do it. I used to have to; I had no other way of surviving. *Ninety-two in the Shade* was reviewed everywhere in the nation 95 percent positively. It was nominated for a National Book Award, it was on the front page of the *New York Times Book Review*, it had two or three full-page ads, and it sold ten thousand copies. I made about $12,000 on it. I never saw anything beyond my advance. In fact, I probably still owe the publisher money for that book. The piety with which the literary bystanders tell you that you must not do movies is hard to accept in the face of the requirements that a family can impose on you.

CA: Your novels have attracted some academic attention, including treatment in a 1986 book called *The New American Novel of Manners* by Jerome Klinkowitz. How do you feel about the critical attention?
McGuane: That one, for example, I saw and read. It fascinated me in the same way you would be fascinated if you wrote something and someone intelligent came over to your house and said, "Would you mind if I spoke to you for forty-five minutes about what you've done?" Other people have perspectives on what you've done that you would like to have yourself but can't have because you did it. Sometimes I'll look at that sort of thing and actually wonder whether I intended all the things that are being ascribed to me. At other times I feel that my work is being misread. But my feelings are never hurt by that kind of critic because they're always trying hard to come to grips

with what you've written; it's not something that's dashed off. It seems to me that earns them some respect.

CA: There's sometimes the criticism that your female characters don't seem as real, as fully developed, as the male ones. Do you find them considerably harder to write?

McGuane: Anything that's not me is harder to write than something that's like me. I wonder what Ellen Gilchrist would say if she were asked the same question about the men in her work. I find them to be more wooden than the women in Hemingway's novels. But the question rarely comes up that way because it's not currently the subject of sexual politics. For me it's harder to understand women than to understand men. I have lots of women in my family; I have three daughters, and as they get older I find out more about them. But I've always been a sort of typical male. I've always liked to be with other men; I have the same pack instincts. I probably *am* a more reliable observer of men's activities than women's. So I'd say that the criticism is probably true.

I would like to think, though, that I'm getting better. I did a fishing story for *Harper's* that came out this last spring, and the editor for it was a woman who told me that she was a feminist and that she had been warned not to read me because of the two-dimensional female characters in my books. Because she was doing the piece, she felt she should read more of my work, which she did, and she said she didn't find the criticism to be true at all. It's going away, thank God. But you can get framed, too. A book reviewer came up to me at a writers' conference where I spoke and said that a woman had asked him to review my last book for her paper. She said to him, "Do you know this fellow's work?" He said yes. And she said, "He's a male chauvinist pig novelist. Whatever you think of this book, you are to give it a bad review." Well, I don't think that's fair. Even if I *am* a male chauvinist pig novelist, that's not cricket.

CA: Setting is very prominent in your writing. One feels the steamy atmosphere of Key West reading *Ninety-two in the Shade* and sees the colors and shapes of the western landscape reading *Something to Be Desired*. How much effect does your own location during the writing of a book have on the writing process? Can you write better in one place than in another?

McGuane: When I used to wander back and forth between Key West and Montana, which I did when having the children in school didn't prevent me from doing it, I noticed that I'd do most of my writing in Montana and most of my living in Key West. Also, places that are heightened the way Key West is, the way New Orleans is, the way New York is, are intriguing to novelists. The novel is basically a social form. A novel is always being strained outside of its contours when it's made to portray a kind of solitude or nakedness. Knut Hamsun was able to do it beautifully, but it's rarely done very successfully. In fact, Chekhov, who wrote some very rural-looking stories, was careful to populate them as densely as a ghetto. I love places as such, though strangely enough I don't like to travel. But my wife is from Alabama, and the last ten years I've spent quite a lot of time in the Deep South. I like being a stranger. I like seeing a scene as though I were a floating camera, trying to guess what happened and who's there. I'm really sensitive to that, no matter where it is. If I went to Pittsburgh, I think I'd feel that force of lives lived in a very peculiar way in particular places, and what effect the setting had had on them.

CA: Reviewing *Panama* for the *Washington Post Book World*, Phil Caputo said that you had done in that book "something unusual for authors in mid-career: written an autobiographical novel." Do you consider the book more or less autobiographical than your other novels?
McGuane: I think it's more autobiographical, although if you were to try to track that idea down to the actual incidents of the novel, it wouldn't meet with much success. In that it was a howl of ludicrous despair, it was autobiographically sincere.

CA: Was *Panama* a personal triumph for you even though it didn't do well in sales?
McGuane: I've been all over the compass about that. It's got a funny history for me. For a long time I was sure it was the best thing I'd written. Now I think it's kind of an interesting book on the shelf, but I'm not sure it's the best thing I've written; it operates from too narrow a base to satisfy me right now. But it was such a crazy stroke from where I stood that it had a way of widening the possibilities, and I'm still very grateful for that. A progression had been seen in my first three books, and there were a lot of people who liked that progression and had imagined in their own minds what book four would be like. I had even done that. And so I saw to it that the fourth book was a complete departure from the earlier books. I think I really needed a departure. It takes ten years to get through three books, and that's a long time

to be doing anything with something like a pattern in it. I wanted to stretch my wings a little bit. From that point of view, I look back on *Panama* as a great refresher, and I still like it a lot. I probably have more vociferous fans of that book than anything else I've written. While it got some of the worst reviews I ever got, it also got the best reviews I ever got. It got a great review in the *New Yorker*, where I had never gotten much attention before. There was no middle ground in the reviews: the negative ones were so outraged. I think Jonathan Yardley said it was proof that I should never write again.

CA: Was it pleasing in a way to have done a book that stirred much emotion, pro and con?
McGuane: Looking at it from some altitude, I can say yes. At the time it was like being in a gang fight. It was so unpleasant. There was always something in the mail that was insulting and hurting. It was really painful to go through that. But there was something good about that too, because once I had survived it, I cared a lot less about what they thought. That was another freeing up.

CA: *To Skin a Cat*, a book of short stories, was published in 1986. Was doing the stories a challenge you deliberately set for yourself?
McGuane: Not in a strict sense. I had some things that had accumulated in my mind over a period of years that weren't novels, and I wanted to write them. Superimposed on that was the feeling that I wasn't sure how to write short stories, though I'd read them all my life and read critically about them and loved them. That book took much longer than any novel I've written. With a short story, you can start out with a forty- or fifty-page manuscript and end up with an eight-page manuscript. There are at least two stories in there that took longer to write than my first two novels. Short stories are hard, but when they're right, they're so wonderful. They've got something that poetry can have, a vision much beyond their physicality.

CA: You are also a polished essayist, as the pieces collected in *An Outside Chance* attest. Have your essays attracted a new set of readers, people who aren't so much fans of fiction?
McGuane: They are my contact with average people, people who are not interested in experimental fiction or whatever. One of the pleasures of my career is that I have never had a book out of print. I've never had a best-seller,

except when *Ninety-two* made the bottom of the best-seller list for one week, probably through a skew in the graph. I've never had big sales, and I've always had to do other things to make a living besides just write fiction. But the books have never gone out of print. The nice thing about that is that, after almost twenty years, each of them has acquired a readership and I hear from those readers. It's kind of like having a grocery store: you have your clients out there, and some of them like their beef well marbled and are glad that you keep what they want. It gives me a good feeling having those readers. But *An Outside Chance* has readers completely different from the readers of my fiction, sporting people who are frustrated by the things they read in *Sports Illustrated* and *Field & Stream* and wish somebody would take their activities more seriously, which I do. I'm glad I have that book out. Most of my friends are very nonliterary; they're ranchers, people who live around here, commercial fishermen down South, farmers. Sooner or later they'll say, "Tom, just what is it you write, anyway?" And believe me, I don't give them *Panama*, especially if they've been letting me hunt quail on their farm. I give them *An Outside Chance*.

CA: The pieces of your life seem to have settled well into place since the personal turmoil of the 1970s. Would it be accurate to say that writing, however important to you, is one part of a whole that includes ranching, travel, family?

McGuane: Writing is really the keystone. I do too many other things. In fact, I'm guilty about that. But I'm really incapable of being happy or even making a normal contribution to my personal and family life unless writing is a daily thing I do. That's what I am, a writer. I may be a lousy one, I may be a great one, but I am a writer. Sometimes things happen—we'll travel, or this summer we've had endless house guests—and I'll go for a couple of weeks without writing. I'm just miserable then. I've ranched now for sixteen years, and I don't know whether I'm a rancher or not. I've ridden cutting horses for twenty years, and I don't know whether I'm a cowboy or not. But I do know I'm a writer, and knowing that one little thing is a kind of ballast. I'd hate to be without it. It's very important not to let the literary stockbrokers get to you too much, or they can take that away from you. John Steinbeck died having won the Nobel Prize but feeling that he was a fraud, that his life had been a waste and he had not left anything to his family or his country. That was because book reviewers had decided he was an idiot, and they told him that in all the newspapers right toward the end of his career. He believed it, and he died in misery. *Travels with Charlie,* which was a sweetly charming travel book, was his gravestone, critically. The reviewers savaged it. When Melville died, his wife put on his gravestone, underneath his name and the dates, *Writer.* And everyone thought it was so touching that there was someone still around who thought he was a writer. The only people who can take that away from you are reviewers, and you dare not give them that power.

CA: What would you like to do in the future, in the writing or otherwise?
McGuane: I'm working on a novel now that appears to be longer and, I hope, better than anything I've ever done. You're always in the position you were in when you first started: you're not sure another page will come, you're not sure you can finish it, you're not sure it will be any good. At the same time, the exhilaration of occasionally glimpsing that it might be *very* good is an excitement that never diminishes. I just want to keep doing what I've been doing. I just want to be better at it. I'm as excited about writing fiction as I was twenty years ago. It's the only thing I'm absolutely sure I have any ability at—and I haven't been fired.

In Pursuit of Crazy Language
Judson Klinger / 1989

From *American Film* XIV.6 (April 1989), pp. 42–45, 63–64. Copyright 1989, The American Film Institute. Reprinted with permission of the American Film Institute.

Thomas McGuane is accustomed to rough weather. He's lived and ranched for the better part of twenty years on the wide, open rangeland of southwest Montana, and nothing much surprises him. But what's going on outside his window today is, to lift a line from one of his books, "worse than real different." A fierce winter Chinook is blowing gusts up to a 100 miles per hour, forming impenetrable snowdrifts in a matter of minutes.

In his book-lined study is a desk occupied by a lap-top computer and the manuscript of his latest novel, *Keep the Change*. The window overlooks his ranch, and, if it weren't blowing snow, we would be able to see six thousand acres of soft hills, wide river valleys, snowcapped mountains, and a huge sky that's seven clean shades of blue.

When McGuane's novels arrived in the early seventies, the country was wallowing in post-sixties disillusionment. Nihilism was the philosophy of the era, ennui was the mood, and James Taylor was the soundtrack to it all. Many novelists of the time chose to reflect that mood with cold stories about detached, alienated characters, written in a controlled, minimalist style. McGuane's writing, by comparison, stood out like a hot pink hearse in a funeral procession. In *The Sporting Club, The Bushwhacked Piano* and *Ninety-two in the Shade*, his outrageous wit, hallucinatory prose and comic-romantic-violent vision drew critical comparisons to everyone from Faulkner and Hemingway to the Marx Brothers. The characters that filled his novels were half-crazy, unforgettable people who spoke the most skewed, arch dialogue you'd ever read. But none of his books sold terribly well, so by the mid seventies, like many a novelist before him, he hired out to Hollywood as a screenwriter.

McGuane's literary reputation had grown quietly, but with his immediate success in Hollywood, his "gonzo cowboy" lifestyle acquired real mystique. A tall, rugged outdoorsman with a black-Irish streak, McGuane ran wild for a few years: he carried on with famous actresses, crashed a Porsche at 140 miles per hour, drank and fought with both fists. Still, somewhere along the way, he managed to write his best novel, *Panama*—as well as almost a dozen screenplays.

His intricate, offbeat comedy, *Rancho Deluxe* (1975), starring Jeff Bridges and Sam Waterston as laconic, chain-saw-toting rustlers in Montana, has become a cult favorite in, among other places, prisons. McGuane then directed an adaptation of his book *Ninety-two in the Shade*, which he brought in on time and under its roughly $1 million budget. It featured a dazzling ensemble of Peter Fonda, Warren Oates, Margot Kidder, and William Hickey, and bears the distinction of being one of the few major studio films released with two radically different endings. "That's called not having the final cut," says McGuane. Barbra Streisand was impressed enough by *Ninety-two* to ask McGuane to direct *A Star Is Born*, but he wisely refused the opportunity.

McGuane's best-known screenwork is the high-budget Western, *The Missouri Breaks* (1976)—which might have been called *Dueling Egos in the Sun*—starring Marlon Brando and Jack Nicholson. The emotional turbulence he gathered on that movie, and on *Tom Horn* in 1980, drove McGuane out of show business and back to the literary life.

His chosen homestead of Livingston, Montana (he was raised in Michigan suburbia), attracted many other show-business friends like Peter Fonda, the late Sam Peckinpah, and Warren Oates. Remote as it was, Livingston was still crowded enough that he and his wife, Laurie, recently moved out to a spread at the foot of the Absaroka Mountains, a twenty-minute drive from the nearest town. There he raises cattle, trains championship-caliber cutting horses and writes books (*Nobody's Angel*, *Something to Be Desired* and *To Skin a Cat*). And, in need of timely injections of Hollywood cash to maintain the ranch, he has lately been contemplating a return to writing and directing movies. The producers have never stopped calling.

A Tom McGuane screenplay is always news, and two of his projects are currently stirring up dust. The Mount Company is preparing his Civil War–era comedy, *Flying Colors*, and *Cold Feet* is about to be released by Avenue. Directed by Robert Dornhelm (*Echo Park*), and starring Keith Carradine, Tom Waits, Sally Kirkland, and Rip Torn, the script was a collaboration between McGuane and novelist Jim Harrison, who have been close friends for thirty years, since their college days at Michigan State.

McGuane's choice to deal with Hollywood on his terms, from his pictur-
esque outpost, is considered nothing short of heroic by the legions of
unhappy screenwriters who have chosen instead to lock themselves in eight-
by-twelve rooms all over the Los Angeles basin and wrestle with compromise.

"At the age of forty-nine," he says, "I don't want to spend a lot of my time
in situations about which I'm cynical.

"I think that the respect the industry's given writers has been so minimal
that it's created a situation in which good writers are going to keep that writing which produces their self-esteem elsewhere."

Sitting in an armchair by his stone fireplace, McGuane is a soft-spoken,
friendly, at times effusive host and a natural storyteller who slips effortlessly
from the subject of contemporary Italian literature to an old Andy Kaufman
comedy routine. With his wit and biting irony, he comes off as sort of a one-
man Algonquin round table.

JK: You've lived up here in Montana for twenty years and managed to have a
successful screenwriting career, in spite of the industry saw that it's hard to
sustain a high-level career without living at least part-time in Los Angeles.
TM: You know, there used to be an American fantasy not so long ago that
everybody would go off to Colorado, live in a log cabin and have a computer
terminal. That's one of the fantasies that came after the Abraham Lincoln
fantasy of cutting fence posts and becoming president. But nothing happens
unless people are actually in a room. It's like AA tells people: it doesn't matter
what your motivation is, it's important that you get your body to a meeting.
It doesn't matter what you *think*. You know, fuck your brain. Your brain got
you into trouble in the first place.

JK: Unproduced screenplays usually have a very short shelf life. How did
Cold Feet get made twelve years after you wrote it?
TM: I have to credit Robert Dornhelm, who ferreted this script out of some
musty closet, liked it, and wanted to do it. Cassian Elwes was the original
producer on this thing, and somehow or another it went to Avenue. So its
long shelf life is sort of an accident.

JK: Did you or Jim Harrison rewrite the shooting script?
TM: I rewrote it. The original Buck was very unlike the character whom Bill
Pullman played. He was an almost pure denizen of the seventies [*laughs*].

He was right out of the whiniest of the Eagles music. He was a bit of a doped-out photographer who was working in New York and hanging out with models. We couldn't wait to get him by his little pointed ears and lift him out of the script.

JK: What was the inspiration for Tom Waits's character, Kenny, the health-conscious hit man in *Cold Feet*?
TM: I went out to Los Angeles one time and met some people who were hit men. And, you know, we think about the sort of hideously awful human being who would be a hit man. Literary types like to talk about nihilism and things like that, but hit men are as devoid of what we call "the human" as it's possible to be. I mean, they literally see the taking of life as a job. But since their dossier is so completely strange, we assume they would stand out sharply from the culture around them if we could ever get to meet them. In point of fact, they're just like everybody else, and they even have these little fetishistic hobbies. I got interested in this workout boom, this health-conscious era that we live in, and I happen to know that these guys have the same kind of petty fetishes as the people at *Self* magazine. So the irony of someone who makes his living killing people, and whose real interest is in health, sort of appealed to me.

JK: Reading the screenplay, I assumed that Rip Torn had the part of Monte, rather than Keith Carradine.
TM: That's what I wanted. Rip Torn would have been a terrific Monte. But the feeling out there is that people Rip's age have sex less often than people Keith's age. And since movies, in this country, have become a basic tits-and-ass medium, at some point in the process of going from a script to a film, the question of what's sexy becomes the ruling issue.
     I'm almost prepared to think that what the American movies want to be about is fucking and shooting, and that you're simply fighting city hall to write about anything else.

JK: You can't really be that cynical, can you?
TM: I'm overstating to be humorous, but my experience, over and over, has been that sexiness is imperative, and to ignore that is to court heartbreak. Why else would you cast Gregory Peck as Captain Ahab?

JK: I know of one major producer who won't consider any screenplay that doesn't contain at least one gunfight with Uzis.

TM: We had a situation like that in *The Missouri Breaks*. Nicholson felt that he never got to "go through with anything"—that was his phrase—and that Brando had all the action stuff. Jack was kind of intimidated by Brando. So when Brando left the scene, Jack suddenly came on strong and wanted changes, right now. Arthur Penn called me and asked me if I was willing to make changes on Jack's behalf, and I said no. So they brought in Robert Towne to help the ending. [As a result] you have this extraordinary moment where the father is getting a haircut in the ranch house, and Nicholson comes in, and the father's got a gun under his barber apron, and so there's this thing where Jack gets to shoot the father. Towne wrote that scene.

JK: In the shooting script of *Rancho Deluxe*, there's a scene in which Harry Dean Stanton's character is weeding a garden. But in the film, he's vacuuming giant rugs on the ranch lawn—the famous "Hoovering-the-Navajos" scene. How did that change come about?

TM: There was a production problem—somebody got hurt or something. That scene, which I love, I wrote about twenty minutes before they shot it. I had to write it that morning, but I can't remember exactly why. That's what's nice about those situations—in that air of necessity, you really get some great ideas.

JK: That scene has the kind of arch, lyrical, comedic language your early novels and screenplays are famous for.

TM: I wish there was a greater call for it, frankly. You know, Paul Schrader, among other people, has criticized that side of my writing.

JK: Right. He said that your movies have so many great lines that you start listening for the great lines, which breaks the narrative thread. He also thinks too many great lines make a movie unrealistic.

TM: In general, I think what he says is true. But I think the age of the kind of writing that Paul Schrader's done—that modernist, flattened-out kind of writing—is passing. I like very charged language. I wish we could all write this incredibly vivid stuff, because art is not life. I like language that makes me crazy, that's like tidal movement—it sweeps you into some other district.

JK: Since you consider yourself primarily a novelist, is it worth it to put yourself through hell over a screenplay?
TM: I think it's kind of a bad sign. Cocteau said, and I'm always quoting this: "A writer should never do anything hard."

JK: After serving as the location for both *Rancho Deluxe* and *The Missouri Breaks*, this little town, Livingston, Montana, was the focus of a lot of media attention as a late seventies "in" spot—a new artists-celebrity colony, with your ranch as the hub of the action.
TM: I used to be quite a bit more sociable than I am now, and I didn't mind being the center of this kind of . . . commune. Twelve years ago or more, I kind of outgrew that. It wasn't what I wanted to do anymore. It's interesting, you know, wildness kind of takes the place of work. I had worked pretty hard most my life, and I had a period, much shorter than commonly supposed, where I just kind of ran the streets. But that, sooner or later, will devour work. The work I like to do requires long-term concentration—every day, good hours. It doesn't quite fit that chaotic lifestyle.

JK: So that lifestyle was exaggerated in the press?
TM: Yes. I did have friends who were always welcome. But what happens is, the nation is so utterly gaga about celebrities that, though you and I may know that Jeff Bridges is a normal human being who's fun to have around, if it gets in the papers, suddenly the two of you are in this intense *life drama*, where celebrities *encounter* on the high plains of Montana. Then, in New York, they get quite worked up about it, because they're all foaming to get out of that septic hellhole where they live.

JK: How often do you go down to L.A. to pitch ideas or discuss projects offered to you by producers?
TM: I haven't done either one for at least a decade. I certainly would, you know. I'm thinking now that I might want to do something again, and I'll do whatever it takes. I wouldn't direct a movie unless I was going to stay and be in their faces until the thing was done. You don't want to phone it in on any level.

I had a deal with Sydney Pollack that fell apart during the [writers] strike . . . we were just going to make a movie. We weren't going to dog-ear it by running around town and boring everybody with an outline. We were just going to get on the same wavelength, and then I was going to try to put my heart and soul in it because I had all this *freedom*. But that's the closest I ever came to a movie deal I'd really loved to have had.

Sydney has hired a number of good writers over the years and not gotten good screenplays from them. He asked me why I thought that was, and I said because people who get into his position, generally, are masters at controlling the agenda. When you control the agenda of an artist, you cancel his being an artist.

JK: You once described Brando, Nicholson, and Penn as being "Kissingeresque in moving other people around for their own plans."
TM: Movies are always described as a "collaborative medium," but all the key players are famous for being uncooperative. The higher up the ladder they get, the more they specialize in controlling the agenda. By the time you got all those guys together, you were closing in on a very, very narrow unoccupied field of control. At that point, it appeared to be absolutely Chinese, the minute gestures that would shift power around the situation.

When I was first working with Arthur, I strongly felt his attention to the matters of the screenplay. As soon as the first movie star arrived, I was startled by how my status in the project just evaporated. I remember one day Arthur and I were talking about something that was intensely interesting to me, and Jack Nicholson came in, and suddenly Arthur seemed to be incredibly interested in how *blue* Jack's eyes were. And Nicholson's standing there like this little balding fireplug, and we're really trying to think about how blue his eyes were! At that point, my interest in the project literally went out the window. I said to myself, "What am I going to do next, because I ain't gonna do this anymore."

JK: You seemed to have lost your enthusiasm for filmmaking after *The Missouri Breaks*.
TM: I'd have to say that I'm only *now* getting over *The Missouri Breaks*. I wrote it as something that I could direct, that would star my old buddies— Warren Oates and Harry Dean Stanton and those kind of guys. It was going to be an ensemble movie about a little gang of outlaws who outlived their time.

Then, all of a sudden, this star casting came in, and it went from being prospectively a very interesting genre movie to this kind of *monster*.

JK: Forty years ago, Westerns were an American Myth exported to the rest of the world. A lot of foreigners still think Americans all wear cowboy hats and settle their disputes with gunfights at high noon.

TM: I'll tell you—it's worse than that. The Western is the *only* mythology we've ever produced. I'm alway surprised that the commonly exploited mythological-origin story of America is not the Civil War, which is the thing that sets America apart from all other nations. But for some reason or another, the myth of the cowboy, which [John] Milius sees as the final version of the Aryan Herdsman Myth, is the one that's been our central myth. And for some reason, it seems to have disappeared.

Nobody wants Westerns anymore. I'd love to write another Western. More than anything.

JK: What are some of your favorite Westerns?

TM: I love just about everything John Ford did. I love a lot of the early Sam Peckinpah movies: *Ride the High Country* and *The Wild Bunch*. I absolutely loved *Hud* and *The Last Picture Show*. To me, *The Last Picture Show* was so good, I remember exactly where I was sitting, what day it was and what the weather was when I saw it.

JK: Didn't you get into a fistfight with Peckinpah that started out as an argument about Westerns?

TM: That's a funny story. What happened was, we were at a table of really boring people, one of whom was a journalist, but we didn't know she was writing about us. And Sam leaned over to me and said, "What can we do to get out of here?" I said, "Why don't we pretend we're having an argument, stand up, and say, 'Let's step outside,' and we'll step outside and leave." So I made some phony remark to him, and he *exploded*. Scared me to death—he was such a good actor. About two months later, an article comes out in a magazine about how Peckinpah and I had this fatal falling out and stepped outside for a fistfight in a parking lot. All we wanted to do was go home.

JK: You once called your script for *Tom Horn* "the Western to end all Westerns." **TM:** Gee, what an arrogant youngster I was! I wonder if I said that before the movie came out? Because I really did try to write this killer Western. It was this enormous thing, a two-hundred-page screenplay. It was this huge, inclusive version that I wrote by myself before Bud Shrake became part of it.

JK: How much research was involved in *Tom Horn*?
TM: Enormous research! God. Endless research. By research, I mean a lot of fascinating reading about the period. [Horn] lived in a hugely interesting era. He was an abused child out of a Pennsylvania Dutch family. Spoke German as his first language. He jumped on a freight wagon and ran away from home. Ended up in Santa Fe, learning Indian languages, working as a translator. Went through all of the bloody and disillusioning things that happened in that era to the Indians among whom he lived, and ended up being deprived of the usual civilized morals of the day—ended up being a very dangerous character. I thought it was a great story, seen that way.

I wanted to do that project for years and years. Tom Horn was the perfect subject, and Steve McQueen was the perfect actor for it. I thought he was a terrific actor. He was not any fun at all to work with as a producer.

JK: You had a terrible time with him, didn't you?
TM: Yeah. His word wasn't any good. He woke up in a different world every morning—absolutely no continuity from day to day.

I went out [to L.A.] with a long script to meet with him, and he didn't want me to change a *word* of it. He made me promise I wouldn't change anything! By the time I'd been there two days, he didn't like anything in it. But this was a guy who just smoked dope twenty-four hours a day. The most wide-open pothead I've ever been around.

I didn't know what kind of ill health he was in at the time. But he had a nice side. It was like being around a thug: there was a terrific side to him, and then there was a side you absolutely couldn't trust. Apart from that, I thought the camera loved him.

JK: When did he turn the script over to Bud Shrake?
TM: The night my phone rang out there in California at about three o'clock in the morning. I picked it up, and I seemed to have a heavy breather on the other end. And this voice said, "You can take your macho bullshit and go back to Montana." I knew Steve and I were not as happy as we'd once been together.

JK: Who has the film rights to *Nobody's Angel*?
TM: It was bought by Warner Bros. There was some kind of a development relationship between them and Robert Redford's company, and I worked

with Redford fairly closely till we did a script and at least one revision—and really enjoyed it; he's very bright. Then it just went into that vast, intricate filing system which is the prospective films of Robert Redford.

JK: Why do you think so many of his projects are condemned to development hell?
TM: I think that he has the same problems that anyone faced with an infinity of choices has. What an infinity of choices produces in most cases is indecision. Indecision and procrastination are probably the two greatest sources of unhappiness known to man. I actually think that procrastination and boredom are the two great evils of modern man.

JK: Was Redford planning to play Patrick Fitzpatrick [the book's hero] and produce and direct?
TM: Yes, as I understood it. He plays his cards very close to his chest, even in the most intimate work meetings. So you really never know what he's thinking of doing.

Again, it's a strategy meant to maintain the infinity of choices. The infinity of choices might make you unhappy, yet you spend all your working time to make sure the infinity is maintained. It's unbelievable. I wish we did see more of him. He has come up and visited us, and he's really a good fellow.

As opposed to most actors I've known, I would have to say that Redford is pretty much of a grown-up. He could go on with his life in a very high-powered way without acting at all.

JK: As one way of getting back into directing, have you considered taking a script through the Sundance Institute and having Redford produce it?
TM: No, I never have. To be perfectly honest, I think writing novels is a more important thing for me to do. In terms of my usefulness on earth, it's a higher degree of usefulness for me to figure out how to write these unremunerative novels.

JK: What qualities do you hope for in a director?
TM: The thing I like in filmmakers is the same thing I like in novelists—I like the sense that they have some sort of personal vision that is independent of their second-guessing markets. When you're watching a marketeer masquerading as a director, it's an unsavory spectacle.

JK: And who do you like?

TM: I thought Hal Ashby was a marvelous director. I like Nick Roeg. I have an appreciation for big, strong-minded directors who sweep all the materials into their own uses. That's why Ford seems to be such a model. Bertolucci has such a tremendously strong view of things, and Altman, at his best, has that, too. I know he's sort of fallen on hard times, but I think his films are just terribly interesting. *McCabe and Mrs. Miller* seems to me to be a model of new cinema. I love Terry Malick. I thought *Badlands* was superb. I know everyone else thought *Days of Heaven* was boring; I couldn't see *anything* boring about it. I loved it. Malick's talent is so enormous, it's kind of like watching Raymond Carver work. He has to come back, or come back to the place he's welcome. Maybe he should be a writer.

But my all-time favorite American director is John Huston. I look down the list of the films he made and get a warm feeling.

JK: I've heard that Malick's absence is partially due to the fact that he had a hard time handling the compromises and emotional abuse that come with the territory.

TM: You know, I think it would really be healthy if writers would just get a little bit tougher—slightly more savage in our dealings with the other elements—and start fighting for stuff.

JK: It seems as though you've done that more often than a lot of writers.

TM: But to tell you the truth, I feel guilty about not doing more of it. I'm sorry I didn't go over to the Red Lodge and break a fucking chair over Robert Towne's head when he was in there fucking up the end of *The Missouri Breaks*. I'm sorry that I didn't tell Jack Nicholson that when you make deals like that, you deprive yourself of your own claims of being an artist—that you're just another filthy little hustler like the ones you complain about. I'm really sorry I didn't do it. But next time, I will do it. Next time, I'm gonna be absolutely right in people's faces, from A to Z. You have to care enough to do that.

Publishers Weekly Interviews: Tom Mcguane

Mark Harris / 1989

From *Publishers Weekly*, September 29, 1989, pp. 50, 52. Reprinted with permission of *Publishers Weekly*.

"The heir to Hemingway"; "Captain Berserko"; "macho pig"—Thomas McGuane has had plenty of labels to live down and just as many to live up to in his nine-book career, and none of them seems to do him justice.

Barely thirty when he burst onto the literary scene with *The Sporting Club*, he saw his star as a novelist soar with *The Bushwhacked Piano* and *Ninety-two in the Shade*. Lyrical, coruscating, and subtly political, his books made him a media darling—the counterculture cowboy. By 1975 he was writing *and* directing the film of his third novel, and careening toward celebrity and its gossip-page trappings: affairs, divorce, remarriage (to Margot Kidder), another divorce, remarriage, prodigious drinking, and a reputation for excess in just about every area but his lean, acute prose. But with his fourth novel, *Panama* (1978), the critics who had made McGuane a hit "couldn't even remember what they had in mind," he recalls. The crash-and-burn reviews were more personal than literary; they took the author to task as much as they did the book.

But McGuane's private life has long been stable, alcohol- and trauma-free, and his critical fortunes have resurged in the last decade. With the novels *Nobody's Angel* (1982) and *Something to Be Desired* (1984) and the short story collection *To Skin a Cat* (1986), the author pursued his concerns with an ever-stronger and more reflective voice. His first novel in five years, *Keep the Change*, just out from Houghton Mifflin/Seymour Lawrence is likely to keep him on the ascendant.

A hunter, avid fisherman, and cutting-horse champion rider, McGuane meets *PW* on a stopover in New York City before continuing on to Labrador to fish for Atlantic salmon. Settling in for dinner after a long day of flying, he begins with espresso: "I need to get some IQ points back." Six-foot-two, long-limbed and darkly tanned, he approaches what he wryly calls "deep middle age" with undiminished enthusiasm and good humor.

Born in 1939 and raised in Michigan, McGuane felt the desire to write early on; his first attempt at a novel came at age nine, and "by the time I was a junior in high school, it was all I could think about," he recalls. As a young man, he thrived in the company of other writers; his classmates and friends have included Edmund White in high school, Jim Harrison in college, and William Hjortsberg at Yale Drama School, where McGuane took an abortive stab at playwriting.

Until his late twenties, McGuane lived nomadically, spending time in Salinas, Key West, Spain, Italy, and Ireland. In the late sixties, longing for a more permanent home, he settled in Montana, where his cattle and horse ranch in tiny McLeod now houses a blended family that includes his wife Laurie, their young daughter, and, intermittently, three older children from earlier marriages.

Professionally, he's roved almost as much. First published at Simon & Schuster (where "editors kept leaving *me*"), he decamped for Farrar, Straus, where he stayed for three books with Michael di Capua. What he calls "a business dispute" precipitated a move to Random House, where, he says, "I was just not at home." His last two books have been with the Seymour Lawrence imprint, first at Dutton and, with *Keep the Change*, at Houghton Mifflin. There, he says, "I'm off on another happy relationship, and I hope this one lasts."

Although its tone—a precisely calibrated balance of sensitivity, restiveness, passion, and irony—is a departure from much of his previous work, *Keep the Change* will be instantly recognizable as a McGuane novel to his loyalists: its territory, thematically and geographically, is purely his own. With a hero returning to his western roots to puzzle out his feelings for two wildly different women and a conclusion brought on by no more than a careful unfolding and discovery of desires, the novel reverberates with his past writing to offer a wholly new effect. And characteristically, it's trim—under 250 pages.

"I know it's not exactly in the tradition of post–World War II American writing," says McGuane, "but I think that you should use as few scenes and paragraphs and words to achieve your effects as possible. If you're building fishing rods or shotguns or yachts the standard is lightness that is as much as possible commensurate with strength. I think that's a universal aesthetic, and the kind of rich overwriting which has become the standard in a certain kind of American fiction is really a mistaken idea. Accretional monument-building as a style is not one I've ever liked."

Unsurprisingly, McGuane's redrafting consists largely of excision. "For me to write a book that ended up being four hundred pages, the first draft would have to be two thousand. That's part of the excitement of revising, to find something that stands on its own strength rather than depending on the buttressing I thought it had to have."

As for the labels, McGuane ingenuously brushes most aside. The Hemingway comparison (in terms of both writing style and productive/destructive lifestyle) has dogged him throughout his career. Of that persistent identification he says, "either I'm outgrowing the issue or it's going away." On the antics in the 1970s that won him the "Berserko" sobriquet: "By comparison with today's dour, money-crazed climate, it does look like it was one great party. Everyone was in a slightly more festive mood. But in the seventies, I also published four or five books, wrote about eight screenplays and about forty articles. I was getting a lot done."

Only the accusation of insensitivity (or short shrift) to women in his prose still rankles him, although he laughs when discussing the female editor who'd been "told that I was one of the macho pigs—me and Harry Crews and Jim Harrison." (After reading McGuane's works, she reported to him, "I don't think you're a macho pig at all!")

While not fond of answering for his characters—whose records with women are fairly unenviable—the author admits that "I don't think I'm ever going to make a certain type of women's literature proponent happy. A lot of women are extremely angry. For those people, who are conscious of the depth of the bad debt that has been owed to women for a long time, almost anyone [can] have some of the features they associate with the enemy. It's like having a German accent in 1919. But I have three daughters, and I'm extremely sensitive to what I perceive as their rights in the world."

A hallmark of McGuane's writing is its sense of location; the physical world is deeply important to his characters and his prose. Most frequently, it's been the town of Deadrock (a fictional gloss on Livingston), Mont. "I require that writing seem to belong somewhere," he says. "If it's floating and I can't attach it to the earth at some point, frustration sets in." Is he a late-arriving regionalist? "I object to the term officially. But in a funny way I sort of like it. Finding people who think of me as a Montana writer reinforces my wish to have succeeded in putting down roots there."

In recent years, McGuane's home state has been the site of a flourishing literary and cultural community—Richard Ford, William Kittredge, James Crumley, David Quammen, and a host of other writers, actors, and artists make their homes in Paradise Valley and Missoula. While McGuane jokingly refers to the Montana literary renaissance as "five guys with hardcover sales of eight thousand each," he admits it pleases him. "I love Montana, but at the same time there's a certain kind of cultural deprivation that I would like to see changed. People who are born and grow up there love it so much they don't ever leave. They aren't liable to produce Márquez characters, and you go around sort of pining for that, wishing that they'd be just a tad more flamboyant."

McGuane's ranch, which keeps him completely busy for about half of every year, has taught him that "there are other circadian rhythms besides the semester system. Like it or not, you get tied into seasons, not just seasons of the planet, but breeding seasons. . . ." During the winter months, when the ranch more or less runs itself, McGuane's schedule is an idyllic-sounding confluence of writing and reading, done in "a comfortable little log house. You're there, you can't go anyplace else, and you can just make a pot of coffee, go back to bed and read and read." His passion for literature seasons his conversations, and his enthusiasms are generous and global: Chekhov, Cheever, Raymond Carver, Joyce Cary, Graham Greene, and uncountable others. Although he's more reserved in criticism, his assessments can be mercilessly pithy: with scalpel precision, he dismisses a contemporary's prize-winning novel as "Micheneresque."

For a time in the 1970s, McGuane was a prolific if almost consistently dissatisfied screenwriter whose credits included *Rancho Deluxe, The Missouri Breaks, Tom Horn*, and his own *Ninety-two in the Shade*. Last spring his name turned up on the cult comedy *Cold Feet*, which he had written with Jim Harrison in 1976. "I literally couldn't remember what it was about," he admits, and adds that he has no plans to return to film writing. "It's menial work," he says.

McGuane begins his novels with a sense of outline and structure, but all of the big issues in his fiction are resolved in the writing itself. "It's nice to decoy oneself by making outlines and planning, but all the writing you're able to keep comes up just the way phrases come up for musicians. But for some reason, you have to pretend that it's plannable and go through a certain number of mnemonic devices just to get started."

The process was somewhat different when McGuane was younger; writing *Ninety-two in the Shade* in 1973, he says, "I felt as if I had a fuel tank strapped on my back; I felt we were on the cultural nosecone of America, and I had to write about it." While many of his contemporaries became casualties of the era, McGuane survived, and views those years without sentiment or cynicism. "In the mid-seventies, we didn't think in terms of taking a life raft on a boat. A kind of Whitmanesque optimism was afloat," he remembers, "and it's definitely gone. Even then there was a sense that it might end in tragedy, and to some extent it did. There were irreversible misunderstandings between generations that were never repaired, and left an unhealed wound in American life."

That belief resounds in many of his novels, in which wars between sons and their fathers are brutal, futile, and fought unto—and after—death. But the fierce cynicism of some of his earlier writing has given way to something more ambiguous, and perhaps hopeful. "I like the more recent novels better," he says bluntly; when he "squints into" his older novels, he "wants to change everything and start rewriting. You say, gee, I wish I saw everything from a constant stance, like a lighthouse. Going back to a 1955 novel is a little like looking at a 1955 Ford—kind of cute, but tailfins just don't mean today what they did then."

In December, the former angry young man of the American West will turn fifty. With his family life "semi-euphoric," McGuane can pour his boundless energy into his fiction. "The only thing that fills up the work hole in my sphere of need is writing," he says. "Between me and me in the dark of night, I consider everything else a fib, even my ranching. I love to do that—it gives me a physical grounding in the world and an orderly way to say, I'm not gonna use the old head now; I'm gonna get in the pickup truck and go look at fences. But then I say, That's enough now. My real job is as a writer and I've got to get back to work."

Thomas McGuane

Gregory L. Morris / 1989

Reprinted from *Talking Up a Storm: Voices of the New West* by Gregory L. Morris, pp. 201–12, by permission of University of Nebraska Press. © 1994 by the University of Nebraska Press.

Tom McGuane is a writer whose work is marked by as much color and variety as is his life. He has succeeded as a fiction writer, as an essayist, as a screenwriter, and as a film director. At the same time, since his arrival in Montana in the early 1970s, McGuane has turned himself into a thriving cattle and horse rancher, as well as a champion cutting horse competitor. Born in Michigan in 1939, McGuane early in his career wrote with a dark exuberance of the Florida Keys and of his home state. Over the years, however, McGuane has gradually turned both his life and his fiction in a westward direction; indeed, his film *Rancho Deluxe* has become something of a cult classic in the region, providing the modern American West with an ironic and not-always-generous mythology.

McGuane now lives on a ranch outside the tiny town (a post office and general store, combined) of McLeod. Though this interview took place in writing (completed in late 1989), I did have the chance to meet with McGuane at his ranch—though only after an earlier missed connection when I ended up having a beer and a burger at the Road Kill Café in McLeod, served up by a bartender named Sam. (Sam was a woman who played out the almost archetypal Western story: a divorced mother working to complete a teaching degree, with plans to head for Alaska—plans, I learned later from McGuane, she had followed through on.) The day of my visit to the ranch, McGuane showed me first his office, in a small log building on the banks of the West Boulder River. Inside, the first item McGuane pointed out (clearly with great pride) is a recently received Trout Unlimited Award, for his efforts in promoting the trout population near his ranch. McGuane is a writer amazed and pleased at the durability of both his person and his work; he is also a rancher who has found full and comfortable accommodation in the lifestyles of the writing-and-ranching self that is Tom McGuane.

Gregory Morris: Do you still believe in the notion of "America as region," as undifferentiated space? Do you note any significant differences or changes in that "American space" you describe in your fiction?

Thomas McGuane: Yes, I do still believe in America as the basic region; I think we are, if anything, less and less segmented. It seems to me that we're entering the eerie new world of mono-space in America, a kind of vast media neighborhood, which may have some as yet undiscerned virtue.

GM: In your work, you seem noticeably ambivalent about the American West, about both the Old West and the New West.

TM: I certainly am ambivalent about the American West or any other region that attempts to bestow virtue through a kind of blessed nativity. I am a Meritocrat. The values of the "Old West" worth clinging to are the earlier American values worth clinging to and those are the systems and practices that derive from self-reliance. I do like to jar the complacency of the so-called New West. In my ranching, reading, conservation efforts, and writing, I would like to remind the West that the Golden Rule is still far superior to shooting first and asking questions later.

GM: Do you feel you've replaced the Old Myth, the "Old Rugged," with a New Myth of the "New Rugged"? Do you think the New West capable of spawning new myths, new legends? Or are the Charlie Starkweathers the best we can do?

TM: I do think that an area like this which retains a freshness of energy per-haps lost elsewhere has a chance to create if not new legends, at least new exemplary tales; but they will have to make sense within the very acute demands of current coexistence if they are not to be discarded immediately. The Code of the West, by current standards, is mere thuggishness.

GM: Do you have any ideas on the resurgence in Western American writing, especially in its fiction? It seems that serious writers of the American West are enjoying a new popularity, a new visibility.

TM: I don't know where this resurgence of Western writing is coming from. We are still in the frontier period here and this good new work is almost all the work of settlers. At bottom, writers nearly always work from optimism or the gaiety Yeats ascribes to tragedians. The West, generally, is a rather unde-pressing place to live. Maybe that's it.

GM: Is Montana still your "adopted home," as you described it in your essay "Roping, from A to B"? Do you feel less of the adopted son after a few years there?

TM: Yes, I feel settled here finally. I've been here a little over twenty years, raised four children here, voted and paid my taxes here. Sometime not so long ago it sank in that I've lived here far longer than where I grew up and it is certainly now home, I am happy to say: that was a lot of work.

GM: Your vision seems to have grown less ironic, less satiric over time. Does the putting down of roots in Montana have anything to do with a greater affirmativeness in your fiction?

TM: There are some areas from which I have lifted the pressures of satire through a kind of forgiveness. We do live in a time of a sort of furrowed-brow earnestness in which it is considered that irony is somehow a bad thing. I think irony is generally a good thing. Edmund Wilson once counseled people to cultivate a universal irony and he may have been right. Having said that, I do think that a tone of affirmation is definitely growing in my work from a variety of sources, like healthy children, happy marriage, love of the place in which I live.

GM: When I speak of the "greater affirmativeness" in your writing, I'm thinking specifically of the stories in *To Skin a Cat*: stories whose voices are generally sincere and unironic, whose characters are down-to-earth, whose visions are clear-eyed and sure. Yet the title story seems a throwback to your earlier fiction, seems an anachronism among the unironic kinds of stories.

TM: It's just a different story, though it is the oldest one in the collection, in my sort of Nathaniel West mode. I don't think it's important to produce a matched set, like china; and I often think of doing more sharply experimental work in the future.

GM: Did your novel *Keep the Change* fall into any sort of natural pattern, any sort of logical development of your fiction over time? Did that book differ, in any significant way, from previous novels?

TM: *Keep the Change*, in terms of its approach, is a perfectly evolutionary development of the books that preceded it. In fact, it is a key to the books that went before. It has some very systematic approaches to theme; and I'm amusing myself to see if anyone figures them out.

I'm pretty much going to duck your question as to how that book differs from early books. I don't think authors answer that one interestingly. Their strategies for preferment show through too clearly. I prefer seeing myself living and writing my way through life as a writer!

GM: When envisioning the West, do you feel (as Patrick Fitzpatrick feels in *Nobody's Angel*) that the Southwest was the "first part of the West with gangrene"? And has that gangrene spread farther north?
TM: I do think that a kind of corruption spreads across the country from the Sunbelt, a kind of hegemony of warmth promoters. Winter in the Northern Rockies has the same effect that tide has on the beach: it does tend to clean things up on a regular basis.

GM: If America is, indeed, region, do you see yourself as a typically or particularly American author? Do you think your work travels well? Do you have to live in, or at least be familiar with "Hotcakesland" to understand what it is you're driving at?
TM: I suppose I am typically American. I have had a fairly good reception overseas, especially France, Japan, and Holland. *Keep the Change* has been sold in ten countries and I am getting the feeling that something rather larger is happening for me out there. For a long time, I was told my work was "too American" for European consumption. This seems to be more of an English reservation than anything else, part of their ongoing fetish that we are screwing up the language.

We *all* live in Hotcakesland; it pours in through every opening: it is the absolute triumph of commerce over every other value; its effects range from the drug war to the hole in the ozone layer. Anyone who doesn't agree with me is wrong.

GM: Thinking about some of the criticisms of your work, do you feel you're working toward a fairer portrayal of women in your fiction, toward some sort of sexual aesthetic? Do you see insuperable problems between the sexes, problems that render impossible any sort of reconciled, harmonious relationship?
TM: I'm understanding women and other things which are not me better than I used to. The question implies a current political pressure rarely

applied in the other direction. It is important to remember that I am a novelist, not a sociologist. Sure, the once-named "war between the sexes" may go on forever. Still, I raised my three well-adjusted daughters to be self-reliant and to apply the Golden Rule. That's about all you can do.

GM: Perhaps as corollary to these concerns, it seems that the American family does not come off well in your fiction. Do you see the family as a casualty? Is the coherent family, too, a modern impossibility?
TM: Without a chain of command—I don't care who is the captain—the nuclear family will have to go. As for the American family not coming off well in my fiction, where exactly does the American family come off well? Certainly not in statistics.

GM: Could the failure of such relationships be in any way the result of the emphasis you place upon the individual, in that anyone external to that individual is viewed as secondary, as less than significant, as a nonsignificant other?
TM: The modern deindividuated novel, the ensemble novel, the group portrait, the heroless novel is as incomprehensible to me as it would have been to the Greeks or to Shakespeare, or to Saul Bellow!

GM: You seem, also, to dismiss religion as a source of belief and affirmation in your work; religion is, in fact, scarcely visible in your fiction. Characters seem to locate themselves and what little meaning and faith they can discover, in places other than institutionalized belief.
TM: I do have an inchoate pining for religion. I see spirituality in the processes of natural renewal, in creation as it were. And I do think my vaguely Manichean worldview derives from my Irish Catholic heritage. In fact, I am very comfortable considering myself an Irish Catholic, implying, as it does to me, a superimposition of the life of Christ upon earth-worshipping pantheism. Like Flannery O'Connor, I frequently portray people in purgatory, hence the irreligious atmosphere.

GM: Thomas Skelton says in Ninety-two in the Shade: "There are no great deaths anymore." Do you believe this to be true? Have we lost some basic, human capacity for the heroic, and for heroic loss?
TM: You must admit that the feeling that there are no great deaths any more is somewhat insistent. I do think that we have undermined the self to the

degree that a long fall is inconceivable. I hope that is reversible. We go on pining for the Billy Sol Estes and Jim Bakkers and Richard Nixons to assure us that our national social life at least has some verticality. You need only to reflect on the death of Lincoln to sense the chasm between the trivialized present and the resonating individual lives of not so long ago.

GM: You recently turned fifty. Does reaching that age seem in any way momentous to you? Are you surprised to have lasted that long, given the paths your earlier life often took?
TM: Fifty. Yes, it seems momentous but I don't know just how. One is drawn to round figures. One remembers such a short time ago being eighteen and thinking fifty the last word in superannuated. I'm not surprised to have lasted this long and I haven't noticed any limitations yet based on age, except some tolerable morning aches.

Mailer said that a novelist at fifty is at the height of his powers, and I feel at the height of my powers. I don't know if I have matured, but I do know I have a more deeply layered sense of the human condition than I once had. Again, it is important to remember that literature is not sociology. Maturity may not have any particular merit in literature anyway. The greatest relief that has come my way, probably with age, is that I no longer feel as pained at being misunderstood as a writer as I once did. It doesn't hurt that I have numerous loyal readers who aren't having the same problems that some critics have and who have kept all of my books in print, nearly unheard-of in a writer of my generation working in the unfashionable backyard of the continent.

GM: Do you still believe that "dropping six or seven good colts in the spring is just as satisfying as literature"? (Now that you're raising cattle, of course, the question should be about your calves.) Do you still feel—or perhaps feel even more strongly—that "art is no longer as important as life"?
TM: I don't know about the life/literature split any more. They are both so absorbing and exclusive if given free rein. I still raise horses as well as cattle. The cattle business has taken me closer to the day-to-day actualities of Montana life, but the aesthete in me wonders about raising animals to kill. What has changed is that my family life seems so all-important. This is a little bit like wondering which is more important, gasoline or cars. The center of my life is writing; it is that without which I cannot be of much use to anyone or anything else.

GM: You mention that you "grew up amidst an oral tradition." Do you feel that influence is present in your fiction?
TM: I don't know about the influence of storytelling on my writing. I don't think of myself particularly as a storyteller. My passion is language and human perception, not necessarily in the form of stories.

GM: You say elsewhere: "I'm trying to remove the *tour de force* or superficially flashy side of my writing. I'm trying to write a cleaner, plainer kind of American English. . . . I feel I have considerably better balance than I have ever had in my life and I don't care to show off; I just want to get the job done." This remark was made at the beginning of the 1980s. Now that that decade has closed, how would you assess your success in this pursuit of an "American English"?
TM: I would still stand by this statement except to say that I think I am beginning to see possibilities for a new elegance in the American language. I am not so hell-bent on plainness as I may have been recently. In fact, I've been thinking of gradually easing up on the old high horse once again, possibly in the form of a comic novel.

GM: Your work in film seems to reflect your concern for the American West, a concern that spans both the Old and the New West. For instance, in *Tom Horn* and *The Missouri Breaks*, you deal with the historical West, and in the former film with a specific historical figure of that West. In your screenplay for *Rancho Deluxe* you managed to create almost a myth of the New West, the film having attracted a cult following in some areas of the West today. Is this all just coincidence? Or have you found yourself becoming a chronicler (on film) of the American West by choice?
TM: It's a bit of coincidence, though it seemed to me that the West needed some revision; not just the corny cowboys-and-Indians West, but the pompous or backward-looking or nativist West of Wallace Stegner, Vardis Fisher, and even A. B. Guthrie.

GM: Relatedly, you seem to write of that historical West only when you're writing for the screen. Do you ever feel the urge to write historical fiction for print?
TM: I don't like historical fiction, ignoring for now the exceptions that prove the rule (Tolstoy, Stendahl, et al.). I do love almost more than anything to read history, however.

GM: Do you ever feel, then, the urge to create a particularly *large* work, something like McMurtry's *Lonesome Dove*? You've said, for example, that your revision process often whittles down your work—work that originally might have been conceived upon a larger scale—into something more moderate, more contained.

TM: Writing historical fiction does seem to be one foolproof way to get large right now. I like McMurtry a lot, but *Lonesome Dove* is not a good book. I often wish I could write a long book, though few of the books I love are long. Having said that, I would note that the felt need to write "the big book" has injured more writers in mid-career than anything else. In our culture, a certain respect is paid to bigness without reference to anything else. Sharp careerists in postwar American letters have gone straight into the whopper business and stayed there, to their great benefit. A recent member of this school, John Irving, has shown in [*The World According to*] *Garp* that you can toss any damn thing into the stretched old hide of the American novel and thereafter have as your principal problem only the hauling of loot and medals and commendations. I've sometimes thought of writing a novel to my own taste and then have the family fatten it up over the winter by seventy-five thousand to one hundred thousand words, as a sort of cottage-industry approach to literature, cutting them in fairly of course.

GM: Unlike many other contemporary fiction writers, one thing you haven't had to do is to teach within the academy. Why?

TM: I just think that teaching is a job itself, maybe even more on a collision course with writing than a more mainstream job. There is certainly something teachable about fiction writing; the trouble, though, is that students today are not often widely read, and they don't want to remedy that, which makes it sort of hopeless. Many writers work in the academy because it's a hell of a lot easier to be a writer-in-residence than to work for, say, Boeing or the Burlington Northern Railroad; and it's also a hell of a lot easier than subjecting yourself to the workplace brutality of the movie business.

GM: I know you look for places, landscapes, that are the "ragged edges," the "blurred edges" of our American region. Are you still looking for those ragged edges of our continent, for those edges that cut, that are messy, that make your characters bleed so?

TM: I think those ragged edges lie well within the world I know. No further searching required. A serious writer learns, sooner or later, that a sufficiency of material is always right at hand.

Lastly, it is well to remember that even Henry James, who thought out the obligations and systems of the novel more thoroughly than anyone else, concluded that the only real requirement of the novel is to be interesting.

Go West

Renaud Monfourny / 1990

From *Les Inrockuptibles* (Paris), no. 24 (July/August 1990), pp. 100–3. Translated into English by James H. Lee. Reprinted with permission of *Les Inrockuptibles* and Renaud Monfounry.

No matter what he says, after having lived ten intense and extreme years, after having been adored in Hollywood, Thomas McGuane has moved to the country and today takes great pleasure in the American countryside. The man has several sides, the writer is always a sleepy read, but when he takes over, it's his humor and his sense of the tragic that push him to the top. The writer-rancher—one would say the gentleman farmer—is the soul brother in writing of Richard Brautigan and Jim Harrison.

TM: I don't understand why there's this sort of legend around me. I think that certain generations or people born in a particular era are more exposed than others to the stories told about them. I must be one of those, because I've read some stuff about myself that is absolutely not true, pure legend without any basis in truth.

RM: So what part of what they say is true?

TM: It is true that I've had a life that's, shall we say, wild. I've been an author, a director, I've spent quite a bit of time in the world of movies, and I've been married more than once. When I was in Hollywood, I took quite a lot of drugs, I drank an unnecessary amount . . . It's this attitude that creates an atmosphere of legend, because people think you're going to die, and that excites them. But if you don't die, that hurts the legend (*laughs*) . . . The problem is that all this gossip has nothing to do with your work. I'll take an extreme example: Keith Richards. The most important thing to know about him is his love for his work, that's most important. Now, you sometimes read that Keith works all the time and that he's totally passionate about rock'n'roll, about his art. But that's not the interesting story for the newspapers. To come back to your question, it's hard to answer directly, it's as if you ask me, "Tell me about your life, now," it's impossible to answer that (*laughs*) . . .

Twilight

RM: In Hollywood, weren't you in the same position as John Fante, writing without ever seeing your projects come to fruition?
TM: There's some of that. When you work in Hollywood, you live a terrible life: most of what you produce is, for no rhyme or reason, tossed. You live in a sort of twilight zone. The case of John Fante is interesting because I learned that he's very well known here, that he used to sell fifty thousand books a year, but no one, absolutely no one, knows him in the United States . . . I don't know what he was doing in Hollywood, so I can't compare our situations, but if he felt terribly frustrated, we have something in common . . .

RM: Like him, you too are very proud of your roots and you throw them into your books. Aren't you more at ease in the American *mold*?
TM: My Irish roots are a source of constant energy. In Ireland, my grandparents were these people who came and went, and told stories in a charming language. They gave me the first positive impulse to do something with language in my life—to be a poet, to write songs, to be a novelist—because I understood that words were a resource. Every American artist feels that he's a bit of a stranger in society, because it's organized in a completely nonartistic manner. America has always been materialistic and close to war. Fortunately, on the other side there's always been a constant influx of people interested in culture, in literature, or in music; it's therefore much less difficult to "assert yourself" than it was back in the fifties, when I was trying to make a name for myself. But there's no need to have Irish blood to feel this profound malaise of an artist. In America, Marlon Brando and artists like him are considered lazy.

RM: How were you led to have this "scandalous" life?
TM: Only in the interests of exploration, by excitement, to know new heads and new energies. To be near people who seemed to me, and who still seem, interesting. I know it was a way of life that was looked down upon, but it still pulls me in (*laughs*) . . . I didn't go to Hollywood to be in show business, but because Los Angeles was the place to be for rock, cinema, or painting in the seventies. It was also the place to be, a crazy town too, with cocaine negatively

affecting everyone's lives, it was a magnet like nowhere else now. I went there to make a living, I couldn't live on my writing. My books brought me maybe $2,000 per year, even in Montana, what could you do with that? I had an underground reputation, but that didn't pay the rent (*laughs*) . . . However, I didn't complain about having to live off of Hollywood, because it was nevertheless with my pen. And that was better than working in a factory or being a lawyer.

RM: Still, it seems that they knew you more by your liaisons and your escapades than by your work . . .
TM: False. It was writers who wanted my work and who worked as reporters to get by who peddled gossip to the newspapers. It's my word against theirs, but they used to really exaggerate (*silence*) . . . I was married to the same woman for thirteen years, that was never written about, why? In this business, journalism consists of selling papers to uneducated simpletons. To make a weak product for cretins, you need idiotic news. That's the secret of American journalism. Me, I was just happy to live and to find some friends, Jeff Bridges or Marlon Brando, whom I adore. It's an absolutely delightful group of people, extremely funny and creative. Contrary to what they say, there are some really nice and interesting people in the movie world: actors, directors, technicians. There are lots of smart people, but most people are so envious that the only satisfaction they can get is to shout everywhere that people in the movies are superficial idiots. They're jealous because they'd like to be in that world, they feel better in their own imperfection with these offensive statements. It's hard to adjust to having the life of a non-entity . . . Look at the English, it's exactly the same, they're always buying scandal sheets, spending millions just to make fun of the people they envy.

RM: So what was it that made you decide to burn your bridges with Hollywood?
TM: When you're evolving, you try lots of things. Some work, you continue with them; others don't, so you abandon them. It's hard to live your dreams. And, a whole part of our culture has disappeared. What was happening in the United States back then no longer exists, there's no more exciting, happening situations or uncommon lifestyles. Rock, for example, has changed. Los Angeles was a center, there were the Eagles and those sorts of bands who lived and recorded there. It's no longer a magnet today, just a town where you use their

facilities, their equipment. I didn't just decide to leave Hollywood one day, there wasn't any noticeable break, like the newspapers would have you believe. I always wrote novels, I've always worked on my ranch, and I've always done rodeo. Besides, at the end of this period where I was supposed to be crazy and hung out to dry, supposed to be in Hollywood to do drugs and chase actresses, I became the Montana state rodeo champion. How could I have done that if I was living the way they said I was?

RM: Was becoming a rancher tied to a desire to get closer to nature?
TM: I've been in Montana for twenty-five years now, that's where I live, where I vote, where I pay my taxes, and where I educate my children. I have four children who've been raised there and the oldest ones are at the University of Montana. So this is my life, and it's very good that a good part of my life had been close to the natural world. But that's not an end in itself. Too much nature is boring, you want to seek people out and talk about other things, want to see paintings and concerts. The ideal is to live in the country and to get out of it from time to time. I live in a pretty place, not perfect but very nice.

RM: Do you think that your rural lifestyle has given you a better appreciation of the American way of life?
TM: No, because where I live, the people aren't famous, they don't buy BMWs with air conditioning, tons of toys for their kids, or $800 sweaters. They live from day to day, from one year to the next. It's a different world. I quickly understood that they had different values and other ambitions besides winning an Oscar. They live their lives with their families, their friends and try to understand what's happening around them. My life is exactly like theirs.

RM: Still, every chance you get, you criticize the values of middle-class America.
TM: I'm not comfortable with them, but . . . I love my country, it impassions me because we're still building it. I didn't want my country to invade Vietnam, I don't want it to deny rights to the blacks, etc. Millions of people think like that, and we try to win, to impose these ideas . . . Reagan, I would frankly have liked to hope that he had more brains. He became president because Carter—who represented the Democrats—was so bad that he

created a void in which Reagan got himself elected. And we've had ten years of totally unparalleled materialism; as in France and in the rest of the Western world, there was nothing else but money. No one in the West can feel innocent in front of this greed. And the most disgustingly greedy people on the cultural scene are the rock stars. Mick Jagger and Paul McCartney are among the one hundred richest people in England. No one attacks their wealth, they only criticize the wealth of industrialists. Because in our collective imagination, rock'n'roll means trashing hotel rooms, spending money, and using women and drugs. People criticize bankers because it's their class that is supposed to abuse the world financially and economically. No one takes himself outside of this convenient perspective and takes a purely human point of view.

RM: Reagan is hated, but still he was elected, then reelected . . .
TM: One of the problems with my country is that the left has never produced an effective politician. Because of that, it's gotten used to losing. Me, I had voted for Carter, but he was a miserable president, he put himself in front of the whole country when things were going bad and said "I don't know what to do." That's the reason that people voted for Reagan. He gave solutions, even if they were bad, it's what people were expecting because they couldn't stand Carter's ineffectiveness anymore. In addition, there's a very strong conservative movement in America, the people who worshipped Reagan are the workers, the rednecks. During the period in which he was cutting back on liberties, breaking unions, he went to working class bars to have his picture taken drinking a beer with the guys . . . It's almost as if, in the American conscience, there was the desire to be told what to do.

Darkness

RM: Do you use humor, which is always very present in your books, as a weapon?
TM: Uh . . . yeah. I think that's a traditional Irish approach to take on the competition, to undermine your enemy with ridicule. You have to use the weapons you have in your arsenal against ineptitude. But this humor, I often combine it with a sense of the blackness that comes from my Irish Catholic education, in which there are sinister visions of a horrible black hell, the kingdom of the sinners is an infernal place. I don't believe it, but that fed my

education, the mythology of my childhood. And then, I had read Faulkner's stories about mankind, and I realized that the predominance of the human race in the universe is not necessarily good. All the other animals have been shoved from the face of the earth by and for man, it's hard to keep on saying how extraordinary the expansion of the human race is and how great man is. At this time, you can ask yourself if man's destiny didn't develop in the shadows.

RM: Is that why your heroes are anti-heroes, especially in your stories where they rush to their fall?
TM: I don't have any theory, my writing isn't motivated by a concept, but that's how I see things. The stereotype of my hero is on the path of his fall, of his extinction, but it's a process that goes back to Greek drama. And I don't think there's an oppressive, urban environment for this sort of anti-hero.

RM: Do you feel that you belong to an American tradition of nomad writing, like Hemingway or Bowles for example?
TM: There are a lot of Anglo-Saxons who have knocked about, in writing. Bruce Chatwin, even though he's English, is the perfect example. For Americans, there has always been a movement towards the West, it's in American stories. Thus, all our fantasy and our romanticism are nomads. And you just try to figure the "how to stay in one place" because that's not normal for us. In reality, I don't get around a lot, but I often dream of traveling in British Columbia, in the South Pacific, or in Argentina. Even when that doesn't happen, there's always the idea of movement in American literature. We don't have a sense of the place, like Europeans. If you ask an American his nationality, he may very well answer French, or Irish. There's a sort of confusion maintained about places, that comes from a sense of movement characteristic of Americans.

RM: What drove you to hitchhike around Europe?
TM: I wanted to discover the world, to write, to take notes. For an American writer, it's almost an obligatory formality to do Europe, it's nothing special or particularly brave. I had grown up in a very plain and boring country in the Midwest, it was like growing up in a huge field of alfalfa (*laughs*) . . . Nothing special happened to me, I could dream about Europe, where everyone has a past, is cultured and intelligent. It's a myth that still persists. So I left for

Europe, and it's in Italy and in Spain that I stayed the longest. The problem is that sooner or later you feel the need to return to your own culture. I realized that I couldn't be European. Today, expatriation isn't a great choice for Americans, which doesn't stop us from traveling. It's better to try to represent our culture, we're in the turbulence, but there's an energy that I hope is good. Today, America has a personal culture, newly acquired.

RM: You have the feeling though that there were more movements and hopes in the sixties, when the American dream imposed itself.
TM: In literature, there was the beat movement, but my generation, in school, was known by the name of the silent generation. We were destined for office jobs until these movements appeared, around '66, '67. Before that, it was a desert. Today, it's a more favorable period for writers of American culture: I read interesting new authors non-stop. That's why I'm an optimist, even if the music is a lot less exciting since the same thing is happening as in movies: five or six malignant people—like Madonna or Michael Jackson—sell half of the records sold. The damned monsters of the seventies were Van Morrison or the Eagles, but it was better. On the other hand, there are today thirty or so American fiction writers to follow, who have had the possibility of being published. Even if, like everywhere, the editors are looking above all for a best seller and that the book has become a product like any other. There are maybe fifty thousand books published every year in the United States. That's way too much, most don't have any chance of selling because they just have artistic pretension without any quality at all. Americans have very bad literary tastes, they don't even know when the First World War happened or who George Washington was, they just read Stephen King's novels. Fortunately, a parallel elite culture is developing, an intelligentsia that pushes back the lack of culture. You've always had an intelligentsia, but us, we've had brilliant minds—scientists, writers . . . —for whom the life of the mind was the most important thing, but they were lone wolves. There is now a class of intelligent people, like in Europe, who communicate among themselves about things beyond such considerations as sales numbers or about their credibility.

RM: Do you think that there is an underground level of American culture that includes people like you, Tom Waits, Robert Frank, or Cassavetes?
TM: Absolutely. It's not a question of patting yourself on the back, but there is a world apart with individualists who are trying to make something more

interesting than what Steven Spielberg, Stephen King, or Michael Jackson are making. Without losing sight that this sort of cultural intelligentsia is based on what you have here. For example, John Fante has recognition that comes from you, he's respected here but totally unknown in the United States. Inversely, I've never understood why you love Jerry Lewis, it's an enigma (*laughs*) . . . Jacques Tati is who makes me laugh, he's absolutely marvelous. My first book, *The Sporting Club*, is an imitation of Tati, the structure is a bit copied from *Les vacances de M. Hulot* . . . I discovered him by chance, as I like everything funny, I went to see one of his films and I just gaped, it was sublime.

Ingratitude

RM: You've used a phrase of Antonio Carlos Jobim as the exergue for your book *The Man Who Lost His Name*: "I took your picture with my Rolleiflex/And what has developed is your enormous ingratitude."
TM: (*Smiling*) . . . It's sort of the subtitle of the book. One of the great sentiments of my hero, and it's a general feeling, is that the world is ungrateful towards us. I like the idea that in the course of a lifetime, you discover that the role of the world is not to be friendly towards us. It's in this spirit that I imagined this book. In the beginning, I found this phrase to be very funny. I like this surreal craziness of a camera showing ingratitude. And if I found that in one of Jobim's bossa novas, it's that I create my vision of the world through all cultural products, not just through American emanations.

RM: Still, those are what you hold near to your heart, like rodeo and ranching.
TM: It's just a lifestyle I've chosen. I might have preferred living in New York, but I chose Montana. And I do what there is to do there, I wasn't going to sit down in the plains and watch time go by. In Montana, business numero uno is ranching. Since I adore horses and physical excitement, I started doing rodeo. I learned to make lassos (*he mimics at length while whistling*) . . . There are a lot of figures to learn and to reproduce, it's just like in the movies. And you've got to learn to get over your fears, because it moves very fast. But nothing's out of reach. It's also by accident that I got into it, in Montana, you do rodeo more easily than harpsichord concerts. If I had decided to live on the coasts, I could have been a sailor. Life's a series of accidents. Also, I've always believed that it's better for a writer to not live in a cultural context.

That way, you deal with information that comes from a virgin place, rather than what other artists regurgitate: images, scenes, words that belong collectively to the world of art. I spent my life among people who don't read, who don't go to movies, who don't paint, and who don't write poetry. Their life is their poetry, they try to put poetry into their everyday acts, in the way in which they lead their horses or make a fire. There's some esthetic that they try to accomplish, it touches me, I appreciate that attitude. I like gestures in which you feel a human understanding and which are done with elegance, even the simplest. I'm looking for poetry in the everyday gestures of life.

An Interview with
Thomas McGuane

Lynette Zwerneman / 1996

From *Firestarter*, April 1996, p. 12. Reprinted with permission of Lynette Zwerneman.

Just back from the Paris Book Fair, Tom McGuane was kind enough to converse with *FIRESTARTER* on the subject of writing.

FS: What first brought you to Livingston?
TM: This was a very different world in 1968 . . . During high school, I had been working on a ranch in northern Wyoming and I kinda thought I was going to end up there. Because I liked that country. I was looking for a place that was a normal town near some of the things I wanted to do (I love fishing) so I could finish the book I was working on—my first book, *The Sporting Club*. Livingston was, and is, an attractive town. I didn't really have a plan of where I wanted to live, I only had a plan to write. Things accumulate and you just end up someplace. There's a lot of places I could have lived happily. As far as starting all over again, I'd probably be living in New Zealand, or southern Argentina . . .

FS: What were the elements you were looking for?
TM: A place where I could afford to live and I could write in peace. Which might have a nice little public library, which Livingston has. It was an uncomplicated life then. You didn't need much stuff.

FS: We've met several young writers who moved to Livingston after reading your work. In a sense you have became a literary icon, a source of inspiration. Does that surprise you?
TM: I think that's part and parcel of just getting older. In all seriousness young people look to older people. They like elders. It's hard to have them in this culture. I think I felt it myself as I was trying to figure out what writers

were doing. I came along at a time when the older writers were really pretty interesting. In the late fifties and early sixties the established older writers were Ernest Hemingway, John Steinbeck, and William Faulkner.

FS: Were they influences?
TM: Well, they were certainly people whose lives I thought about. It's gotten much more diversified, or dissipated now. In a funny way, writers are not as prominent as they once were, yet there seems to be more of them. And the pie is divided into so many more pieces, between books and movies, etc.

FS: What does it take to be a writer?
TM: It's a love of literature itself . . . a love of reading . . . a love of books. That's certainly the first thing, without one cannot go on.

FS: Do you think it's harder to be a writer now?
TM: At the Paris Book Fair, we talked about those very things. Joe Heller said he thought it was much harder now. And I think that he's right. It's probably a little easier to get published now than it was, because publishers are spitting out a lot of books. But it's harder for young writes to make a reputation for themselves because the whole scene is so fragmented. It was harder for my age group than it was for Joe Heller's.

FS: What were you attempting to do when you started writing?
TM: The literary world I grew up in included this sort of black humor that was very much in the air. There was Vonnegut, etc. . . . I've always been interested in comic literature. That's part of what motivated me. Plus, I've always been a reader. I think I became a writer in order to justify my reading habits.

FS: It has been said you've created a new genre. How would you classify your writing?
TM: I don't know. I just came from Paris where there was a panel of French scholars sitting around trying to explain exactly what it was that I was. I just had a real strong view of how I wanted to write, and also a real strong view of my limitations. I don't think I've ventured too often into where I didn't sense I had capability. I think that pretty much anybody's style of writing, just like a running back's style, becomes inherent in the way you do things. What I

think was original for that time, was that people really weren't writing about my kind of stuff. They weren't writing about people wandering around Montana, and the Florida Keys and all those other places. That wasn't considered the stuff of literature.

FS: Interestingly enough, the winners of our Short Story Contest are all women . . .
TM: Well women, I think have got more juice these days for this job.

FS: But isn't the writing world usually considered "The Boys Club"?
TM: Oh, that's completely to the opposite. The boys, I think, are to the back of the room now. This is not a blanket statement, but I think that in general women are really much more energized right now as literary persons than men.

FS: Any suggestions for writers?
TM: In terms of their work, and I can't pretend to be an expert on how everybody does it, but generally it seems to me that most writers I've known who've gotten anywhere with it have had a couple of things in common. One, they were avid readers and very excited about how others wrote. Secondly, for one reason or another they were people who perversely decided that they were going to be writers, whether it was a good idea or not. They did not say "let's try this for a year, then let's try something else." And they were not going to be dissuaded by somebody telling them that they did not have any ability.

FS: Is that a common experience for writers?
TM: Well, yeah, people often don't get encouraged. But looking back over my contemporaries, for those who just decided they were going to do it and weren't looking for a lot of support, it worked. With a very high degree of predictability. That seemed to be a much greater factor than talent.

FS: Were you ever discouraged?
TM: I was often discouraged because I was considered a bad student. I didn't get much encouragement from teachers, but I did get encouragement from other people who were writing. I didn't think I was really good at anything else. I put all my eggs in that basket, and had to live with it.

FS: Has your writing become more optimistic?

TM: I think that's true. I don't feel quite as threatened. There was a period when a *New Yorker* reviewer said that I viewed all of life as a "highly organized nightmare." And I think probably that I did think that at that time. But I don't anymore. I have a lot of positive things in my life now, kids that I am just nuts about, and I'm also happily married. I have a lot that I am very grateful for.

FS: What do you want people to know about writing?

TM: One of the great things about writing is that you never really know exactly what it is you're doing. I've been writing for almost thirty years and I still have the same insecurity I had when I was nineteen. And that actually turns out to be one of the really positive things about writing. One of those things that never turns into part of life's dreariness. It's always kinda frightening, it's always out there, and it always has that sense of risk and excitement. And it never really loses its value.

FS: Thank you, Tom McGuane.

Thomas McGuane

Jim Schumock / 1999

From *Story, Story, Story: Conversations with American Authors,* by Jim Schumock, pp. 82–96. Reprinted with permission of Black Heron Press.

Thomas Francis McGuane was born in Wyandotte, Michigan iñ 1939. He is the author of eight novels, beginning with *The Sporting Club* in 1969. Next came *The Bushwhacked Piano,* followed by National Book Award nominee, *Ninety-two in the Shade,* whose film version he directed. After a hiatus in Hollywood, he returned to the novel with *Panama.* Since then, four successive novels, *Nobody's Angel, Something to Be Desired, Keep the Change* and *Nothing but Blue Skies* have inhabited the fictional Deadrock, Montana. He has also written a book of sporting essays, *An Outside Chance,* and a collection of short stories, *To Skin a Cat.*

JS: You've given rather broad credit to your literary fathers, among them Malcolm Lowry. Do you think there's any novel more read by novel writers and less by novel readers than *Under the Volcano?*
TM: That's really an interesting way to put that. There's no doubt that it's essential reading for modern writers. It's one of the books you read and go back to your own work and say, "Now, what changes can we make in what we've been doing." A serious writer could scarcely go through that book without contemplating changes in his own work.

JS: In *Ninety-two in the Shade* Tom Skelton talks about having a one-man intentional community. It seems a number of your major characters seek that.
TM: It must spring from some deep place. I do see my protagonists as being on some kind of survival mission, probably a byproduct of my paranoia and the paranoia of the fifties and sixties when I was coming of age as a writer. This sort of siege mentality seems to be going away in my writing for some reason, maybe as I'm getting more comfortable in my own skin.

147

JS: Writers I would be tempted to call American secessionists—Robert Stone, Walker Percy, and Ken Kesey—have characters who, like yours, were trying to bounce contemporary America off the edge of their own psyches.
TM: I think that's true. I particularly feel close to Percy and Stone in their approach to things. And I do know that the indicator species in the culture always seem to be those marginal or outlaw types, or falling-apart types, who seem to show the ailments of the age right on the surface of their own hides.

JS: In *The Sporting Club* you have two well-born characters, Vernon Stanton and James Quinn, in total conflict with the underpinnings of American society at that time. Do you think dissent is a high American value?
TM: I think dissent is the principal American value. I'm not sure there are many substantial nations that were founded on dissent, but this is certainly one of them.

JS: There's a high degree of contentiousness in Quinn and Stanton. Is it because they sense they can learn more by subjecting people to that kind of stress?
TM: You're right in identifying an opportunism in that approach to life. And I think there's something about the characters that attract me that is put off by stability. They either seek chaotic situations or convert the stable ones into chaotic situations, and that's just part of it. It's also, frankly, part of the strategy of the common novelist: the picaresque figure who disturbs things for his own purposes.

JS: Rather than becoming expatriates, your characters tend to become internal emigres in America.
TM: I do know that I have, and my characters have, this emigre instinct, but the sheer exoticism of American life is endlessly fascinating to them and to me. This continues to seem to me to be the most foreign country that I know of, and its internal workings are so fascinating there's never seemed to me a lot of reason to go elsewhere for the atmosphere that I was looking for in fiction.

JS: What was going on in your life that favored the writing of *Ninety-two in the Shade*?
TM: The biggest thing that favored the writing of that book was the sense I had that I was in the face of a breaking wave in American culture. And I

didn't understand it, or really know what it was, but I knew something was going on, and I knew I was in the middle of it. And I knew that I could address the reader as I wrote, that there was something speaking through me that was almost the feeling a zealot might have, or a convinced politician might feel. I'm not trying to elevate its status with this description. I just know that I could feel the shove of culture behind me as I wrote that, and that allowed me to supercharge the text to any degree I wanted. But there was just such a fuel tank there, and a very distinctive feeling in the writing of that book that I never had before and I've never had since.

JS: Your blue-collar characters often have a Greek monumentalism about them: big thoughts and big questions. How do you achieve that?
TM: Well, I think they do that themselves. I think that every class of people has its capacity for arias and strongly-expressed emotions and it's often in an untraditional mode. But it's there among blue-collar people as much as anybody else. Some of their laconic habits make it a little harder to get to them, let's say, but, especially in rural America or in the South or parts of the West, they are very well able to express themselves in highly charged ways.

JS: Tom Skelton's father in *Ninety-two in the Shade* has preceded him into eccentricity and madness. What made you give him such a father?
TM: The eccentricity part of it interested me in the braveness and poetry of his father's vision. I wanted to give him a good father, by my lights, and I gave him this very peculiar person who's not probably viable but has, to my view, great merits and some of the generational strengthening that Skelton needs to live according to this emerging code in his life.

JS: Do you think these characters see life as more preordained than allowing for acts of free will?
TM: Maybe their author, at that point, saw their lives as more preordained than they did.

JS: How would you describe the bare bones of *Ninety-two in the Shade*?
TM: The bare bones of it is about a person going home to make some sense out of a life that has seemed to him to have come apart at the center and to find that, to pull his existence into some kind of orderly fashion, he's going to have to take on some personal codes that are perhaps more formal than

anything he's ever contemplated before. While these are the right and only thing for him to do, they are part of the tragic paradox that costs him his life.

JS: How did your move to Montana change your life?
TM: It was an accretional move. I went there with the remains of my Stegner Fellowship back in the sixties. I'd worked not too far away across the line in Wyoming when I was in high school. Even then, I thought that eventually I would make a plan and go to another place. But, I just got comfortable there. I had a young child to see to, and a wife, and our well-being to look after. We found a pleasant community that sustained us, and when I sold my first book I just decided to stay on until further thought. But the further thought never came, and twenty-five years have gone by and I have four children who've been raised there, and it's my home.

JS: Any regrets about the move?
TM: None at all. I would say that it has been a great place to have raised a family. The only disadvantages are those of a small and uniform population. It's a little hard on a novelist who thrives on human variety. That's its only disadvantage.

JS: Patrick Fitzpatrick, the protagonist in *Nobody's Angel*, is a dissocialized warrior. He fits the mold of many of your characters in his tremendous worry about just what American life has brought him.
TM: I suppose that's just a characteristic I impose on my protagonists. Fitzpatrick typifies a certain kind of Montana dilemma which is that people find these formal away-from-home jobs because they can't find work at home. Very often people go into the military from Montana, not because of their personal views, but because they must find some way of surviving outside of the place where they grew up. However, I did see him as a heightened figure and therefore he took on some of the dilemmas and colorations of the age.

JS: Fitzpatrick seems to be going through some of the difficulties you suffered through with your family. Is he a character to whom you feel particularly close?
TM: I certainly did at the time. I think that some of the unresolved issues of grief about my own family losses were imposed on him and, in fact, gave that book its doomed quality. A quality that I'm happy to say at this remove seems

strangely dense, but at the same time it was the atmosphere of my own life and I really couldn't escape it, even write my way out of it. So that's there apart from my will for it to be there.

JS: A number of your characters seem bent on gaining acceptance from their fathers even if they're not still around. Did you achieve that acceptance from your own father?

TM: I'm sure if I pressed you, you'd have to admit to me that you've had this dialogue with your father that goes on fairly regularly. It's just something that men have. It's our cross to bear, this unwitting and unwilling conversation with our fathers, even long after they've died. I'm sure my father did that with my grandfather. I certainly have been discussing things with my father since his death in 1976. It's something you never get away from.

JS: Were you raised a Catholic?
TM: Yes.

JS: What mentions you make of it in your work are few and minor.
TM: We did not have a religious household particularly, though I was educated by nuns. But I think there are two kinds of Irish Catholicism: one is the real intense, regular mass attendance kind; the other is where it's a received part of your culture. You've more culturally a Catholic, very often, than you are religiously a Catholic.

JS: What brought you with such expansiveness to *Nothing but Blue Skies*? It's longer than anything else you've written?
TM: Lots of things. One was the conviction I had that, contrary to official views, Montana was as much in the soup of American excess in the eighties as any other place. That was part one. Part two, the conviction that for a long time now, Americans have been on one drug or another, with predictable results: discovery of the drug, passion for the drug, the hangover, the remorse, and the look of the new burnt-earth landscape that lies ahead. We had the real drugs in the sixties and seventies. In the eighties we had this rediscovered drug called money. And this one came under government auspices with the faint feeling that it was patriotic to indulge. But when the drug had run its course in the culture and people were backing off the narcotic, we were in the same situation we'd been in in the late seventies, in these Hotel California–noir atmospheres

that descended at that time. And our situation now is the familiar sense of cultural thinness: nothing to live for, spiritual bankruptcy, and the collapse of our most intimate institutions, like the family and our problems with our cynicism about government and all those kinds of things. I wanted to reduce that to a personal story. And I didn't want to do it with a furrowed brow. I wanted to do it comically, and humanely. So that was the background, the general praxis for the writing of this book.

JS: Frank Copenhaver, the middle-aged picaro at the heart of this novel tells lies of mammoth proportions.
TM: Desperate people do desperate things, including lying about everything. And what Frank has done which has been rather crazy is to have taken the important things in his life and put them in front of parking meters at the margins of his life, put in all the nickels and then gone about pursuing follies and trivia. And on the recommendation that this is the only game in town, let's play it, he has gone and played the principal American game, and it hasn't worked out for him. And the punishment is the meticulous collapse of his life and happiness. That's what springs the comedy in the book.

JS: How do you balance the need for love with the fear of domestication?
TM: Fear of domestication? Well, it's a kind of breathing process. You can't breathe in, if you don't breathe out. And the domestication process turns into the sick version, codependency, whatever it is, if you don't find ways of letting a lot of blue sky and fresh air into your life. So you're always trying to titrate one to the other and carburete the two. You try to have a stable and respectful partnership with other people—members of your family—at the same time not become so housebroken that you have no new information for them or for yourself, where you begin to build anaerobic atmospheres that characterize the average household. But that's something that requires daily study and, in fact, it's never stable. It's something that you just have to work at all the time. I'll go home, for example, tomorrow and I'll read and write and try to work on a new book; and it'll be exhilarating for a while and it'll go through an arc, it'll descend on the other side. I'll get bored, my family will get annoyed with me, someone will suggest a trip. I will take the position I'm being kicked out of my own house. Finally, I'll see the need for the trip or the experience myself. I'll go do it; we'll start back at the beginning of the arc. That's how it goes.

JS: Several characters in *Nothing but Blue Skies* are what you call "hippies in a heartbeat." How does that inform their life in contemporary America?
TM: Basically, these people are subcutaneous hippies, but masquerading through other parts of their lives without revealing this. I just think that many of us came through a sustained experience in the so-called counter-culture and then vanished below the surface of quotidian American life. We've never really relinquished those views that we acquired in "bootcamp"; but they're not there in equal intensity with everybody and they're not there as intensely on a daily basis for those of us of whom that's true. Still, it's a very informing and guiding force in our lives. And, in the long run, as there are millions of us, it's going to impact American culture, and somebody's going to go back and figure out how it happened. But my part in this is to be a little bit plainer in saying that we are a slightly separate society within American society and we're going to aggressively play our part in evolving this culture.

JS: In this novel, as in several others, you have your main character taking on a hired hand. Why do you put hired hands through such hell?
TM: Just as there are deluded people in the entrepreneurial class, like my pro-tagonist, there are also in the working-cowboy class people who don't really want the job. They have their own romance about that work, just as Frank has about being a capitalist. As a result, their hold is tenuous and they're always on the cusp of violence or rage about being in that situation, and they're naturally in conflict with their bosses. The fact is that hired hands on ranches usually arrive "looking for a quit," as they say. They've got a job expectancy, from their point of view, of about ninety days because none of them really wants to stay. They naturally want to move on, and they're part of the deliquescence of the ranch culture, which is falling apart. That used to be a real profession. There were lifetime-admired, respected ranch hands. Now, it's mostly angry temporary help.

JS: When Frank's friends see him falling apart, they come to his aid. Do you have good friends you rely upon?
TM: I do. Although, I'm—more than I like—I'm a somewhat reclusive per-son, and I don't hang out as much as I did ten, fifteen years ago. My interest in literature and writing is such that I'm never really very far from it and I don't do a good job of socializing.

JS: Over the years you've subjected various characters to untold miseries but you don't let up on Frank Copenhaver. You keep putting him to new comic tests.

TM: I've always been a great admirer of Buster Keaton and am fascinated by his attempt to logic his way through things while these enormous, deterministic forces reduced him to human jelly. And I've been challenged by the broadness of fooling with the elements of the ridiculous. They gave me pleasure and a sense of rightness as I did it, and, of course, with the model of the great Keaton staring at me from heaven, I felt reassured that I was on the right track.

JS: One of your early characters lamented that we go through life with a diminishing portfolio of enthusiasms. How do you forestall that for yourself?

TM: You have to continue to work harder for the perceptions and discoveries that renew life, and they are harder and harder to come by as you approach "veteran status," particularly as a big part of my life is my reading life. And I'm always looking for those books like *Under the Volcano* and *The Moviegoer* and *The Sun Also Rises* and Flaubert's *Three Tales* and *The Sportsman's Sketches*—books through which you pass and are altered. And, as you get older and more experienced as an artist of any kind, you find it harder to find those things which will transmute your approach. But that's the exciting part of the search. And that's the thing that will fight off this pattern of diminished enthusiasms.

JS: You say that you won't let the *New York Times* discourage you from writing. Yet this book didn't receive a very favorable review from Jay Parini in the Sunday book review. What's your take on the literary establishment at this point?

TM: Well, that's an interesting case. Actually, the *New York Times* until this book has been quite kind to me. Jay Parini's just another reviewer. He might have been reviewing the book for the Houston paper or the Indianapolis paper. They have people as qualified as him reviewing. When it comes out in the *Times,* however, it acquires this ballistic quality that is sometimes hard to dodge. This book has probably gotten the best reviews I've ever gotten nationally. So far, it's probably been reviewed in thirty or forty papers and more than half of those have been what are called "rave reviews," but they've almost all been really, really positive. And I had that one negative review, but that negative review, which was in the Sunday *Times Book Review* really gets around to bookstores and has a lot to do with the impression of how the book has been reviewed to everyday readers. The Monday *New York Times*, the weekly *Times*, in the industry in New York is read with more seriousness than the Sunday *Times* because I think it's less assailed by literary politics. The Monday *Times* was a rave review, but people don't know that. And the trade reviews, *Publishers Weekly* and *Kirkus* were all extremely positive. But you have a hard time escaping that one bad review because all the bookstores have the Sunday *Times Book Review*. They're sort of complicitous in this tremendous power that one newspaper has over us. The author of the review of my book in the Sunday *Times* had a book in the marketplace at the same time. That book got a terrible review in the *Times*, and it has not gotten good reviews much anywhere else. I don't think the *Times* should give a book to be reviewed to someone who has a book coming out himself; I think that's plainly crazy from an ethical standpoint. But you just have good things and bad things happen while you're publishing a book, and in the long run a book has to take care of itself in that it has to find a readership. I think this book has certainly gotten out enough that it has a fair chance to discover a readership, and if it's going to have one, people are going to have to read it, like it, and tell others that they ought to read it. That's really what makes books go round, and that's the immutable thing about the book culture that to some degree or another can't be interfered with. We've all also seen books come out and do tremendously well and never get reviewed at all.

JS: Your brother-in-law, Jimmy Buffett, was on top of the bestseller list with a novel of his own. How do you see the bestseller list?
TM: Actually, I was thinking of Jimmy in this reviewer syndrome. His book was on the bestseller list before anybody reviewed it, which kind of under-mines the power of book reviewers. Jimmy's interests are not in literary fic-tion, they're in pop fiction, and the bestseller list is a free-for-all with Kirk Douglas and Jackie Collins and all sorts of people who are really not literary people. It's an inaccessible place for writers like me. I've never had a bestseller; I wonder if I ever will have one. The blessing that I frequently count is that I've never had a book out-of-print. I started publishing in the sixties; it's now the nineties and I'm extremely grateful for that, and I owe that just to read-ers, the "common reader" as Virginia Woolf called them: this person who's been euchered out of the academic fiction and the NEA fiction and that kind

of committee fiction. I think there's a third market there. First, you have this
officially sanctioned art fiction which functions without readers—readers
aren't required for that process. Then you have pop fiction, which takes care
of itself with its own economics. But there's a third stream which is serious
literary fiction that's meant for readers: readers and writers continue to commune as they have in centuries past.

JS: You're a voracious reader. Are there many writers whose work you value
in contemporary times?
TM: I think there are really a lot of good writers around right now, and some
wonderfully distinct, individual voices in a time of wholesale homogeneity. I
don't know how I would live without all these beautiful voices coming out of
the American land right now. It's what makes it conceivable to go on.

JS: Who are you reading right now?
TM: Barry Hannah and Jim Crumley and Jim Harrison and Susan Minot as
well as the "highbrow realist" standards like John Updike and Anne Tyler and
all those people. Tim O'Brien and Robert Stone. I also read Frederick
Barthelme and I read everybody who makes any claim to be serious: William
Hjortsberg, my old friend in Montana, and Larry Woiwode. I read Larry
McMurtry pretty religiously; I read John Nichols. I've gone back to reading
some of those postmodernists I grew up with, like John Barth and John
Hawkes and Robert Coover and all those guys who were around in the sixties
and seventies. And I read Beverly Lowry. I think that's a pretty good short list.

JS: Have you ever read Robert Boswell or Lorrie Moore?
TM: Not Robert Boswell, but tell me about him later. I've read all of Lorrie
Moore. I like Lorrie Moore.

JS: If you knew you were to be stranded in a cabin in the Montana mountains for the rest of your life alone and could only take along two books and
one piece of music, which ones would you take?
TM: I know the piece of music would not be "Pop Goes the Weasel." That I'm
sure of. I'd take *The Brandenburg Concerto*. The books would be the *Collected
Works of Shakespeare* and *Dead Souls* by Gogol.

A Passion for Ranching, Fishing, and Writing: A Conversation with Thomas McGuane

Christine June / 2000

From *Bloomsbury Review* 20, no. 4 (June/August 2000, Annual American West Issue), pp. 13–14. Reprinted with permission of Christine June.

Thomas McGuane burst upon the literary scene thirty-one years ago with his first highly acclaimed novel, *The Sporting Club*. There followed a number of brilliant works, including *The Bushwhacked Piano* and *Ninety-two in the Shade*, the latter of which was nominated for the National Book Award (and should have won). Critics compared his unusual talent in those years to that of the early Jack Kerouac and Ernest Hemingway, and the 1965 MFA graduate from Yale University soon moved successfully into screenwriting (*Rancho Deluxe, The Missouri Breaks, Tom Horn*). Since then he has, in more than a dozen major works, established himself as one of the premier working writers in the American West, standing as a peer in the company of such luminaries as Jim Harrison and Larry McMurtry. With biting realism and occasional satire, McGuane has provided, in his novels, screenplays, and essays, a rich series of insightful looks at western life. He has a strong and ever-loyal cult following, similar to the quiet hordes of readers who have steadfastly followed, for example, the writings of the late Edward Abbey.

Before moving to his current ranch, Thomas McGuane lived in the environs of Livingston, Montana, an area just north of Yellowstone National Park that, like Carmel, California, or Taos, New Mexico, has become a thriving bohemia of creative spirits, including landscape painter Russell Chatham; writers Doug Peacock and Tim Cahill; film actors Peter Fonda, Jeff Bridges, Dennis Quaid, Meg Ryan, and Andie McDowell; and other celebrities, including Tom Brokaw. McGuane is known, in this community of friends, for his magnanimity. He is the person, for example, who introduced once-struggling artist Russell Chatham to affluent collectors such as Jack Nicholson and the Fondas. Similarly, writer William Hjortsberg has credited McGuane with helping him to land his first book contract. Later, it was Thomas McGuane who persuaded Robert Redford to read Norman Maclean's *A River Runs Through It*, a work that Redford later turned into a film featuring a then little-known actor named Brad Pitt.

McGuane is also a devoted husband and the father of four children, and raises quarter horses at his ranch on the Boulder River. When not writing, he enjoys rodeos (cutting-horse competitions are his specialty), sport-fishing (from high-country brown trout to tropical bone fish), and big-game hunting. His two most recent books—*Some Horses* and *The Longest Silence*—speak, respectively, to his passions for horses and fishing. Over the last thirty-one years McGuane has created a life that has been productive, authentic, and close to the earth. Like certain mountains, he stands out on the landscape, and people are drawn to him as they are to those mountains, knowing that talents of considerable stature always provide commanding perspectives on nature and life.

The Bloomsbury Review: Could you tell us a little bit about your life? Where you grew up? Your family?
Thomas McGuane: I grew up in Michigan in an Irish Catholic household—which is a particular culture—but my family was all from Massachusetts. So I had a little schizophrenia about where I really grew up because my mother was so committed to Massachusetts. She'd always take us back there to my grandmother's house as soon as school was out. So I grew up with one foot in Irish-Catholic milltown New England and the other foot in Michigan. I went to work on a ranch in the fifties in Wyoming, and that was a decisive moment in my life. I knew I was going to move to the West as soon as I was out of school, and that's pretty much what I did.

TBR: How long have you lived in Montana?
TM: I've lived in Montana for going on thirty-three years, but I was in the area working and traveling for ten years before that.

TBR: What is your life like on the ranch?
TM: Busy. There's something going on constantly. We run three hundred cows, and we have about ten mares and another seven or eight saddle horses. We raise a lot of alfalfa hay in the summertime, so there's always something going on. I couldn't begin to do this by myself. My wife is a very skilled ranch

manager; she could run the ranch by herself. And we have good people help-ing us. We usually crew up at branding time, and there are people on the pay-roll the rest of the year. We've learned to expand and contract according to the needs of the ranch.

Things have changed for us now that our kids are grown. We have four children, and they're all doing their thing, so it's just my wife and I at the ranch now. Things are pretty quiet. We raise competition quarter horses and travel to cutting contests, probably about thirty a year. We're big readers. I spend a large part of my time writing—a normal rancher wouldn't be doing that. I find a way to cram it in, but it's definitely a case of cramming. We're just slightly overloaded at all times.

TBR: What sort of horse do you most prefer to work with?
TM: Quarter horses. Quarter horses are like Labrador retrievers. They are a universally used horse. People who raise cutting horses look for talent wher-ever they can find it. I have an outstanding cutting horse right now. He's not particularly well-bred to do anything—he came out of a west Texas feed lot. It's just his individual talent. Quarter horses are great performance horses. We also raise rope horses. I basically just like the friendly ones. I'm a mare person, and most of our horses have been mares over the years.

TBR: There is a vibrant community of writers and artists such as Russ Chatham who live around Livingston. Was that one of the attractions for living there?
TM: I think Russ moved up to Livingston initially to visit me, and it certainly is an attraction to have such people around. Russ is a wonderful painter and cook and an outstanding fisherman. Then there is my friend Bill Hjortsberg, a writer friend who lives up there now. We went to college together. My visi-tor friends included Jim Harrison and others who come from different parts of the country from time to time. I went to school with most of them. Jim Harrison and I went to Michigan State together. I haven't lived in Livingston for about fifteen years, so I don't see quite as many of the new wave of very talented people, but there are marvelous writers living there. Now we live in the middle of nowhere.

TBR: I heard that you had been in Zion National Park recently, and are exploring the Colorado Plateau country. How does that high desert land-scape compare with the Yellowstone country where you live?

TM: There's something going on in the desert that I've never really been able to quite understand. We've hiked in the desert for quite a while, and there always seems to be an anchoritic feeling in the air. I don't know if it's because you're reduced to such minimal supplies—things like water and shade become so important—as well as the uninviting aspects of desert life. You can hike in the desert and love it and be inspired by it, but you don't really want to live there—I mean in the real desert. It makes you think about place in a somewhat different way. You're not going around house-hunting; you're not trying to domesticate a landscape with a shade tree. You have to look at land in another way, and that sinks in and gives you a spiritual, liberating experience. It's not surprising that the early Christian figures were all desert people. It seems to be the right setting for that. It's hard to imagine in even more modern times a writer like Carlos Castaneda setting his book in the forests of Minnesota. It's impossible to imagine, right? But I live in a transitional area; I don't like living in heavily timbered country. I live in the sagebrush uplands with the mountains in the distance, and we have a big horizon. You can see a long way anywhere around our place, and that's where I'm most comfortable.

TBR: You recently wrote *Some Horses*, a book devoted to your love of horses. Have you always been a horse person?
TM: Not really. When I was young, I disliked horses. I can't remember why, but I wasn't around them much growing up in Michigan. My sister was a very good horsewoman, and I had a girlfriend who was a serious horse person.

When I was seventeen years old I went to Wyoming. I became comfortable with horses and got to like them. I could see what they were for. Some of them would help you, and some of them wouldn't. You've just got to get into their personalities a little bit. Then I bought a couple of cheap 4-H kind of horses that I used as hunting and packing horses in the Beartooth Wilderness in the sixties and seventies. They just grew on me over the years. I guess I have become obsessed with them—I mean, not obsessed, but I spend a significant amount of my time with horses.

TBR: How would you describe *Some Horses*?
TM: I would say that *Some Horses* is a non-technical book comprised of stores that involve horses, things that have happened over the past thirty years. There's a writer in Wyoming—Alyson Hasy—who has written a book

about horses. She said a friend of hers told her that "riding a horse consists of one nervous system taking over another." I think the enchantment of horsemanship lies in this incredible closeness—the relationship between person and animal—when you're really not sure where one leaves off and the other begins. It's not exclusive to horses by any means, but there's a magic there for some people, and to people who are open to that magic it's very profound.

TBR: Have you ever been injured by a horse?
TM: Yes. The year before last I was injured pretty good. I was bucked off hard and broke a bunch of things. Was hurt for about a year. I think that was a little age-related too.

TBR: How did you come to be a writer?
TM: I'm not sure. My mother and father were both avid readers, so I grew up in a household with lots of books, and there was a family magic about the printed word. I read adventure books when I was young, things like *Kon-Tiki*, and I associated writing with an adventurous life. I'd like to say that it was my pure poetic love for the language. I certainly imagined that a life like Tolstoy lived or Jack London lived or Thoreau lived was part of it. I also just like to read so much that writing became an extension of my reading life. It seemed the next logical thing, and it's still that way for me. If I have a cold streak and just can't write, I forget about it for a while and go back to reading only. At some point or another, reading refuels the writing tank. It's either that there's something you can't find so you want to supply it yourself or that the general excitement about literature makes you want to participate in it at another level.

TBR: Do you have a book or an author you turn to in times of difficulty?
TM: Chekhov. The reason I always turn to him is that his writing leads from perception to perception. There's nothing in his writing that is bad for a writer, in terms of influence. I mean you're not going to start imitating him as you might with Faulkner or Hemingway or Tennessee Williams. When you read Chekhov, the only lesson you get out of it is the excitement of having extra perceptions about characters. That excitement sometimes leads me back to myself if I'm stalled out on writing.

TBR: When and how did you first start publishing?

TM: It was the late sixties. I had been writing constantly for ten years and couldn't get anything published. I was at the end of my rope. I wrote a novel and sent it to Jim Harrison, who was living around New York. He knew people in the publishing industry and passed it on to an editor at Simon & Schuster. And to my astonishment Simon & Schuster accepted the book, and it was sold to movies. It was a low-level bestseller. It was a bestseller in Japan. A lot of good things happened for that first book. Then I was off and running—zero to sixty in one minute. I hadn't even published a short story at that time, so it was much-needed encouragement.

TBR: Would you have any suggestions for someone who is just starting to write?

TM: Nothing very surprising; it's just that writing, in my view, is the by-product of reading. So I would say to someone who doesn't really like to read that they ought to reexamine their enthusiasms. I would say the only two things that I know—at least the things that have worked in my life as a writer—are to read constantly and spend lots of time with other writers. There's something about the way writers, especially young writers, train each other through conversation and selecting books and recommending books and pursuing the enthusiasm that's enclosed in the love of literature. That's the best kind of training for young writers.

TBR: Which contemporary writers do you most like to read?

TM: Right now, I'm completely swept away by a writer named Alice Munro. All I've been doing for several months is reading her work, which stands head and shoulders over anyone else I've read in a long time. So, it's a fairly simple answer for the moment. Otherwise there are hundreds of other young writers and contemporary writers that I read. I read them all—friends and the ones who aren't my friends.

TBR: Many of our readers are writers and might be interested on your approach to writing. When you begin, for example, to write a novel, do you have the plot and characters already formulated in your mind, or do you use a different approach?

TM: A friend of mine used to say that writing is entirely improvisatory, and I must say that my experience has tended to support that. I often have a plan for where a book is going and who the characters are, but it never turns out to be true. It's just a way of getting started, but is illusory. I usually start with a vivid image or a strong feeling about something—a place, relationship between people—and I pursue it. After that, another energy joins in the quest, and you are in almost a musical stage of improvising. The end result is that what you've written will certainly require a lot of revisions, because this approach makes for lots of false leads and red herrings.

TBR: What is your assessment of the current state of the publishing world?
TM: I don't think I'm really qualified to talk about that. I know there are things about it that are not very reassuring. I wouldn't call it a "publishing world"; I would call it a "literary world," at this point in time. I got a very strong feeling about this a few years ago when I was chairman of the fiction panel of the National Book Awards. I read every thing published that year that was serious. I got worried about whether there was a strong relationship anymore between what Virginia Woolfe called "the common reader" and writers. I think that writers are fairly safe in the academic environment now, but I worry about their actual intercourse with the real public. People used to be impacted by writers—writers had an audience. I don't see much of that anymore. But for the most part, writing seems to be relegated to a branch of the academic world.

TBR: Do you have any suggestions as to how the situation could be improved?
TM: I don't know. There are so many things that people would rather do than read books. I don't think that's getting any better, but I do think that there's an irreducible minimal readership for serious books. There is an esti-mate that thirty or forty thousand people out there simply like to read good literature. They like stories, and they like them in book form. They don't want them on a screen; they don't want them on fax paper. They want to read books. That group never seems to go away. They are the people who support independent bookstores and people like me and other writers.

TBR: I have read that you feel we have a responsibility to Mother Earth.
TM: I have served on a good many environmental boards and have done a lot of environmental work. I'm particularly interested in finding channels of communication between the agriculture and the environmental communities,

which are somewhat estranged right now. I'm on various conservation boards, trying to do that without falling into the class arrogance that a lot of environmentalists seem to have drifted into, which I think is bad for everybody. I'm a member of the Montana Livestock Association, which is a large body of anti-environmentalists, and I'm on four environmental boards. It seems that a lot of people aren't talking who should be talking and would probably talk pretty well if they just gave it a try. So my goal at the moment is to try, in my small way, to create a bit of a bridge between the two communities.

TBR: It's easy to see your love of animals. Do you participate in or believe in any animal rights movements?

TM: My wife is a member of PETA (People for the Ethical Treatment of Animals) and has companion dogs. She goes to retirement homes and hospitals. That's probably why two of my daughters are PETA members. I wouldn't put myself quite in that category, because I'm in the cattle business. I'd have to say I have a moderate position on the issue of animal rights. I'm not a vegetarian, but it's very important to me how animals are treated, including livestock. That's a very, very strong issue.

One of my daughters cofounded the first no-kill animal shelter in Montana. She did fundraising for that, and she's only twenty-two years old. Our family is somehow or another involved in this animal well-being issue, either formally or informally. We do have some contradictions in that. I mean I've roped and rodeoed for thirty years off and on, and those things have a troubling component. I'm trying to work my way through all that.

TBR: Are you troubled by any unfulfilled ambitions?

TM: I have a lot of fire in the belly. I've resigned myself to the fact that I'm going to have to live through to the end of my life with a long list of things that I'm never going to get done. I think, though, that my ambitions have become more reasonable. One of them seems to be slowly coming true, and it hasn't been easy. My wife and I were both previously married, and we have children from both marriages. And we brought up all of them. We have a family unit in a way—not a unit, that's too strong of a word. We have a family presence in Montana. Our kids live in different towns and are active in different ways. My son is a very well-known bladesmith up here. My youngest daughter just started college here, and my second oldest daughter just moved back to Montana from Seattle. And there are two grandchildren.

I'm excited about this larger family in the landscape where we all live together. I would have to say that making that a success, right now is my number one ambition.

I also would like to write a better book than I have written before. I think that all writers feel this way—that every book is kind of a failure. You have an ideal book in your mind, and you never get there. That never changes. But if you don't run out of energy, with each book you know more and you have a better chance of getting there. So the prospects of writing the book that you really want to write are constantly improving. You keep trying.

TBR: What are your current literary projects?
TM: I have been working on a novel for years, and I've written probably four hundred pages of it. I don't seem to be in any panic to finish it, and whatever short-term rewards there are in writing, I've had them: the usual array of good reviews and bad reviews, prizes, rejections. I've been through the evolution that all writers go through, and now that doesn't excite me anymore. The only thing that is really exciting is to write better, and I'm trying with all my might to be a better writer. That's always the drive. Then there's the excitement of discovery when you set out on this improvisatory adventure, and, to your own astonishment, you sometimes do things well that you couldn't have foreseen if you hadn't gone on the adventure. Things simply happen. You can't plan them. Writing is so much like that.

TBR: Is there any question you've never been asked in an interview but you always thought would be helpful to your readers?
TM: I think that writers, particularly young writers, are assailed by such a lack of confidence in what they're doing that they assume that they're not very good. What I would tell writers everywhere is that this feeling of anxiety and fear and lack of confidence is something you have to accept, because every writer feels it. Writers, I have learned, often fake confidence in their public personae. I want to assure people that it's an anxiety-ridden profession—that's one of the sources of energy. And it's one of the things that might be a good reason for not doing it. But don't think that because you're fearful in your every attempt that what you're doing is not good, because that's not true.

Interview: Thomas McGuane

Robert Birnbaum / 2002

From The Narrative Thread, on the Identity Theory website (www. identitytheory.com), May 24, 2002, pp. 1–12. Reprinted with permission of Robert Birnbaum.

Robert Birnbaum: In preparing to talk to you I looked you up on an Internet search engine and more than half the entries were for your fishing and horse books.

Tom McGuane: Well, I'll be darned.

RB: Not a lot of references to your fiction.

TM: That might be a symptom of the fact that I haven't published any fiction in a good while. Those two books that I did—I can't say that anyone particularly wanted to do them—I had a two book contract at Knopf and I did the fishing book with them and—I'm not sure—but I think maybe they felt they had to do it. It went through seven hard cover printings.

RB: Wow. Aren't they happy?

TM: I know. Then the little horse book got as high as number six at Amazon. They were surprise performances for both their publishers. And they are doing pretty well in paperback. You know there is something to be said about pulling together that sort of thing, these things that you only do when passion strikes. You sit down and write while it lasts and eventually, in this case many years, they turn into books. It's not my main thing, by any means. Are we taping yet?—

RB: Yes we are . . .

TM: . . . I'll change nothing. Let's say you have something you care about. There was a wonderful book by a West Indian writer about cricket. You probably know this book. It's a kind of a Communist book in a way.

RB: Oh, by C.L.R. James.

TM: Yes, a fabulous book. That's at a very high level. I don't think that any book that deals with cricket or fishing or horsemanship, you can't just sit and draft it. Maybe you go to fifty cricket matches and then something comes to you and you sit down and write twelve pages. And you do that sort of thing for twelve years—in the case of my fishing book—for thirty years. Eventually the corpus of a book emerges, that needs to be repaired and revised and redone and there it is. But those kinds of books couldn't be written in any other way. You can't just sit down and write them.

RB: Maybe there is some kind of Library of Literary Oddities there? You on fishing and horses, the James book on cricket, Eduardo Galeano on soccer, Jim Harrison on food . . . probably you get twenty or thirty titles by writers about subjects they are passionate about.
TM: You know fishing is the most published subject outside mathematics there is. Did you know that?

RB: No. Why is that?
TM: Just because it's such a non-directional daydreamer's game. It bites at the language process.

RB: So why did you write a novel? (*laughs*)
TM: I didn't write one until I felt strongly about some things. It was interesting the last time I saw you I got this great review from Fredrick Busch. The best review I think I have ever gotten for a book. I had this kind of funny experience with that book [*Nothing but Blue Skies*] which was that it got great reviews everywhere except the Sunday *New York Times*.

RB: Which in the publishing world seems to be the most important.
TM: Yeah, it's in every independent booksellers desk. What was strange about it was Jay Parini, the guy who wrote the review had a book out at the same time, We were on a book tour at the same time. Tom Brokaw called me and said, "God, we couldn't even do that in TV." Competing merchandise. My son-in-law Walter Kirn is a novelist and his first book came out and he got a bad review in the *NY Times*. He was out on book tour, he made one stop and his publisher called up and said go home and cancelled the tour. All based on that. You could have a book reviewed in the *LA Times* by Saul Bellow and get a rave review and it wouldn't make much difference but a graduate student in the *NY Times* can kill you.

RB: So your last book got good reviews except one.
TM: Yeah and it overcame that review and did pretty well. But it was a book my publishers were thinking could be kind of a break-out book because there was a lot of enthusiasm before the book came out from places like *Publishers Weekly* and *Kirkus*. It sold better than anything I ever wrote.

RB: What would a break-out book be for a writer who has been around for a while and been well received?
TM: They were hoping to have a best seller of some kind. I'll never have a best seller. I'm just too weird to have a best seller (*laughs*).

RB: Well, you do seem to be a writer who is more focused on writing than the business of writing.
TM: Well, I think that's true. There are really built-in limits to this. I saw V. S. Naipal's last book, the first printing was twenty thousand books. I mean he's a great writer and we know that and the world knows it. A book on shopping addiction, they'll run off a hundred thousand just 'cause they are in the mood.

RB: Who west of the Hudson River or out where you are is a best-selling successful writer?
TM: Nobody. We all feel we are a little bit invisible to the Northeast Corridor. That it's hard for us to persuade people in the East that interesting lives are lived beyond. I remember H. L. Mencken's famous remark when people were praising Willa Cather—who truly is a great writer by any standard at all, most readable and so on—he said simply, "I don't care what happens in Nebraska." And that's pervasive and there is just no sense fighting city hall with this issue. I go back to a thing John Barth said to me when I was very young. He said, "You want your book to do well enough so that you can publish another one."

RB: The Woody Allen strategy of filmmaking.
TM: It's a legitimate strategy. It means you can go on and have a career if you don't starve out—I have always been able to find other things to do, other ways to make a living. Worked in films, I did a lot of journalism at one point. I've had some success at ranching and so I really have no complaints about it. We all are filled with complaints—let me be honest—but I don't have an overwhelming one.

RB: You're not bitter.
TM: I'm not bitter.

RB: Tell me about the title of your new novel, *The Cadence of Grass*. It has a buddhistic ring to it. Does it signal a writer coming to a different place in his approach to fiction?
TM: One of the things, I think, that dawns on you living where I do—maybe you don't have to live in some place where you are so dominated by weather and those things as we are, seasonal issues and without over-interpreting those, you go through two periods. The first period is that you are making an effort to make a life in this place, and the indifference of the landscape sort of drives you crazy. You can tell that the land doesn't care whether you stay or go or flourish. And then you get this feeling of being relegated to what nature is going to do. And you begin to like it. You like the feeling of living in a cycle that is more important than you are. And that that has a kind of rhythmic quality and an eternal quality that is reassuring. That's a little of what that title is about.

RB: And yet the story reminds me of a Carl Hiaason/southern Florida story. You have serious whackos here in some odd situations.
TM: Yes, I know. They are serious whackos. Of course there's the voice of the person who is not remotely like that, Bill Champion. I consider him a stick in the flow. Something to reference. At the same time you always have the burden to write an interesting story.

RB: Was your detailed description of the horsemanship and riding—was that gesture directed at Eastern readers?
TM: No, no, no. For some reason the concretia that is associated with these kinds of ritual processes is something that has always appealed to me. I used to fish with a guy who had an old wooden rowboat. He was a great fisherman. I was always trying to figure out why he was such a successful fisherman. He did everything in a ritualistic way. He had a bailing can that was an old Maxwell House can, cut off in this perfect way. Always went *there*. Oars went *there*. After you anchored the anchor went *here*, the line was coiled *there*. The whole outfit wasn't worth a hundred dollars. It was nearly all he had, but it was so deeply ritualized that it had a kind of glow. I don't know what this all means but there is a lot of that in horsemanship. It's part of its appeal in a

way. All those things the vacarros did, hang up their bridles with the reins hanging down. Most people would just throw the reins over the hook where they hang everything. Well, if you hang 'em like that when you go to ride the horse, they've got these two weird curves in them. So the vacarros would hang their reins hanging in opposing directions. They'd pull the bridle down on the horse and the reins would hang like they are supposed to. There are thousands of little things like that associated with horsemanship or fishing or aviation. I think it's a mistake for people not to have a good bit of that in their lives. A good bit of reassuring ritual—empty ritual being the thing to be avoided.

RB: That assumes that people have something they really care about beyond folding their newspaper in a certain way.
TM: People do a surprising amount of it—getting the leaves out of the gutters and the things they do with their lawns and when they repaint their house and how they keep track of stuff. One of the things you notice in Japanese literature, there is nothing that is not ritualized by those folks.

RB: Do you read a lot of Japanese literature?
TM: Yes, quite a bit. Before I left on this trip I read Lady Sasheen's *As They Crossed the Bridge of Dreams*. It's a wonderful melancholy little book, that's almost a novel in a way. I love Japanese literature. My son is a nut for it. My son is a bladesmith and he studied in Japan.

RB: Meaning he makes blades for knives?
TM: He's a knife maker. He's a great knife maker. His heroes are all Japanese blacksmiths. He went over there and lived for a while. His house is full of Japanese literature. He's always pressing it on me.

RB: So he makes the steel and forges the blades?
TM: Yeah, he does quite well at it. He won the New York Bladesmith Show last year, the biggest one in the world. He's self-taught. He studied under a man in Japan—they have these characters called national treasures, individuals are called national treasures. This man was a national treasure, in his seventies and Thomas worked with him for a while and the man told him in a very direct way, "You can be the best in the world." He forges steel, Damascus steel. His knives are art quality knives. He's usually about a hundred knives behind in filling his orders.

RB: What does he charge for them?
TM: He gets as much as $5,000 a knife.

RB: One-of-a-kinds?
TM: Yeah.

RB: How many does he make in a year?
TM: Fifty. But not all at that price. He makes ceremonial swords and those are even more. He makes cooking and hunting knives that are less. His specialty are these complex folding knives.

RB: Where does he live?
TM: In Montana. All my children live nearby.

RB: That must be great.
TM: It is great.

RB: How often do you venture from Sweet Grass County?
TM: I get out, I guess. I'm kind of reclusive when I'm there. In fact Bruce Weber, the photographer, had a place up there for a while, said I was the most reclusive person he'd ever known. Which I don't think is quite fair. When I'm there I'm just so happy at my ranch, as you would be. It's a beautiful place, full of books. Lots of dogs and horses. I'm not suffering there by any means. But we get restless from time to time. Usually in the middle of winter we'll go some place, do something very conventional. I took all the kids to Florida this year, went to the beach.

RB: Did you go fishing?
TM: Oh yeah. And then I make fishing trips. My cousin and I—he lives here in Massachusetts—we've been fishing together for fifty years. And we're still going fishing together. We started with little hand lines fishing for chogees, off the pilings, and this year we're in the southern Bahamas fishing together. We've always done it.

RB: You are on your way to NYC. What's that like after months and months in seemingly splendid isolation?
TM: We'll soon find out. I haven't been there in ten years.

RB: Ten years, wow. Do you watch television?

TM: Yeah, I watch hockey games. CNN. I'm really a print guy, though. Even to the point of reading newspapers on the Internet. I'm pretty excited when I can get a real newspaper and whip around with it. My wife—it frustrates me sometimes—she just won't keep up with the news unless she sees the six o'clock news at night. As soon as we go traveling and she can get her hands on a real newspaper, then she is fully informed again.

RB: What's your local newspaper called?

TM: I live between two local newspapers, the *Billings Gazette* and the *Bozeman Chronicle*. Neither are bad papers. They are extremely local in focus, which is fine because you can get the other stuff pretty easily. I get up in the morning and read the *NY Times* everyday. But scrolling through it is not the same deal.

RB: Let's get back to what caused you to reenter the stream of fiction writing? Pieces of this new novel appeared in various publications . . .

TM: As I went along some things struck me as being stories, two or three were in the *New Yorker*, one of them was in the *Harvard Review*, another was in *Grand Street*. I was writing this damn thing for such a long time. I would want to publish something periodically and something would jump out that would look like a story. I reentered it because I was preoccupied with some thematic things. Without pretending to be a feminist, I really started getting the idea that one of the things that was kind of septic about our lives was there were always these alpha males camped at the middle of our lives. It might be the Ford dealer in Big Timber or Ariel Sharon. It might be Yasser Arafat or Robert Mugabe or George W. Bush. It was always this pattern and I began to think, "Well, you know maybe that's what's wrong with everything." Halfway through writing this novel Montana elected for the first time a woman governor and she was a complete monster (*both laugh*). Her campaign slogan was, "I promise to be the lapdog of Industry."

RB: No!

TM: Yeah (*laughs*). She's a Neanderthal. Right-wing Republican. So my theory, which was you could take a random sampling of women and drop them all in key positions and everything would get better—and I still kind of believe that—but she's taken some of the wind out of my sails.

RB: Evelyn [in *The Cadence of Grass*] is pretty admirable. I don't know about her mother.
TM: There are only two characters who have my approval in this book, Evelyn and the rancher Bill Champion.

RB: What about the cross-dressing . . .
TM: . . . oh yeah, he has my approval. I have basically two versions of "the bad male." One is the old imperial ego guy, like Sunny Jim and then Paul, who is sort of the antichrist. As somebody who was raised an Irish Catholic I had to make the devil sort of appealing because that's what we believed.

RB: Perhaps I didn't read closely enough. Did Paul Crusoe actually kill the motorcyclist or was he taking the rap for Sunny Jim as he later claimed?
TM: Paul's responsible. I heard a new version of that. I was at a rodeo a couple of weeks ago and this old guy, he was a rancher—a no-good guy—had died and I ran into his neighbor and we were talking about him. He said that this guy [the unpleasant old rancher] when he was growing up, he and two other guys went over to the Paradise Valley in the Upper Yellowstone, were stealing cattle and hauling them to Billings and selling them. They got caught and two of the boys were the sons of well-to-do ranchers and the third one was a poor kid. So the parents of the well-to-do kids said to the poor boy, "If you take the fall for our sons and go to prison, your ranch will be paid for when you get out." I knew that guy that did the time. He did seven years in the penitentiary and he's been ranching for thirty now. Probably was his only shot at ranching.

RB: Was it a good deal for him?
TM: Probably from his point of view it was good deal. Because it's been at least fifty years since you could go to work on a ranch and end up having a ranch. It's basically an economy that belongs to hereditary land-owners and there is no way into it. Except if you are somebody like me who comes in from left field.

RB: Is it a money-losing business?
TM: Yes. Net net, sans subsidies, Montana agriculture is about 300 million below the line. The whole thing, all of it.

RB: Are you done with movies?
TM: Yeah.

RB: Do people still call you?
TM: Yes, and every now and then I get tempted to do it. There are some appealing things about it. Writing a novel is like doing the Appalachian Trail by yourself. You're out there, nobody to talk to, nobody knows what you are doing, and if you have this great burst and you want to run out of your office and tell about this great scene, nobody is remotely interested. When you work in film there are always people around and you can interact and that has its appeal. But it's changed very much since the days I worked in it. I did a project about five years ago at Universal that didn't get made and it was really the best script I'd ever written. But it was done at the same time they were doing *Titanic* and all the smaller things just shriveled up. What I noticed when I was out there was that the atmosphere had changed and it was a much more committee-oriented bureaucratic kind of thing. It was like going to work for Merrill Lynch. You can't walk in and pitch your idea to two guys and have them say, "Let's go for it." That isn't ever going to happen. Everything is in development and the downside of it is that it's wildly time consuming. Projects like [Jim] Harrison's *Legends of the Fall* was in development for fourteen years. You are just watching your life go by. The temptation is that it's almost the only way you can make a living writing unless you are associated with a university.

RB: It doesn't strike me that very many writers are in it for the art of it.
TM: I was in it for the dough. No other reason.

RB: When you did *Ninety-two in the Shade*, wasn't it what we would call today an independent film?
TM: Well, it was United Artists. It was off-shore financing, Sir Lew Grade financed it.

RB: It seemed like you had your own way.
TM: Yeah, I did. But the budgets were so small. We had a million bucks. They basically said "You have thirty-six shooting days; if you get a brain tumor you still have thirty-six shooting days. You have a million dollars. If it's a million and one, we hope you have a dollar bill with you." You knew what the deal was.

RB: Then you wrote *Rancho Deluxe* and then came the epic *Missouri Breaks*. [with Jack Nicholson and Marlon Brando]
TM: Oh God! As the producer said, "The pus actually got on the walls." (*both laugh*) It was a nightmare.

RB: What do you see looking forward in your life?
TM: If there is a complaint I have about my life, I'm a little bit overloaded in a way. I'd love for life to thin it down for me just a little bit. But we seem to get up in the morning and have a wild run and pass out at the end of the day.

RB: When you were a subject of magazine articles in the seventies and perhaps eighties, there was a scene out in your neighborhood. In the nineties Russ Chatham the painter started Clark City Press. What's going on out there now?
TM: Well, there never was to the degree that it seemed to be. Somebody would get the idea that there was and then *People* magazine would wear out a rental car by the time they constructed the idea of an urgent scene happening there. There is a bit more of one in Missoula, which is about a five-hour drive from us. It would be like you going to Portland, Maine [from Boston]. That's a little bit more of an urban thing. There's a wonderful new book called *Breaking Clean* out by a woman who left a ranch up there named Judy Blunt. It's really a good book. She's the newest addition to that scene. Bill Kittredge and Jim Welch and there are some very estimable writers living there. They live in town and they have the Oxford Bar they all go to. It's very different over in southwest Montana where I live. [Jim] Harrison's just moved there, just last month. So he's there. Russ Chatham is there. William Hjortsberg, he and I went to college together, he lives close to me. Tim Cahill. Walter Kirn. There are others, I'm just not thinking.

RB: The university writing program has a good reputation?
TM: Yes, it does. It's the second oldest one in the nation.

RB: Where did John Edgar Wideman teach?
TM: At Wyoming. I taught there last year.

RB: Are you going to continue to teach?
TM: I'm not sure. I liked it so much and I got so involved in it, it was the only thing I could do. I had some pretty interesting young writers. But probably

not. It's an "either or" for me. I can't just do that and get involved in their projects, which I did, and see them on and off hours and then go home and want to work on your novel. It's out of the question.

RB: Your classmates at Stanford were Robert Stone, Larry McMurtry, Wendell Berry?
TM: People were still kind of around in the community when I got there. A lot of the people would get that Stegner fellowship and stay around Palo Alto for a while so the effect of them would still be there. Kesey was around, Robert Stone was still in the neighborhood. Larry McMurtry, James Houston. There was a lot going on. Stegner didn't have much to do with it. He thought we were all crazy hippies. He actually told me that he thought it was the end of civilization.

RB: The program?
TM: No, the people. We were just hippies and he couldn't process that.

RB: Is there a movement to identify a western school of writing, in the way that southern writing is marked?
TM: That attempt is in place. I don't see a lot of merit in it, frankly. (*laughs*) I get asked about that, "What about the Montana school of writing?" I have this filthy little trick I play. I answer, "It would be like talking about the New Jersey school of writing." They all burst into laughter. I say, "Wait a minute. We've got Walt Whitman. We have William Carlos Williams. We have Allen Ginsberg. We can put Bruce Springsteen in there. We can put Stephen Crane. Maybe New Jersey writing is not as negligible as you horse-laughers think it is?" (*laughs*) Anyway, I don't even believe in American writing. I've heard myself saying that a lot. The problems of writing, the issues of writing are really universal. They are the same in Mexico, the same in Yugoslavia and the same in Montana. And getting away from that notion you are headed down the twisted road to local color and other things.

RB: There are certainly claims that there is a New York kind of book. In Tom Wolfe's controversial essay [*Stalking the Billion-Footed Beast: A Literary Manifesto for the New Social Novel*] he scoffed at writers who weren't doing what he was doing . . .

TM: . . . lots of research. He does believe that strongly. But almost no one takes him seriously as a writer. Actually I think people are too hard on him. He does have some merits as a writer. I used to love his essays. I think he has polarized people against him with these preposterous sweeping statements about what everybody else is supposed to be doing.

RB: And there is his attack on Mailer, Updike, and Roth . . .
TM: I remember that attack. It was based on their sales figures being below the targets. What an attack for an artist to launch.

RB: What writers do you stay in touch with?
TM: I'm not a big letter writer. [Jim] Harrison is a great letter writer. He is in touch with everybody on earth, it seems. I hardly see anybody. What's happened to me is, not by design, I went off in this kind of remote place and I actually started doing what they do there. I've been running cattle for thirty years. So almost everybody I know is a rancher and somehow associated with that. That's not to say that makes me into a real rancher. I'm just a real writer. But we are talking on a daily basis who do I see. I see people who are ranching or training horses.

RB: Do you keep up with the literary world? Is there a good bookstore in your locale?
TM: Yes, there is a good bookstore and I keep very much up. The bookstore in Bozeman is on the *NY Times* list for the best seller list. It's a good bookstore. I read reviews. I do all these things that you probably shouldn't do. I keep up. I like to know what's coming out and if it interests me I get and read it.

RB: You did mention something about forestalling old age. Any profound observations about growing old?
TM: Well, no, and I feel like I better get them. Because here it comes. I'm so active that I haven't had some of the problems that other people my age have had, yet. But I'm going to have them, I know that. The fact that nothing has really changed in my M.O. for about thirty years, it's going to change. One of these days I'll get some kind of weird health report or something and it will scare me. Something that will make me change what I do. In fact if Advil weren't so plentifully available I wouldn't be lying to myself like this. There's no doubt I have more aches and pains than I used to have. You know, I get up

at five everyday and I'm on horseback half the day and then to other physical things. That's not going to last too much longer but that's going to be okay with me. I noticed this spring when I got a really good case of the flu, it was just a great time for me. It reduced the scale of things. I thought, "God, I can really concentrate on reading." I didn't feel very well but I put the blanket over my lap and I got a big pot of tea and I read all day long. I haven't been able to do that. I thought, "Gee, it was nice having the room cleared a little bit."

RB: Are you giving a lot of thought to what you are going to be writing? What are you going to write next?
TM: Yeah, in fact I have some things outlined in my head and it's one of the things I am really looking forward to this year. I have been working on a novel—since I finished this one—it's always about a year out on these things. You never quite put your shoulder to the wheel until the current one is on its way. I've got this novel I can't wait to get back working on. I get enormous gratification out of the process of writing. We're taking about approaching old age. I've learned that is the reward of writing, that is, doing it. It's not a particularly reliable reward because you are often not able to get there. You are not able to write as well as you want. You are not able to feel inspired or energized. But it does come. It is the only reliable reward. Everything else is subject to these crazy outside things. Fashions that are going through . . .

RB: What do you mean that you are not able to write as good as you want?
TM: I have this set of criteria of how it's supposed to be. I don't have long spells of glee about what I am doing but every now and then—you work your way and you actually write better than you think you can. And those are happy times. The novel is a very rigorous kind of master. It's not lyric poetry. You have a lot of traveling to do getting from point a to point b. Any sustained narrative has sheer mechanical problems and all sorts of things have to be dealt with.

RB: Are you happy with *The Cadence of Grass*?
TM: I'm pretty happy with this one. I had the odd feeling at the end of this book I was just fine. Whatever happens. That's as good a feeling as is available to me. I wasn't waiting to see. I said to myself, "There."

RB: In the scheme of things, you think of one book at a time?
TM: That's right.

RB: Do you keep a notebook?
TM: Well, I am always scribbling things down that might get away from me. I have a pile of papers that are just scraps or just images that seem evocative. I always imagine it's like going through sagebrush and there is the mouth of the cave, like every little kid's fantasy. You can barely crawl in there and there is this big chamber on the other side. It probably has some hideous Freudian side to it. There are things that seem to be tags for some greater reality beyond, even though you don't know what that is. Like in Melville, the movement of a whale's tail at the surface which is just a theme in the ocean implies the tremendous bulk of the whale—you are always looking for those kinds of things that imply something beyond. And you often have no idea what they are. Sometimes you write them out and you find there wasn't anything there at all. No whale.

RB: How far do you get before you will discard something?
TM: I've gone a long way on some projects and thrown them out. When you sit down to negotiate a new contract with a publisher and the publisher asks what you are working on. You try to give an idea what the book is going to be. I'm always careful to include the caveat that this thing could go up in smoke two years from now, I don't really know.

RB: Hmm.
TM: You have to know that, otherwise you will just doggedly do the bad ideas.

RB: Okay. Thank you.
TM: Uh huh, thank you.

Not Really Ranching

Bill Kohlhaase / 2002

From *Tributary Magazine*, July 2002, pp. 12–13. Reprinted with permission of Bill Kohlhaase.

The answer to why a decade separates Thomas McGuane's last two novels is as complicated as one of the charming scoundrels who populate his eight previous works. Rumor had it that the writer, rancher, and former movie director had grown tired of the publishing business.

"That was part of it," McGuane says from his ranch in Sweet Grass County. "We have to drive everything we do through this aperture of New York City and I get tired of dealing with all that it requires. And we have such a busy life. I've got four children in the area, three grandchildren, a falling-down ranch to prop up. It's not that I've been sucking my thumb waiting for a better day. But writing another novel just got de-emphasized. My first book came in the sixties and it seemed appropriate to take a break at the quarter-century mark. And it gave me time to write about some things that I love. I didn't care if they were important to the publishing business or not."

There is another reason for the gap of ten years between McGuane's last novels, a reason that reflects the struggle between the old and new West, a reoccurring theme in his own life. Tired of being tied to a desktop computer, he wrote his latest novel, *The Cadence of Grass* (Knopf), out in long hand. "I felt like I couldn't write unless I was at the computer terminal and I didn't like that feeling. So I wrote this last one out by hand. But I can't live with my writing. I just got a thin laptop. I'm hoping it will supplant my bad handwriting."

Images of old and new Montana sit side-by-side in *The Cadence of Grass*. An ornate, mechanical cash register stands next to an electronic box used to process credit cards. A woman tries on a sexy black evening dress while wearing manure-stained boots. There's a dried-out ranch and a bottling plant that produces "ECO FIZZ."

Much of the novel is set in and around Bozeman, and it's here that the old-new contrasts are most apparent. New homes gnaw "through old grain fields toward the Bridger Mountains, one after the other like caterpillars."

Cattlemen sit next to "hippies" at a hole-in-the-wall diner that's surely the Stockyard Cafe. One of the book's central characters picks up a misguided, anti-government malcontent at a music bar that resembles the Filling Station.

The Cadence of Grass revolves around a family patriarch's attempt to control his heirs, even after his demise. The death of Sunny Jim Whitelaw brings out the dysfunction in his family. Sunny Jim, in life a strong-willed dapper Dan, leaves the Whitelaw bottling plant to his wife and daughters on the condition that daughter Evelyn and ambitious son-in-law Paul drop their plans for divorce. Everyone who stands to profit scrambles for influence and wrestles with desires. Evelyn is at the center of it all.

Letting a woman take a leading role is a change for McGuane, whose past books focus on doomed bad-boys and ne'er-do-well males. While these sorts play a role in The Cadence of Grass, it's Evelyn, and to a lesser extent her sister Natalie and their mother, who are the focus of the book's central themes.

Creating a novel around a woman is something McGuane's family life helped inspire. "I have three daughters and a wife and I know more now, maybe, about how women are different than men, how they think differently. I think all this made me move [Evelyn] more to the center of the book than I might have before."

Reviewers familiar with McGuane's history of troubled male leads have focused on Paul Crusoe, Evelyn's estranged rattlesnake of a husband, a character straight out of McGuane's earlier books. Paul, with prison time for manslaughter under his belt, is having an affair with his parole officer. He wants to see the ranch subdivided.

McGuane agrees Paul is important, but as second fiddle to his estranged wife. "I just read one review out of New York that said Paul was the main character. I think of Paul as the antagonist, if not the anti-Christ. Evelyn is the protagonist. She's the central consciousness of the novel."

While the inheritance scenario shapes the story, it's the side-trips, in which McGuane takes his characters out of their element and into the Montana landscape, that are most revealing. These excursions, as when Evelyn drives off lost in a blizzard and is taken in by a strange, isolated farm family, could easily stand alone. In them, McGuane makes his best points about changing cultures standing shoulder-to-shoulder in our part of the country.

McGuane has seen a host of generational and cultural shifts during his thirty-three years in Montana and his own life embraces facets of both old and new cultures. "Life in the West is changing. There's a changing arc of relationship between the generations, a new century with a move into a new society. If there was a generational conflict in my grandparent's day it wasn't that they were moving into a new society. They continued to lead the lives their parents led.

"Now [in Montana] we have the famous dichotomy of old and new West. It's the demographic things that are assailing us, things like the population turnover. We see people growing up on ranches who want to join rock bands. They're making a bigger leap than the generations before them."

McGuane's previous novels dating back some thirty years make good use of old and new West conflicts. In 1992's *Nothing but Blue Skies*, old and new Montana values battle to a draw as the book's anti-hero, Frank Copenhaver, a businessman involved in livestock and real estate, tries to win back his estranged wife and bridge a generation gap with his daughter. Ten years later *The Cadence of Grass* sees old and new ways seeking an uneasy truce as its characters pursue Sunny Jim's legacy.

McGuane often turns notions of western stereotypes and old-new conflict inside out. In *Nothing but Blue Skies*, Frank Copenhaver's young daughter runs off with notorious, not-so-young property-rights advocate Lane Lawlor, a crank who stirs audiences with declarations of "Montana is not a zoo" and ". . . why do these out-of-staters want us to have a system in Montana which has failed in Russia?" Lawlor wants Montana to dam its waterways at the state line. "If you are unlucky enough to run into someone who wants those rivers flowing elsewhere," spouts Lawlor to a captive audience, "gut-shoot them at the border."

McGuane doesn't exactly deny that Lawlor-types exist. "There's this footloose libertarian movement running through the West and running through the administration and I don't think it bodes well for the natural world," he says.

McGuane says that the polarization between Montanans is as great as he's seen it during his time here. The tension surfaces in *Cadence* when Evelyn, stuck in a blizzard, doesn't know if she should trust the four men in camouflage who advance on her snow-bound car or flee.

The state's changing demographics, he says, explain why Montanans are split between native and new-comer, old and new economies, roads and roadless supporters. "There's lots of ill will between the sectors. More than half the state is losing population. And the other part is not changing numerically so much as qualitatively. The media doesn't address these issues. What they talk about is celebrities. They don't talk about tax flight, or the kids who've been through our schools. They don't talk about the new waves of

Christian fundamentalists. Instead, they focus on some movie star settling in. It's a non-reality for the folks in Montana.

"Clearly we have to find common ground among the various factions in Montana, though I've not found a lot of progress in that direction. Some of the disagreements we face are insurmountable. We have this anti-government feeling in Montana agriculture but without government subsidies, Montana agriculture would not stand on its own. I'm not sure how an industry like that can control our culture. At the same time, I don't think the only solution is to leave the farms and ranches and go to work in the tourist industry. There are great mistakes to be made on both sides of the issue."

That includes the environmental side. "The mistaken idea that farmers have nothing in common with environmentalists can be blamed on environmental elitism. We shouldn't have to feel guilty when making our intentions clear or when finding common ground with those with whom we disagree."

Appropriately, McGuane has fueled his environmental activism with opinions that are somewhat pragmatic. He has been on the board of the Craighead Institute and says he's currently involved with American Rivers and the Wild Salmon Center, a Portland-based, international organization seeking to save salmon migration routes in North America and Asia.

"I guess I get involved because I take so much from the natural world in terms of happiness that I feel I should do something in return," he explains.

McGuane's love for the natural world extends to horses, particularly cutting horses, and fishing. During the years between his last novel, McGuane wrote about both. His 1999 collection of essays, *Some Horses*, is a sort of steeds-I've-known that delves as deeply into four-legged behavior as any of his novels delve into human behavior.

This pairing of man and horse, McGuane and Montana, began in 1967 when he arrived from Michigan to work at the ranch of a girlfriend's father. "But I didn't get crazed about horses until I was living in Deep Creek in the late sixties. I always appreciated athletic skills and I thought roping would be a marvelous sport at the time. I just like the animals. It's arbitrary really that it's horses. It could have been cats."

Another of McGuane's essay collections, *The Longest Silence: A Life in Fishing*, is a thoughtful consideration of time spent in Montana creeks, the Florida Keys and other locations around the globe. At the heart of the book is its deep respect for the creatures and the waters they inhabit.

But this isn't heartfelt nature writing. McGuane's cynical wit and dark sense of comedy colors the new novel just as it did his earlier ones. The book's most ironic statement comes from Paul who indulges visions of development: "Money brings us closer to nature," he declares.

"I thought it was one of the most poisonous remarks Paul could make," McGuane explains. "I absolutely don't believe that myself. But it is one of the floating fallacies in our world. Lots of people who acquire nature do it for economic reasons and they don't seem to have much time to go there once the closing's signed. I know ranchers who spend some fourteen days a year on their place."

McGuane wants it known he doesn't consider himself a real rancher. "I make the distinction that what I do is not real ranching. Real ranching is something that doesn't leave much time for writing novels. It's a brutal job. You have to run so many cows in today's world to make it. I personally can't imagine how you'd do with less than five hundred cows. You'd be tied up all the time."

Early in *Cadence*, Evelyn suggests that veteran rancher Bill Champion kept cattle just so he had an excuse to have horses. McGuane, who runs two hundred yearlings and claims to do ranch work every day, says his own interest in ranching is a little deeper than rationalizing a passion for horses. "If you have land in this high desert climate you have to do something to cut down on fires. Grazing is good for that. I've always known ranchers and been interested in cattle culture. But it's partly true that I'm most interested in horses."

At one time, McGuane's interests included movie-making. In the seventies, he built a reputation in Hollywood for his offbeat scripts. His screenplay for *Rancho Deluxe*, a cult favorite, starred Jeff Bridges and Sam Waterston with music by Jimmy Buffett. He directed Peter Fonda, Burgess Meredith, and Warren Oates in *Ninety-two in the Shade*, the story of warring charter boat captains in the Florida Keys based on his novel. He was connected for a time with *Rancho Deluxe* leading lady Elizabeth Ashley and was married to Margot Kidder. He wrote *The Missouri Breaks*, the twisted and infamous Western that starred Marlon Brando, Jack Nicholson, and Frederic Forrest. The film was badly received at release and considered a box-office flop. But time has seen its stake rise, due in part to the fact that twenty-first-century audiences can better stomach the idea of bounty-hunter Brando wearing a dress than audiences could in 1976.

"I don't miss those days," McGuane says of his movie business experience. "But they were good days. In terms of going back to the filmmaking world, it's not there for me to go back to. It's very different now. In the seventies, the business was so abstract. It was the OK Corral. You could persuade people on your knees to do your project. Now it's done by committee. It's like working for Enron."

McGuane says it's difficult for writers in the West to be taken seriously by the East Coast publishing establishment. "I think there are a lot of enlightened people in the publishing industry who know what goes on. But in general it stands to reason that people in the Northeast are interested in their own part of the country. It's like that Saul Steinberg cartoon the *New Yorker* ran looking across New York City to California with nothing in between. That's a very bitter joke. When H. L. Mencken said he didn't care about Willa Cather because he didn't care about Nebraska he referred to a truth. It's why I think people in the East are less interested in the West. Unfortunately, the whole [publishing] industry is back there."

Currently, the East Coast publishing industry is waiting for McGuane's next effort, this one produced on the new laptop. "It will be a very different novel. I've been working on it intermittently for the last six months and should finish in two years. I'm such an improvisational writer that I would be trying to fool you if I told you what it's about."

A Dialogue with Tom McGuane

Beef Torrey / 2005

Edited version of a previously unpublished interview conducted by Beef
Torrey, June 29, 2005, at McGuane's ranch near McLeod, Montana.
Transcription by Gloria Theide. Clarifications added via follow-up email
exchanges. Final transcript by Beef Torrey.

In the summer of 2004, during what has become an annual pilgrimage for
me to Livingston (a.k.a. "Deadrock"), Montana, I had the opportunity to
speak with Tom McGuane about a book proposal I'd submitted to the
University Press of Mississippi (UPM) for their Literary Conversation
Series—*Conversations with Thomas McGuane.* Later that week, I forwarded
Tom the volume, *Conversations with Jim Harrison,* edited by Bob DeMott,
and an annotated list of numerous interviews I'd stockpiled the past twenty
years. By happenstance I ran into Tom at Dan Bailey's Fly Shop the following
day, where we agreed to keep in touch as the project progressed (or not). Our
subsequent sporadic e-mail exchanges were encouraging and Tom later con-
sented to sitting down with me, for—yet another—interview when I
returned next year.

When I arrived in Deadrock late on Sunday evening, June 26, 2005—I
immediately telephoned Tom and left a message that I had made it to town.
Later that night Tom returned my call at the Rainbow Motel, where I was
staying, and suggested that we meet at ten in the morning on Wednesday, at
his ranch near McLeod—it had been a number of years since I'd been to
Tom's place, and then only as a passenger, with our mutual friend, William
(Gatz) Hjortsberg—providing informative and remarkably detailed directions without being persnickety or pedantic.

Just before closing at Martin's Cafe, I celebrated my return by ordering the
customary bowl of shredded pork and noodles, their signature entree. This
unusual, yet tasty culinary concoction of ramen noodles, with a helping of
shredded pork, topped with a handful of radishes, several carrot sticks, and
sliced hard boiled eggs was accompanied by a heaping wicker basket of
saltine crackers, a liberally supplied plate of individually, foil-wrapped *real*

butter and a bottle of soy sauce. This is the staple meal of many a late-night drunk—during its former twenty-four-hour operation as a railroad diner—which I had first been turned on to by Richard Brautigan.

This week is the annual Livingston Roundup—street dances, live music, *the parade* (the long-standing crowd favorite), nightly rodeo, etc., etc. (lots of etc., etc.). The revelry in Deadrock is gradually gaining steam and by week's end will become a rowdy, rambunctious hootenanny.

Over the past twenty-five years life has changed considerably in this quaint, former cow town of Deadrock, just north of Yellowstone National Park. McGuane is credited with prompting the exodus of writers/artists from California to Paradise Valley—bohemian refugees taken in by his charisma, blue ribbon trout streams, stunning scenery, and reasonable rent. Many of its legendary transplants are no longer counted among the living: director Sam Peckinpah, actor Warren Oates, and poet-novelist Richard Brautigan, but the burgeoning literati of young and established writers remain, while McGuane has long since relocated.

Wednesday morning finally arrived, cool and clear—a welcomed respite from the heat and haze I'd left behind in eastern Nebraska. I left the "The Rainbow" at 8:45 A.M., headed for Swingley Road, into what McGuane refers to as "yup and nope country." Nourished by one of the wettest springs in recent years, the valley flourished with sagebrush, blue stem grass, Indian grass, prairie bunch grass, crested wheatgrass, and brome. I crossed Chicken Creek, Poison Creek, Beaver Creek, and Little Mission Creek, spied the Old Crow Mission, and ascended Wolf Hill as I entered the West Boulder Valley; to the west is the regal Shell Mountain. Spotting isolated thickets of huckleberry, chokecherry, wild rose, thimble berry, and service berry bushes, I was bordered on my right with the fir and lodgepole pines of the Absaroka-Beartooth Wilderness.

Nestled in the sun-drenched hillside is McGuane's ranch—one of the oldest cattle and haying operations in southwestern Montana, sprawling along the West Boulder River in Sweet Grass County.

I passed under the overhead gate with a wrought iron "Pinwheel" (McGuane's brand) and over the *Otto* gate; the sign on the right admonished drivers to "Slow Down, Now! Kids and Old Dogs!" I was warmly greeted by the curious canine crew, Zero, Patty (a.k.a. Cow Patty), Gracie, and Shelagh.

The McGuane ranch house epitomizes rustic charm, entirely appropriate to the character of the man who penned the screenplays to *Rancho Deluxe, Missouri Breaks,* and *Tom Horn.*

Shortly after my arrival, Tom rode in on a quarter horse named Vedette, a fine mount with "an even temperament" as Tom attested to. Tom was appropriately attired in standard ranch wear: boots, blue jeans, pressed western shirt, a light woven jacket, underneath a summer straw cowboy hat. His resemblance to the multi-hyphenated Sam Shepard in his prime was striking. Tom was lanky and fit, with a wide, infectious grin, weathered face, huge rugged hands, and a full head of thick grayish hair.

Tom led the way to his study, dwarfed beneath the shade of stately cottonwoods, a stone's throw from the West Boulder River—a 1909 bunkhouse converted into his private retreat—one of many converted outbuildings during the course of his life where he forged his craft.

A fly rod and waders lean against a chair on the porch, outside the front door. To the left of the entry way is a glass-enclosed sunroom with an overstuffed chair, pillows, an ottoman, and reading lamp.

The main room, where we sat ourselves, is walled with filled bookshelves—a bibliophilic heaven. A long writing desk (an old library table) and computer sits in the center of the room. The screensaver was a photograph of legendary "Comanche" (the sole surviving steed of General George Armstrong Custer and his 7th Cavalry at the Battle of the Little Big Horn in 1876, and likely namesake of the aggressive North American Indian tribe with great equestrian skill).

Tom exuded genuine character; he was candescent, candid, affable, and articulate, as you would anticipate and expect. Our interaction was sincere, animated, and lively, punctuated with frequent guffaws—two acquaintances who share a long-standing history, many mutual friends, a passion for literature and a love of reading.

Beef: I'd like to know about your new book that will be released next spring (2006).

Tom: Well, it's a collection of stories. And one of them is quite long. One is sixty-five pages, or seventy pages long. The name of the book is *Gallatin Canyon.* I'm proud of these stories. Several of them have been collected in *Best American Stories.* The *New Yorker* has taken a number of them. I've always loved short stories and probably never really applied myself to them quite as assiduously as I did with these. I spent three years writing twelve stories. And it's been pleasant not being a piñata for the *Times Book Review*, watching those good days go by.

Beef: Whew!

Tom: I liked the fact that the *New Yorker* was willing to publish some of them as I worked, thanks to the fiction editor Deborah Treisman who is exceptionally thoughtful. I was happy publishing my work that way. I dread publishing this book.

Beef: You dread publishing?

Tom: I don't like publishing books. You rarely have the feeling the publishers actually know what they're doing. If you've been in other businesses you are unlikely to be moved by the expertise of publishers who have no idea how to sell books except to put the author on the road. Anyone with a modicum of self-respect will avoid much of that. As Larry McMurtry said, "I don't want to go around the country talking about last year's book."

Anyway, these last three years have been some of the happiest, most consuming years in fiction writing I've had in memory, right up there with the days when I was young and had no publisher. And now, I have the publication of the book of these stories that gave me such pleasure looming in six or seven months. If I never published another book it would be a road to happiness. Unfortunately, this is a disease; it's my life and I'm going to kind of go on with it.

Many of the American writers of recent times who've excited me most have been short story writers. Ray Carver, obviously right at the top of that heap. Richard Ford's short stories. I love John Cheever's short stories. And I loved Updike's short stories. And the great southern women, Flannery O'Connor, Eudora Welty, Carson McCullers. As an Irish Catholic I'm aware of the Irish short story writing tradition, Frank O'Connor, Liam O'Flaherty, William Trevor, and all those people that I kind of grew up reading. Nearly my favorite writer is Sherwood Anderson: *Winesburg, Ohio* really is a collection of stories. That's, I think, probably the best book of the American Golden Age. That, *As I Lay Dying, In Our Time, My Antonia,* and *The Great Gatsby* are really the most perfect books from that era.

I'm working on a novel now, but it's all I can do to keep myself from going back and writing a short story. It takes me a long time to write a short story and I'll draft them and they change and they change and they change and it's very easy for me to spend a month working every day on one story. A lot of my friends can do much of a novel in that time and I wonder if I'm really just treading water. For the longest time I'll feel like there is still work to be done.

Beef: Are you going to be doing a promotional book tour when this book is released?
Tom: I'm not doing a book tour.

Beef: Okay. *To Skin a Cat*, a collection of . . . probably the best collection of short stories, one of my favorites of your stuff . . .
Tom: The title story, not always admired, was a rant. But I saw it at the time as being a sort of a feminist tract, it was a certain male principle gone amuck. I think some of the reviewers thought that I was celebrating this character, but there are so many kinds of dim bulbs out there writing about literature. It's a minefield. Often when you're writing a story you're dealing with as much psychic terrain as a novel traverses and you have to almost do it with the efficiency of lyric poetry. Something has to happen. Gary Snyder says, "Every perception must lead to another perception." And no *pensees* or asides or throat clearing and blowing the spit out of the embouchure. Something has to happen in every line. In a twenty page story you can absorb the material that might have been spent on a novel.

Beef: The interesting thing to me is the *New Yorker* connection . . . I love reading your pieces that have appeared, like "Ice." But to me it's such a highly unlikely outlet, despite the fact that some of your earlier work appeared there as well. How did that come about?
Tom: I've had stories in the *New Yorker* before. Chip McGrath was the fiction editor then. I think he was sympathetic to my work. And then they had an editor in the Tina Brown era who was distinctly not sympathetic to my work. Deborah Treisman is now the editor there and I sent her a story and she liked it and I sent her another one and she liked it. I sent her one, she did not like it. I have a straightforward relationship with her. I trust her judgment. If she doesn't like something of mine, I listen carefully because she always has a good reason which often leads to my making it a better story.

Beef: Speaking of periodicals, Tom, tell me what kind of periodicals you get at your home.

Tom: Like everybody else we're smothered in paper around here. But I have a really very eclectic bunch of things that I read. I read *Sports Illustrated*, I read . . . *Wooden Boat* every time it comes out . . . I read *Performance Horse*, horse stuff. I read the *Quarterhorse News* every month. I read the *New Yorker* every week. I read the *New York Times* every day. I read five Montana newspapers every day. The *Atlantic* and *Harper's*, all the rubbish that semi- and pseudo-intellectuals read, I read. I occasionally read the *New York Review of Books*. What else? I like to read about boats and things like that. So I'll pick up *Sail* magazine from time to time. I'm a magazine junkie actually. I read fishing magazines which are almost universally terrible infomercials. John Updike said that reading should be the best part of your life and I really believe that. My problem is that I'm indiscriminate. We just built that little bay window on the front of the house so in the wintertime we stretch out in there with our books and our coffee and our reading glasses. Reading is the core of my life, not writing, but I read a lot of things that are completely without merit, like cereal boxes, out of sheer fascination with print.

Beef: Would you agree that good writers should be prolific readers?
Tom: It's not always the case. Edmund Wilson used to make fun of Scott Fitzgerald because he was so under-read, but obviously in the best times wrote like an angel and on a bad day he wrote better than Edmund Wilson. I have some friends who I think are very good writers, including a couple here in Montana, who have not read much. I'm occasionally flabbergasted by who they've never heard of. Harrison and I are omnivores. Harrison's got a leg up on me because he's a fast reader. I mean, he can really read fast and retain, too. I've given him books . . . back in the Michigan days . . . "You ought to look at this," you know, it would be a fatty and he would have read it by the next day. I'm a slow reader and sometimes fantasize too much when I'm reading so that at the end of the book I sense I've had some sort of experience but am uncertain as to what it was. In many ways, I'm still the idiot who flunked ninth grade. I'm a daydreamer.

Beef: Tell me what your daily routine is like. You say you're an early riser?
Tom: I'm not a much routinized person. I was almost forty before I developed regular bowel habits. I may have taken a position about it: "I shall not shit by the clock." My horses are the exception: they're fed and worked very regularly. I ride probably 250 days a year. But that's because the horses need

that. Otherwise, I'm moved more by impulse than by habit. My reading schedule doesn't change. I read a lot every day because I love to read . . . I'm following some motif, you know, or something. Right now I'm revisiting all the post-war Italian writers that I like so much. Moravia, Pavese, Silone.

Beef: Isn't Alberto Moravia an unbelievable writer?
Tom: He's wonderful. He's as adventurous and strange as Knut Hamsun. And I'll go on these tears of reading things that are not necessarily good books. I'm very interested in equestrian things. Last year, I read all these books by Arnold Rojas who I knew late in his life and who was one of the last of the California vaqueros. He wrote absorbing books about the old vaqueros, their horsemanship which was quite different from what we've inherited up here. That discursive approach to reading doesn't change, but my writing does change.

I'll try to figure out why something has attracted me. I'll make notes and I'll scribble around and I'll avoid work and then it gradually accumulates. And I think most people probably work this way. You kind of start on something and then it acquires importance to you and it's easier and easier to go to work, right? And so, that's how writing goes for me. I'll start out barely able to spend an hour a day writing on a new book say. And then at some point I can hardly go to the house anymore. I'm just there all the time, day and night. I used to sort of celebrate a kind of a workmanlike approach to writing. Just go there and you do three hours each morning and then four hours each morning and then . . . but I've had a hard time living up to that. And I think of myself as a pretty hardworking writer but it's lopsided. It's asymmetrical.

Beef: Do you have a down time after you finish a book?
Tom: I want to keep writing because the knack part of it is trained at that point. You've become accustomed to translating thought into language, you've been going every day, you're tuned up, you're in shape and you want to go right on and write something else but you don't always have something to write. I would say that's a little bit the case since I finished this book, I'm kind of treading water waiting for my editor to get back to me so we can do the necessary work and park it and go onto the next thing with the real separation that you look for. I haven't really got that with this book yet. But I'll go through the same insecure hell on the next book as I always go through before it gets a little *gestalt* that starts to pull you along. Meanwhile, you drift and call yourself bad names.

It's like that on the ranch. I don't want to go out and build fence. I hate building fence and then you get a few posts in, you get a few wires up and you start to think, let's make it a straight one. And then all of a sudden you get kind of vain about how good your gates are. (*Laughter*) I think there's a huge similarity among all jobs, if you're worth a damn and want to get something done.

Beef: And what would you say those similarities are?

Tom: In all cases there is a run-up period as you develop passion about a particular task, and then that kind of glow period where the thing is gathering fuel around itself, and then the period as you see the end in sight and you feel that short-term syndrome like they have in prison where they know they're going to get out. And you start hurrying a little bit and you have to resist that because you worked in this kind of Apollonian way for a long time and now you don't want to get too impatient just because you can see the end. Then it's over, and you're back in the trough again. I think it's that way for people who build boats or try to put together a good set of cows or bake a cake for Christ's sake. A rancher tries to have a good calf crop and he works himself crazy and the calves are healthy and they've got all their vaccinations and they're well fed and the weaning has been successful, the death loss is low, and you get down to the scales in town and the trucks from Nebraska are all there and you look at all the weight tickets on those calves and you say, "Damn, we did it," and they're gone and they're going down the road and you've got to start again. At that moment, everyone loses all their energy but they get over it. I've raised thousands of calves and they look more like stories every day.

Beef: You have mentioned many of your interests. Are you concerned at all that these outside interests, hunting, fishing, ranching, training horses, in addition to literature, could result in making you a jack-of-all-trades?

Tom: I should be more concerned than I am. I have a primary interest in the world and feel that if the ratio of world to word is high, that rightness and concision are honored, I may safely avoid the often suet-filled oeuvre that characterizes the writer who has no other interests. I think that excellent writers like David Foster Wallace and Jonathan Franzen would be even better if they were less interested in writing. Any writer can disappear up his own ass in a New York minute. You've got to have a life. Otherwise every noun in the book looks like it came off Google.

Beef: Where do you get your inspiration from, Tom?

Tom: Things sort of capture your excitement because of some poetic eternal quality. I was talking to this old cowboy friend of mine who is almost eighty today. We were telling all these funny stories about the neighbors and people stealing water from the irrigation ditch and all the little battles we always have up and down the ditch and those reminded him of some things in the twenties and the thirties. And we're just having one of those real pleasant visits and some of them are based on his great age, his appreciation of things knowing that not much of his life remains to him. Then on the overhead gate to the corrals two flickers landed and they were having some kind of courtship thing. It was real pretty. One of them handed the other one a little bug and we just stopped talking because we know each other really well—he worked for me for ten years— just watching these two birds and we didn't say a damn thing, we were completely comfortable for about ten minutes watching these birds. And at the end of it Bob says, "What a great day," gets in his truck and leaves. (*Laughs*)

I thought about that afterwards, I thought, I don't know how you get something like that down, but that's the kind of the thing you live for, the kind of treasure that falls your way in the course of a day. So, you think maybe you're an artist and you have the capacity to keep that sort of thing from dying entirely. And that will kind of lead you down into the jeweled bower of further labors. (*Laughs*) That's it. But also, you know, writing . . . if I can ever get back to your question. Cheever said that writing is really more improvisatory than anybody admits. And I think that's true. It's certainly true in early drafts. You just set out and really don't know what's going to happen. But you do want to set out in a direction that might be fruitful. Everyone would like to enter a creative trance because it's effortless. But the creative trances are remarkably scarce, though they have produced more than their share of accounts of stories and books "writing themselves." Good luck.

Beef: Explain that process? Do you mind?

Tom: You begin with something that is vivid, something alive and arresting which has a kind of stand-alone quality, which serves as a kind of "now." But it has no value beyond its weightless attraction. Next is "now what?" "Now what" is narrative and it is fraught with perils and rich opportunities to make an ass of yourself. It's a bit like the purported last words of a hillbilly: "*watch this.*" It is why many learn they have no stomach for the game, especially when you stumble and the literati fall upon you with murderous glee.

Beef: Is there one part of writing that you dislike the most?
Tom: First drafts. (*Laughter*) Yeah, they're tough.

Beef: What are your blind spots?
Tom: I have a lot of them, as does every writer. It's hard to admit to blind spots when all evidence suggests they are produced by ignorance. As I am old and corrupt, I will admit to a few of them anyway.

Except for the short stories, which I love, and maybe *Sons and Lovers*, I don't get D. H. Lawrence. *St. Mawr*, often described by the credulous as the greatest horse story of all time, is implausible to anyone who ever rode a horse—just as Malamud's *The Natural* makes little sense to anyone who ever played baseball. I don't think the great H. E. Bates was far off when he described the late Lawrence novels as "hysterical slobber."

Despite mighty exceptions like *The Red Badge of Courage*, I am skeptical of most historical novels, and the current spate of Civil War novels, skillful as they are, has not changed my mind. Imagine a Civil War novel by John Cheever, or Richard Ford. I think writers should write about their own times. This is one thing that fiction can do that is imperishable and which elevates it above all the forms of media. Compare *The Great Gatsby* to newscasts and films of the same years. It's the quick versus the dead and is meant to compensate us for the paltry rewards here on earth.

Henry James and Thomas Mann, for me, stew in similar juices and emit a similar sickliness. James is certainly a master and offers a real reward for surviving his prose; but I'm not so sure about Mann.

Contrary to popular opinion, my admiration for Hemingway is limited to the short stories, *A Farewell to Arms* and *A Moveable Feast*, and I do admire them for their austerity and disciplined perceptiveness. I despise *For Whom the Bell Tolls*, *The Garden of Eden*, *Across the River and Into the Trees*, and *Islands in the Stream*. I'm almost embarrassed to admit that I was unresponsive to *The Old Man and the Sea*.

I have spells of Faulkner skepticism, absent his work from 1929 to 1935. Reading *The Unvanquished* alerted me to the fact that there is much fraud in much Faulkner.

I love comic novels but found *Catch 22* and *A Confederacy of Dunces* tiresome; those two iconic books missed me.

Beef: Can you think of a book no one ever mentions that just swept you away?

Tom: Yes, Joyce Cary's *To Be a Pilgrim*, Knut Hamsun's *Victoria*, Halldor Laxness's *Independent People*, Brian Moore's *Lonely Passion of Judith Hearne*, Vittorini's *Conversations in Sicily*, Cela's *The Family of Pascual Duarte*—not quite unmentioned but insufficiently mentioned. There are others, lots of others.

Beef: You're renowned for just being a superb stylist and I certainly couldn't disagree with that. It's obvious as well that you have a great love for language, and it appears that language is what propels you, as Jim (Harrison) says, "An intoxification with language." Do you still have that just incredible passion for language itself, language for its own sake?

Tom: Yes, I think I do. I remember Stegner was asked, "What do you think of Tom McGuane's writing?" And he said, "He's nothing but a word witch like that Updike." He had a word for all his old students. McMurtry was the phoney historian, Robert Stone, the spoilt Catholic, Ken Kesey was ineducable, and so on. He did say Wendell Berry was of "whole cloth" but that was it for the kind words.

Beef: A word witch?

Tom: Yeah. Saul Bellow, I was very glad to learn, liked that very thing about my writing. I would say that my interest in language is not quite the runaway fervor it once was because I feel a greater need to put it in the service of other things. And right now my interest strangely enough is in storytelling.

Beef: What was it like studying with Wallace Stegner?

Tom: I was on an elevator in the Stanford library with other young writers when we first met Stegner. We were a bit lost at that point and asked him what we would be expected to do. He said, "You can take the money and go to Hawaii for all I care." It was an accurate introduction to this man who seemed so uncomfortable in his own skin. But it was a great blessing at that point to have a year of financial support to write, a bonanza really. My encounters with Stegner were all more or less glancing ones that usually included bad advice. I thought reading the King James version of the Bible was an essential exploration of the English language, but he said it was wasting my time because religion was dead. When he learned I was reading Dostoyevsky, he remarked that that too was a waste of time as "Conrad did it all better." He informed me that all modern poetry was bad and Nabokov, whom he knew, was "just another foreigner." This jingoistic remark fitted aptly with his western nativist obsessions. Like some writers in the university, Stegner's interest was in his own work, and his sinecure at Stanford provided an opportunity for which teaching could only be an interference. Increasingly, college chairs are endowed in his name. *Sic semper academia.*

Beef: So tell me how your style has changed over the years?
Tom: Cyril Connolly said that the book of serious intention which stays in print for ten years is at least a minor classic. And I've got ten of them like that. So I hope one of them makes it! (*Laughter*) But things have changed. I had a spell where I read and re-read everything that Chekov wrote. And I was really moved at how human perception driven by a sensibility which was the arch-enemy of cruelty and meanness, really ought to be kind of at the center of what you're trying to do.

Beef: Speaking of which, what is the future of literature?
Tom: I don't think literature is ever going to go away though it competes less and less well with those forms better suited to the passive consumer. It's not as reassuring a future obviously as it was when I started writing, and when it was a religion. We were still in the aura of modernism and there was a sacred quality about all the arts, which may not be quite as palpable as it was then. I think that it has a pretty secure future though, and I recently read something that indicates that young people are abandoning other kinds of media more and more to be readers. I don't know why we should cite young people, as credulous and ignorant as they usually are, but that's how we invoke the future. Literature is irreplaceable. Now, on what scale it's irreplaceable I don't know. Buckminster Fuller said years ago that we will eventually reach a point in which most of mankind will only be asked to consume. And a very few will be allowed to produce. Clearly, passive consumption is the road of the future for most people, but not everybody. There are always going to be elites who care about better things and this is going to be one of the elites. And as to the future of literature, I only have to read the writers far younger than me who are carrying good torches—Susan Minot, Thom Jones, Julie Orringer, Rick Moody, Lewis Robinson, Tobias Wolff, Andrea Barrett, Nell Freudenberger,

Chris Offutt—among lots and lots of others, and I cheer right up. And writers like Orhan Pamuk who is relatively young give me the feeling that all the possibilities for greatness are still there.

Beef: You're considered a cult hero to a great extent, you have what's called a cult following. What is that? What does that mean to you and who are these people?

Tom: I really don't know who they are. I used to kind of know that I had this kind of counterculture standing which has come back to haunt me because that's what makes tweedy chaps in well-endowed former women's colleges so upset with me. I don't know if cult is the word, but I have readers who like my work or like the way I live or what contribution or form of usefulness I may have taken over time. But I think in an odd way the more I get interested strictly in literature and less in my way of life, that kind of goes away. Because people who sustain cult writers are people who are looking not for clues about literature but clues about how to live their lives and they're interested in what independent people are doing with theirs.

My passion since I was ten years old has been literature. That's what I'm interested in. And I want people to read my books as successful or unsuccessful attempts at literature. Not what kind of pants to wear or what kind of geography should entertain them. Or how I train horses or catch fish.

Beef: Not long ago I was visiting with Yvon Chouinard and he was saying, "Boy, *The Longest Silence* was just the most incredible book. I just loved it." He goes, "I wish Tom would spend his . . ." I mean, "Nobody writes about fishing better." Which Jim [Harrison] has said about you as well.

Tom: Yvon thinks my best book is *Some Horses*. But he also said, "I don't know anybody who reads novels." I've had this conversation with Ted Turner and Brokaw. Tom asked me, "What do you suppose you were doing in 1968?" And I said, "Well, probably I was waiting for Saul Bellow's next novel." He said figuratively, "Nobody is waiting for Saul Bellow's next novel anymore. Times have changed." And I think that he probably believes that since books don't have the sway that they once had that probably fiction is superfluous. I don't believe that and if I did believe it I don't know what I'd do about it. It's what I do. I can write non-fiction, but it never has the traction for me that writing fiction does. Anyway, a book by Coetzee, Sewald, Timm, or Pamuk turns all that on its ear unless you're in some sordid show business mentality where you count box office receipts to determine merit.

Beef: As I'd mentioned earlier during our conversations, the way we actually met was through Richard Brautigan. What are your reflections now of Richard as a writer, as a friend, and has that impacted your life in any way?
Tom: I don't know that it impacted my life except that he wrote some things that I thought were very good. *Trout Fishing in America* is an original, wonderful book. But frankly, I just couldn't understand some of his other books. The last one, the posthumous book, I thought was also very good but mostly it was all downhill from *Trout Fishing in America*. Still, everything he wrote had something that you couldn't find anywhere else. He was a unique character, what Melville would call an "isolato." Richard was an anomaly because part of him was a very normal person, just a guy, who wanted to fish and hang around, but he was so strange with this high squeaky voice and bizarre costumes and appearance. He always struck me as somebody not entirely comfortable on earth. And then he had a celebrity following for a period of time—the Beatles and so on—that he got addicted to and it was quite misleading because when they left him as they always do, I think he felt sort of bereft. If he had kept his sights on writing, for which he had a gift and commitment, if that had been exclusive, I don't think he would have fallen in despair over not being as popular as he once was. He'd wander around seeking places where he was still well known like Japan, looking for the old buzz. The thing that maybe was a real limitation on my friendship with Richard was that I worried about him a lot, I liked him personally, and I wasn't going to do like the Bozeman gang did, when I thought Richard was drinking himself to death, to call him up to go drinking all the time because they liked the companionship and the excitement of this wacky, famous artist. When he would come to me I would talk to him about some of his problems and where this was going to head, which was in my view, untimely death. I wanted him to stay alive. He didn't necessarily want me to point out how much happier he was the year he attempted moderation. I said, "This is working. This is it! This is what you need to be doing." He was cheerful, productive, and fit. But he had terrible demons and was cruelly raised. So, I can't judge him.

And then he'd get up in the morning and his hands would be shaking and he'd make a pot of tea and he'd put this much tea in it and that much whiskey on top of the tea. This is at 7:30 in the morning and it would be like that for the day. And I couldn't look on that and say, "This is all part of the myth, let's really do this!" It was years before I forgave the people who lured him down this road. And I knew what I was talking about, having boozed my way through a decade, getting in bar fights, going to jail, and running from guilt. It ain't that pretty at all, and I don't shrink from giving folks the bad news.

Beef: Speaking of self-destruction, what was your reaction to Hunter's death? Hunter S. Thompson? Had you had much contact with Hunter the past couple years?

Tom: I just had talked to him. I had a very pleasant conversation with him. It was the Hemingway story. Hunter had acquired a public role and he had sycophants around him to encourage him. He had become a kind of a parody of himself. He was a wonderful writer and he loved being a celebrity but, once again, that comes and goes. And he got no support for his good work by the American literary officials, the canon builders working on texts with titles like, "Unpacking Fraught Outcomes." Literature is always there and writing is always there. They don't come and go. If you get addicted to being popular, you're hosed. And he had taken just way too many drugs. He was probably mentally frayed enough that he didn't have the energy and freshness to break new ground as a writer. And he was in poor health. But having said all that, I was totally surprised. I didn't foresee his suicide.

Beef: Your circle of friends includes some very successful people. How has that impacted you?

Tom: I'm a bit of a loner really and I've never been drawn to succeeding by association. I'm not particularly drawn to hanging out with successful people. I probably ought to lose some of this resistance. I'd never been to the set of the *Missouri Breaks*, for example. And I remember Russ (Chatham) and Jim were going up continuously and it was a good thing, in a way. Those are interesting people. Marlon Brando was an interesting person. Jack Nicholson is interesting. Arthur Penn is interesting. Probably I should have gone there and hung out and kind of you know, raised my profile a little bit. I was challenged by the whole uproar. I didn't want that scene. But I've had the benefits of knowing great people, especially in more recent years, like Yvon. He and I have been friends for about ten years. I've learned a lot from Yvon. And my oracle Buster Welch, five-time world champion cutting horse rider and great cowboy/ rancher, has been an inspiration to me for his superb values and resolve.

Beef: Yvon's an incredibly interesting man, isn't he?
Tom: I can't wait for him to get here. I think he gets here Monday. But Yvon and Tom Brokaw and I all became friends in our fifties. And that's kind of an unusual thing because we're really good friends. I mean, the kind of friendships that you would think that would have started much earlier. But before that, you know, my friends have always been people like Jim, Gatz, and people I've worked with here on the ranch. I have a friend Lou O'Connor I was put in the playpen with at age eight weeks. We've been friends ever since. We've hunted and fished and played baseball and soccer together. You know, we've been friends for sixty-five years. My cousin Fred and I have been doing things together all our lives. My school pal Fred Woodworth, still a friend. I'm still regularly in touch with my girlfriend from junior high and my girlfriend from high school, grandmas one and all!

Beef: Were you involved in athletics at all, Tom?
Tom: I played baseball. I played soccer. Baseball was kind of my big deal. My favorite sport. I played football in Catholic school.

Beef: What position did you play in baseball?
Tom: I played third base.

Beef: I read somewhere that you watch hockey?
Tom: I'm a hockey nut. I played a lot of hockey. Just pond hockey. The hockey strike has been going and I've started watching more basketball. My wife loves to watch tennis and she usually lures me in there. Wimbledon is going on right now, and I'll go watch the finals. In fact, I think the women's semi-finals is today with Serena, Venus Williams, and Maria Scharapova. For some reason, the women are far more interesting than the men.

Beef: Tom, you know, I've read nearly every interview of you. What's question that you've never been asked that you always wished somebody would ask?
Tom: I'm surprised I guess probably that at my age people don't ask me how I feel about death. I can't figure out why it doesn't worry me. Maybe when it

gets closer I'll let out a screech. On a ranch, you see so much life and death among animals that it no longer seems unnatural. It's not concealed from you as it mostly is in modern life where death appears as something bizarre and macabre. Next year I'll have outlived both of my parents. Shouldn't I be a little bit preoccupied with this? I mean, maybe I'm living in some sort of psychic fool's paradise. But it's not anything that has concerned me. Sort of being and nothingness. I think partly because I'm not absolutely sure what happens. I don't know if I go up in a silver column of light and look down in sort of mindless merriment at all the troubles people are going through. But I wish I had a stronger view of it. I mean, I remember a year ago Harrison wrote me a letter and said, "I've had kind of a bad year. I was really scared about mortality." And I thought well, that's very healthy and reasonable: you should be. But I don't feel it. And I've had things happen. I had a horse fall at a wide open gallop last year and pile up in the rocks and I remember thinking, "How can I be so detached about this? This might be the end of the line right now. Why am I kind of noting things going by me?" It was a similar sensation when I rolled that Porsche in Texas. Because the kid that was with me said, "This is it." We were going 140 miles an hour, and I'm being a ghost in my own life.

Beef: Tom, what do you . . . and I mean, pride is kind of a goofy word, and probably not the best, but what are you proudest of? As far as, you know, you as an individual, as a . . . and maybe it's different if I ask you as a writer or as a person.
Tom: Well, I'm proud of being gradually, but steadily a better husband. I'm not saying I'm a good one. I'm proud of the fact that I'm a better husband all the time and I'm proud of the fact that I'm a better parent all the time. And mind you again, I'm not saying a good parent, or a good husband, but I'm better than I used to be and I'm getting better all the time. And I think my wife and my children would concur. And some of that is just natural to the aging process. I mean, I was a very, very driven writer.

(*Laurie comes in.*)

So I'm proud about that and I'm also proud of the fact that I was a driven writer. Somebody interviewed Gerald Chapman and asked him what I was like when he was my writing teacher at Harvard and his remark was, "He was so intense it was frightening." Well, you know, you can't live like that your whole life. And also it causes you to neglect a lot of things. And if you're working hard and you're driven by fear of failure and all those things, your peripheral vision goes all to hell. Furthermore, I had a very unsympathetic kind of family who did not give me the sense that my writing was worthwhile work.

I'm kind of proud of my modestly improved performance in my personal life, and I'm proud of the fact that I think that love has become a big part of my life, that I've got love where it belongs: right in the middle of everything I do. I love my life, I love my family, and I love my friends. I love this beautiful country I live in here in Montana. And there are days when the work is going well that I perhaps feel a little justification for my good luck and happiness.

Beef: Let's talk about your father. Do you mind, Tom? Tom, if your father was alive today, what do you think he would say or what would you say to him?

Tom: Well, I would like to think that we would have probably had some kind of *rapprochement* along the way because our positions were sort of hard, and then he died. We never really worked it out. There are a lot of things about my father that I understand better than I used to. He came up hard and he grew up in the Depression. He then went to Harvard as a sort of sample poor Irish kid the way Dartmouth might draft a black basketball player from Newark. And it left him socially embittered because he was despised by the Gentlemen C types at Harvard, the legacies and air-head Brahmins. And he had a bitter beef with the cards he'd been dealt but he also had a huge capacity for work. He was an alcoholic all his life and never missed a day's work. I mean, he didn't miss a day's work in forty years. So he was a very, very hard-working person driven by a lot of things, probably anger as much as anything, and without any vision of a good life, peace, or happiness. But I have a lot of respect for how hard he worked. But he left me for a long time with the impression that that anger should be your motivation in life. You got up in the morning and you said, "I'm going to kick somebody's ass today."

I read an interview with the founder of McDonald's. He said, "If I saw the competition drowning, I'd get a garden hose and stuff it in his mouth." I mean, this was kind of the post-Depression sort of work ideal, you know. Life is short and brutal and if you don't get them they're going to get you.

I was talking to an old friend of mine and I said, "The one thing I hate about running a ranch is having to fire people." He said, "It's them or you."

My old man certainly believed that. I don't think I do. I think there are other accommodations.

Beef: Any regrets?
Tom: Well, you know, the original ones that you didn't save your parents from the dark course which they were heading down and I have a huge regret that I was unable to rescue my sister Marian. I just couldn't get over it. I can barely talk about it twenty-five years later. I have a mixed kind of bag of regret about failing in marriage. I say mixed bag because I adore the children that came from my failures. And now I have an unbelievably good marriage and I'm in the third decade of this jubilant marriage. I might be a more important writer if I weren't so in love with the world, if I stayed home more. I would have written more, maybe written better, I don't know. I have never figured out if you're supposed to live it up or work on your legacy. In any case, I'm not particularly regret-ridden, that's for sure.

Beef: Tell me about this particular point in your life as a writer?
Tom: I'm very grateful for the fact that I've been doing this for a long time. I'm no longer young and I'm grateful to have so much fire in the belly for writing at this point in life. I've probably never been more excited about writing. I look at Philip Roth whom I admire very much and I see all the work he's done since he turned seventy. I was talking to Brokaw the other day about this and he said, "I can remember in my home town in South Dakota when they'd say, 'There goes Bill, fifty years old and he can still get on a horse.'" I just think people are a little different now. Nicholson calls us "the new old." Late maturing, too. My kids are older than Hemingway was when he wrote *The Sun Also Rises*, and they're fairly juvenile still. As was I.

Beef: I was intrigued where you were talking about fun. Fun means a lot of different things to different people, but to actually mention having fun, like, "My wife and I have fun every day."
Tom: Oh, yeah. Well, she's got wonderful energy and I've got pretty good energy. Not as much as she has. But we're excited about our bird feeders. We're excited about our horses. We're excited about our grandchildren and our children. We're excited about cooking. We're excited about the ranch. We both love to read side by side with dogs piled on the foot of the bed. I think

we are blessed. Leave the ranch every morning on a horse and head out. House full of books. Can't beat it.

Beef: One of the things that I always think about when I think of Tom McGuane as a writer—is your sense of humor displayed in your work. Where did that originate?

Tom: I don't know, but it's amazing how many people miss that. *Nothing but Blue Skies*: a lot of reviewers didn't notice that any of it was funny. I'm like, "Fuckheads! It's a comic novel!"

Beef: Seriously?

Tom: That really made me feel alienated, a real instance of pounding sand down a rat hole. The result is I examined that which I'm alienated from, and alienation became something to celebrate.

Beef: Where did your sense of humor come from, what things make you laugh every day? What things do you find funny?

Tom: Well, I will say one thing about my family of origin, they were all comedians and that's a classic Irish-Catholic culture. I was in Argentina and was driving by this little town in Patagonia and this Argentine said, "In that town they're all Irish but they came here long ago. They haven't spoken English in two generations."

I said, "What are they like?" And he said, "Oh, it's stupid practical jokes and fart books in the bathroom." But they were all named O'Malley and O'Toole and Murphy and Collins and so on. My uncle Bill said, "Never leave a room unless everybody is laughing." And I've always felt that sort of entertainer drive. We had sixteen people here for lunch yesterday and I thought I'm pretty compulsive about this, making everybody giggle all the time, and I've tried to kind of keep that in control and maybe make it more embedded. *Bushwhacked Piano* is full of pratfalls, really quite primitive. I try not to do too much of that these days. But some of my favorite books, I mean, my early formative books were almost all comic novels. Dickens's *Pickwick Papers* which I deeply loved. *Dead Souls, Don Quixote*. Fielding, Peacock, Sterne, some of Thackeray, Jane Austen, Mark Twain. Joyce and Kafka are quite comic, aren't they, and Beckett? And I've read all of Evelyn Waugh. I was delighted to learn that Charlie Parker was a big Evelyn Waugh fan. Bird had a first-rate mind.

Beef: If you have a choice would you say life is comic-tragedy or a tragedy-comedy?

Tom: I'm probably a comic-tragedy guy. The human folly about time places mankind in a permanent comedy. The South Americans say, "Everybody knows they're going to die but nobody believes it." Delusion is the final source of the comic. *Poshlust*, so gorgeously explained by Nabokov, is an eternal source of comedy, and that Gogolian ideal, laughter through tears. If Yeats really wanted to cast a cold eye on life, he should have turned to the comedians.

Index

Abbey, Edward, 157
Alabama, 105
Alexander, Samuel, 13
Allen, Woody, 168
Altman, Robert, 119
American Academy and Institute of Arts and
    Letters, 29, 35
Amis, Kingsley, 45
Anderson, Sherwood, 65, 99, 101, 189;
    Winesburg, Ohio, 189
Arafat, Yasser, 172
Argentina, 139, 143, 205
Aristophanes, 48
Ashby, Hal, 97, 119
Ashley, Elizabeth, 37, 184
Assis, Machado de, 4, 10, 88
Atlantic, 191
Austen, Jane, 41, 205
Avenue, 110, 111

Bachelard, Gaston, 10
Badlands, 119
Bakker, Jim, 130
Barrett, Andrea, 197
Barth, John, 17, 23, 24, 54, 89, 156, 168; *The End
    of the Road*, 54; *The Floating Opera*, 24, 54;
    Sot-Weed Factor, 17
Barthelme, Donald, 23, 99
Barthelme, Frederick, 156
Bates, H. E., 195
Baudelaire, Charles-Pierre, 87
Beatles, the, 199
Beckett, Samuel, 205
Beebe, William, 86
Bellow, Saul, 55, 89, 129, 167, 196, 198;
    Henderson the Rain King, 88
Bergson, Henri, 21
Berkeley Writers' Conference, 26
Berry, Wendell, 176, 196
Bertolucci, Bernardo, 119

Best American Stories, 188
Biely, Andrey, *St. Petersburg*, 14
Billings, Mont., 39, 40, 173
Billings Gazette, 172
Blunt, Judy, *Breaking Clean*, 175
Bob and Ray, 14
Böll, Heinrich, 90
Bombeck, Erma, 40
Borges, Jorge Luis, 89, 94
Borrow, George, 88
Boston, Mass., 15, 53, 100, 175
Boswell, Robert, 156
Bowles, Paul, 88, 139
Bozeman, Mont., 177, 180, 199
Bozeman Chronicle, 172
Brandenburg Concerto, The, 156
Brando, Marlon, 11, 27, 32, 96, 110, 113, 115,
    135, 136, 175, 184, 200
Brautigan, Richard, xiv, 23, 24, 74, 134, 187,
    199; *Trout Fishing in America*, 199
Bridges, Jeff, 110, 114, 136, 157, 184
British Columbia, 139
Brokaw, Tom, 157, 167, 198, 201, 204
Brontë, Emily, 41; *Wuthering Heights*, 79
Brown, Tina, 190
Browne, Sir Thomas, 14
Bruce, Lenny, 14
Buffett, Jimmy, 36, 155, 184
Burroughs, William, 12
Burton, Robert, *Anatomy of Melancholy*, 14
Busch, Fredrick, 167
Bush, George W., 172
Butler, Samuel, 17
Byron, Lord, 4

Cahill, Tim, 157, 175
Cairo, Ill., 99
California, 34, 117, 185, 187, 192. *See also*
    Hollywood, Calif.; Los Angeles, Calif.
Camus, Albert, 35